MARTIN SCORSESE'S
AMERICA

Ellis Cashmore is the author of Polity titles *Tyson: Nurture of the Beast* and *Beckham*, now in its second edition. Among his other recent books are *Celebrity/Culture* and *The Black Culture Industry*.

MARTIN SCORSESE'S AMERICA

ELLIS CASHMORE

polity

First published in 2009 by Polity Press

Polity Press
65 Bridge Street
Cambridge CB2 1UR, UK

Polity Press
350 Main Street
Malden, MA 02148, USA

ISBN-13: 978-0-7456-4522-3
ISBN-13: 978-0-7456-4523-0 (pb)

A catalogue record for this book is available from the British Library.

Typeset in 10.75 on 14 pt Adobe Janson
by Servis Filmsetting Ltd, Stockport, Cheshire
Printed and bound in Great Britain by
MPG Books Group, UK

The publishers would like to thank the following for permission to reproduce copyright material:
Page 21, © Warner Bros./ The Kobal Collection; 28, © Warner Bros./ The Kobal Collection; 63, © Universal/ The Kobal Collection; 78, © Columbia/ The Kobal Collection; 124, © Miramax/ Dimension Films/ The Kobal Collection/ Tursi, Mario; 144, © Warner Bros./ The Kobal Collection; 166, © Universal/ The Kobal Collection; 186, © United Artists/ The Kobal Collection; 209, © United Artists/ The Kobal Collection; 241, © Columbia/ The Kobal Collection/ Caruso, Phillip; 252, © Touchstone/ The Kobal Collection.

For further information on Polity, visit our website: www.politybooks.com

CONTENTS

1

INTRODUCTION – GRAND, DARK, AMERICAN VISION

It seems stupid to have discovered America only to make it a copy of another country.

There is a scene in *No Direction Home*, Martin Scorsese's documentary about Bob Dylan, in which Joan Baez recalls Dylan's scathingly reporting how scholars and highbrow critics were in the 1960s deconstructing the meanings of his lyrics and assessing the profundity of his vision. "All these assholes, they're gonna be writing about all this shit I write," Dylan told Baez.

Baez, one-time muse and folk artist in her own right, suggests that Dylan took pleasure from the earnest interpretations of his songs, most of that pleasure deriving from the fact that the interpretations bore no resemblance to what he had in mind when he wrote them. Baez remembers Dylan scoffing, "I don't know what the fuck it's about and *they're* gonna write what it's about."

I guess I'm going to do something similar with Scorsese:

I'm set to write what his films are about, possibly in a way he won't recognize himself. Scorsese might be a fearless film-maker who has steadfastly pursued his own goals, often in defiance of Hollywood traditions. But I'm less interested in him as an individual, more as a creator of a vision. His personal morality, his motives, his intentions, his aspirations rarely reveal a sense of purpose beyond creating art. Scorsese has never said he is trying to create a body of work that will tell us what he thinks of America. But it does exactly that.

Scorsese has the reputation of being a preeminent film-maker. Rightly so. But can he enrich our understanding of America's history, the values that unite it and the divisions that cleave it apart? In a sense, the answer is implicit in his reputation: one of the reasons he is so widely acknowledged is that his work dramatizes and documents America in a way that's both enjoyable and edifying.

We can understand history and contemporary culture through all sorts of creative artists as well as historians and social scientists; their aesthetic and scholarly work always offers a scope, an opportunity to examine something or somewhere. Since 1501 when the Italian merchant and explorer Amerigo Vespucci sailed along the west coast of South America, turned north and looked into the distance, there have been any number of visions of America. The very word "America" is thought to derive from the Latin form of the explorer's Christian name, *Americus*. A land named after its first visionary became the source of countless other visions. Scorsese's America is just one of them.

Despite his popular reputation as a furnisher of thrill-ing and ruthless tales of gangster life, Scorsese is an eclectic director, delving into novels, biographies, historical docu-ments, and especially other films. As well as his chronicling Italian Americans' attempts to chase the American Dream, he has dramatized such subjects as ethnic animosities in the

nineteenth century, the morbidity of living in the twentieth-century metropolis, and the crumbling confidence in
mainstream institutions, such as the family, the legal system,
and big government. He's captured the swarming egotism
of America and the rewards and punishments offered by
attempts either to escape or embrace it. His documentaries are often knowledgeable and enlightening reports on
American popular culture and the struggles that both tear
and repair it. America's history, its torments and its crises;
the people who build it and those who break it. They're all
there. Scorsese has put together a vision of America.

When you stand back and ponder, "What *kind* of America
is Scorsese visualizing?
How can we interpret his **"Scorsese is fascinated
films in a way that allows by reckless obsessives."**
us to see a single image DAVID COURTWRIGHT, *JOURNAL
rather than numerous, OF AMERICAN HISTORY*
fragmented impressions?"
you scratch your head and reflect on the assortment of different subjects, periods, and genres Scorsese has essayed.

Two writers have offered their own ways of characterizing
Scorsese's America: as an obsessive society and one that is
endlessly collapsing and restoring itself, always in the grip of
violent change.

First, David T. Courtwright's summary: "Scorsese is
fascinated by reckless obsessives." Gusting through every
film there is what Courtwright, in his 2005 analysis of *The
Aviator*, calls "the hurricane of obsession." Obsessive people,
that is, in an obsessive society. Scorsese brings this to life
through both his characters and the environments in which
they live and die.

Obsessives sometimes give way to their obsessions, taking
their own lives or those of others, doing things that land them
in trouble or arranging their own lives in a way that doesn't so

much invite problems as drags them in. But most of the time, they just incorporate their obsessions into their lifestyles in a way that nobody else notices. We see them everywhere, probably without knowing it. They're in supermarkets, sitting next to you on the subway or in a plane, working at the desk facing you at work or in the library. They're people preoccupied with something or someone to a troubling extent. Troubling, that is, for them and everyone around them.

Scorsese makes films about them. In doing so, he contrives to make films about the society in which they operate and which gives rise to their obsessions. "From his first feature film, *Who's that Knocking at My Door?*, Scorsese has been an observer of life on the margin," writes Esther B. Fein, "and the movies he has directed since then . . . have studied that viewpoint from different angles, and through different lives."

Gentle psychopaths, tortured lovers, and avaricious gangsters share space with vengeful malefactors and woebegone wannabes, in what David Bromwich calls the "Scorsese Book of the Disturbed." They are united only by the compulsive resolution that fires their pursuits and by the unbreakable spirit that eventually condemns them.

It sounds like a world of misfits. But it's not: *everyone* in America is an obsessive in one sense or another. Everyone fusses over things that would either amuse the Dalai Lama or make him despair: like goods, revenge, or public acclaim. Everyone wants to be a winner of some kind. Success is a very American preoccupation.

Scorsese is a kind of annalist of the obsessive society, where material possessions and physical comfort are valued, where the pursuit of individual improvement is rewarded, and where male prerogative is respected as if a favorite ornament that has been fixed in position for so many generations that we dare not change it.

Why should these be regarded as obsessions? After all, America didn't invent materialism, any more than it created the individual and vested in him – I use the masculine pronoun deliberately – a sense of purpose and desire for self-improvement. Yet, it was in America that these were changed into unquestioned values, principles to guide a population's conduct and to reward as beneficial. In themselves, they aren't obsessions; they become so when they intrude on the mind of independent citizens, motivating them to the kind of behavior that upsets not just other people but the entire social order of which they're part. This leads us to the second way of characterizing Scorsese's America.

In reviewing *Gangs of New York* in 2003, James Parker proposed another dominant feature of what he considers Scorsese's "amateur sociology." Setting aside whether Parker equates "amateur" with lack of scholarly rigor rather than ineptitude, his point is that Scorsese's storytelling condenses complex information into comprehensible narratives about a society that's always shifting. For Parker, Scorsese's work provides us with a model of "threatened or collapsing order."

The "order" he refers to is an arrangement of codes, rules, protocols, and laws in which everything is in its correct or appropriate place and in which people are disposed to act toward each other according to patterns or accepted norms. Orders exist everywhere there are humans: gregarious creatures that we are, we establish and maintain stable and predictable ways of conducting our lives that allow others to do likewise. So why, in Scorsese's conception, or at least Parker's interpretation of his conception, are they under threat?

Parker doesn't expand his point, but I'll make inferences in the chapters to come. Orders don't stand still like buildings: they are continually under threat or in imminent danger of collapse. Some repel or absorb the threats and give the impression of continuity, if not rock-solid stability, while others actually do cave in. Scorsese essays both forms. In *Casino*, we witness the final throes of a criminal order established on the principles of greed, ambition, and capital accumulation. A near-perfectly calibrated system, but with inbuilt hubris, contrives its own demise.

Codes and constitutions creak in *The Age of Innocence*, they crack up in *Taxi Driver*, they renew and restore themselves in *The Color of Money*.

In a parallel universe we find Bob Dylan's onetime backing band reminiscing on sixteen years spent on the road, rising from barroom gigs to packed stadiums, meeting blues legends and entertaining groupies, but sensing, as Robbie Robertson puts it, "the beginning of the beginning of the end of the beginning" as they prepare for *The Last Waltz*.

America is full of orders collapsing, while others emerge. Codes and constitutions creak in *The Age of Innocence*, they crack up in *Taxi Driver*, they renew and restore themselves in *The Color of Money*. Collapse lurks around every corner and new orders are never far away. This is certainly a way of approaching Scorsese's take on American society. And the idea of an entire society racked with obsessive thoughts is also full of promise.

Scorsese has offered pictures of an ever-changing America in which people are sometimes raving, more often just passionate about whatever stirs them. But there's always a connection between the people and the world around them; Scorsese makes us see that it isn't just around them – it's actually inside them too.

Scorsese's characters are often, to use Fein's phrase, on the margin, or what Gavin Smith, Donald Lyons, and Kathleen Murphy call "the edge of America." By elaborately exposing what Smith and his colleagues anoint "chosen people plucked willing or not out of anonymity and inertia," Scorsese shows a society that both commissions and condemns the same actions – in roughly equal proportions – and invites a perspective, or a way of seeing something we might already know but would probably not want to acknowledge.

Richard Blake, in 2005, captured the uneasy relationship by likening the director to a torturer: "Scorsese has peeled back the eyelids of his audiences and forced them to watch the sordid, cruel realities of urban life that most of us would rather not see" (p. 25).

Cliff Froehlich of the *St. Louis Post-Dispatch* believes that Scorsese's films "vary wildly in quality and content." Yet, Froehlich argues, despite the variations, the films "display key traits that distinguish the director's entire oeuvre . . . unified by his recurring themes."

Froehlich doesn't spell out what he sees as Scorsese's "recurring themes." But the challenge is there: what are the themes that repeat themselves, reappearing in different guises time and again, giving Scorsese's films an identity as an integrated *oeuvre?* The obsessive society and its collapsing orders provide shape and direction for Scorsese. But, to follow Froehlich's point, there is an unusually wide range of subjects, and to make sense of them, we need to identify distinct themes. I'll deal with a theme in each chapter, though, as the readers will soon recognize, several of the themes blur into each other, into patterns.

Considering that Scorsese's films cover over 160 years of American history, there is a surprising continuity of style and thematic consistency in his work, though understandable changes of emphasis as he, like the rest of us, has matured. Scorsese's history might be imperfect, but it's provocative and, for this reason, I haven't tried to identify breaks or interruptions: for work of such breadth, there are actually few. In this book, I'm more interested in the coherence of Scorsese's cinema and what it tells us about the way he understands and perhaps wants us to understand America. Next, I'll outline the chapters and, in the concluding chapter, I'll stand back to see how they all crystallize into the patterns.

Chapter two. Success is integral to America. It's almost as if Americans are under obligation not just to be successful, but to exhibit that success. They have found the perfect ideal. Scorsese's elemental *GoodFellas* is a kind of primary film in this respect. In this film, which was released in 1990, Scorsese restored what had been something of a guiding light in his films of the early 1970s. The hunger for achievement, or rather the actions it has excited, has helped shape many films of radically different sensibilities, from *Citizen Kane* to *The Wizard of Oz*. In Scorsese's hands, it becomes an inspiration, though not for the noble. Scorsese heroes are not engaged in a metaphoric search for the great American grail.

The American Dream and the way it motivates the quest not so much for money but for the type of "success" money represents is obviously dominant in Scorsese's America: here, reprobates, fraudsters, extortionists, and miscellaneous other scumbags vie with wholesome, doe-eyed youths whose pursuit of the Dream will end in tears. In fact, everybody's endeavor ends in tears.

This is an America that, for all its democratic ideology and Christian doctrine, upholds a culture in which the vast majority of those who chase the Dream will be broken by it. If there is one brutal argument propounded by all Scorsese's films, this is it. Everyone chases the dream, some by legal means, others by other, more innovative methods. In *GoodFellas* and other films, Scorsese dispenses with simplifications such as law and order, opting instead to see the two as tendencies rather than absolute poles; tendencies that don't necessarily lead in different directions.

Chapter 3. I examine Scorsese's understanding of the sometimes symbiotic relationship between, on the one hand, the forces of law and order and, on the other, the forces of criminality. The gray area in which cops and criminals coexist in mutual tolerance is what really arrests Scorsese's attention. There are no good guys and bad guys in America: just people who see themselves as the former, but whose actions suggest they are the latter.

Lurking everywhere in Scorsese's work is an individual urgently trying to assert, or reassert, his individuality in the teeth of monsters who feed on such peculiarities. Individuals are quirks, oddities, their foibles those of fugitives and eccentrics. Scorsese doesn't make horror films, of course; but he does make films in which corporations, organizations, syndicates, and even whole cities try to swallow and digest individuals in their strivings for uniformity. Never a romantic, Scorsese resists the quieting message that individualism can never be suppressed for long. In his America, it is frequently consumed by larger, more powerful entities that thrive on sameness.

Crime, for Scorsese, is a caricature of power: an exaggerated version of what law-abiding people do en route to becoming powerful. Actions and omissions that constitute offenses and are punishable by law are little different from the everyday behavior of powerholders.

Chapter four. There's no evidence that Scorsese has ever read David Riesman's book *The Lonely Crowd*, which was a study of the changing American psyche in the 1950s. But there is an irresistible comparison: many of Scorsese's insular, tormented, and, sometimes, haunted men could have been cut-and-pasted from Riesman's research. Chapter 4 focuses on how characters such as Travis Bickle exemplify the lonely man in the lonely crowd.

"*Mean Streets* and *Taxi Driver* contain a reality of urban America that I don't think we'd seen before," says Patricia Finneran, director of The American Film Institute's Silverdocs festival (quoted by Kelly Jane Torrance). There are any number of movies about grimy, unstable city life with its ubiquitous violence. But Scorsese offers an unusual angle of vision – through the eyes of existential anti-heroes accountable to no one, not even themselves, segueing from disorganization to utter derangement.

Bryan D. Palmer detects a tension in Scorsese's effort to link the individual with society. "Robert De Niro's drift into pathology in *Taxi Driver*, while powerfully evocative as a representation of social crisis in the 'post'-1960s decade of the 1970s, never manages to shake loose of a fundamentally alienated individuality" (p. 321).

Taxi Driver shares with *Bringing Out the Dead* and *After Hours*, as well as Scorsese's television program "Mirror, mirror," a scope on living in and through the modern metropolis. Specifically, how living in city environments affects the way we think and how we react. At times, there is almost a duel between the public city and the private inner world of its inhabitants. All of the films considered in this chapter can be seen as master classes in the relationships between individuals and their environments. In Scorsese's eyes, those relationships are often confrontational.

Chapter 5. Scorsese spikes most of his work with a shot of racism or ethnic rivalry of some kind, and *Gangs of New York* engages full-on with issues of racism in the New World of the late nineteenth century. As Palmer argues, there is an unsettling conflict in this film. It's unsettling because it's so familiar even today.

Racism resurfaces, in different forms, in several other Scorsese films, especially his not-so-affectionate backward glances at Italian-American ethnic bonding. Issues of inclusion, exclusivity, segregation, and prejudice appear in different guises, which I explore in Chapter 5. Again, the conflict between the demands of individuals and those of the groups to which they notionally belong or perhaps no longer want to belong are addressed by Scorsese in a way that forces us to think of the politics of race and ethnicity.

Many of Scorsese's films reveal Italian-American culture, usually not in the best of lights. His efforts at addressing other aspects of American ethnicity are often overlooked. Yet, ethnic cultures and the racism they either suffer or incite are, on inspection, germane to Scorsese's version of America.

Chapter 6. The conflict between social or public presentation and individual or private lives is imagined in several works, dramatically in *New York, New York* and documentarily in *No Direction Home*, for example. The exploration of Dylan's career offers Scorsese raw material with which to examine public personae – the aspects of people's character that are presented and, in turn, consumed by audiences. It is a theme that surfaces repeatedly in Scorsese. *The King of Comedy* is Scorsese's masterwork in this respect. Was there ever a more penetrating cultural prescient?

Chapter 6 deals with what's been called Scorsese's "fascination with the US entertainment industry": his treatment of fame, the industry that promotes it, and its effects on both the famous and their fans. For Scorsese, the rise of entertainment as an industry rather than a pastime is seen as a sublime development in American culture. Turning entertainment into a product that can be traded on the market was a pioneering gambit in the late eighteenth century, something Scorsese broaches when, in *Gangs of New York*, he features the visionary P.T. Barnum plying his wares among the masses. But, it is in *The Aviator* that Scorsese is able to engage with the very medium he uses to project his own vision.

In the 1920s, American culture changed dramatically. Quite apart from the underworld changes wrought by Prohibition, there were adaptations to new markets in consumer goods. The cults of glamour and celebrity resonate today, of course. In *The Aviator*, Scorsese uses Howard Hughes as his prism to disperse rays of light on the almost fetishistic pursuit of profit in a country that needed, as President Warren G. Harding affirmed, "less government in business and more business in government." Hughes' Midas-like capacity to turn a profit is tested, though not destroyed, during his attempts to muscle his way into Hollywood.

Scorsese's evident fascination with the entertainment industry is nothing to do with introspection: his interest seems to be with externalities – the consequences of the commercial activity that affects entire societies. Everyone in America – everyone – is, in some way, affected by entertainment.

Chapter 7. The family. It's a capstone American institution, of course, though, as with everything else in Scorsese's America, perilously close to collapse. When you think of the multiple challenges to it that have been launched particularly since the tumultuous decade of the 1960s, the family shouldn't really exist at all, at least not in the traditional, nuclear sense. Its ability to change has enabled the traditional family to survive decades of cultural upheaval and still retain its appeal.

Cape Fear was Scorsese's remake of a 1960s film and, as a way of understanding how the portrayal of the family reflects the changed cultural climate, I compare the two versions in Chapter 7. It might surprise some readers that, of the two, Scorsese's version presents the more traditional, even a reactionary, model of the family in America.

Gender is a concern for Scorsese: every one of his films set in America deals with some sort of disoriented or disorienting relationship between women and men. There is little comfort in his depiction. Women are not always, as critics of Scorsese sometimes point out, helpless appendages; but there is a sense in which they are perpetually seeking something in men that men either can't or won't provide. This helps Scorsese's disillusionment with the family.

Every man in every Scorsese film enjoys rights that he hasn't so much earned as inherited. Scorsese shows how this cultural inheritance has shaped the way we understand manhood in America.

Chapter eight. Men themselves are often excessively self-absorbed scions of privileges. Scorsese's entire project has been described by Paul Arthur as a "mapping of masculine prerogative." This sounds an apt summary: nearly every man in every Scorsese film enjoys rights that he hasn't so much earned as inherited. Scorsese shows how this cultural inheritance has shaped the way we understand manhood in America.

So, what does it mean to be a man? Scorsese has an answer of sorts and Chapter 8 examines it. Critics often name *Raging Bull* as his most compelling essay in brutal, red-blooded manhood. It might well be; but in several other films, Scorsese reveals a slightly more nuanced conception of manhood, as we will see. Yet, in a way, validating manhood is in evidence in all Scorsese's films; and, by validating, I mean corroborating, backing up, and authenticating. In every film, men are busily confirming that they are real men. Why? In Chapter 8, I'll start to answer the question, though the full answer is brought into the open during Chapters 9 and 10.

Chapter 9. A criticism often leveled at a director whose mainstay is men is that his women are one-dimensional. Some critics suggest female characters are just men's appurtenances in Scorsese films: accessories that can be proudly exhibited, but exchanged when their use value wears out. It's a common misconception but one that I'll put to the sword in Chapter 9, where I show that Scorsese has a well-developed understanding of the changing role of women in the twentieth century and beyond. It might not be the same understanding as many other artists and writers, but it's one worthy of serious consideration.

Examining the way in which Scorsese has tackled the disappearance of one kind of femininity and the emergence of another takes me to historical works like *Boxcar Bertha* and more contemporary films such as *The King of Comedy*, where we discover women who are either self-conscious mavericks or rule-breaking individualists. They always seem constrained, as we will see. Scorsese's depiction of women who, while not exactly feminists, defy convention and tread their own paths provides an insight into how he sees women in America.

It's a surprise to learn that Scorsese's America accommodates rule-breaking women who make demands, disobey orders, and stop at nothing in their efforts to get their own way. It's not such a surprise when calamities, personal or cultural, intervene. It doesn't matter whether they're singers who want a family as well as a career, celebrity idolaters, ex-hookers, or free spirits trying to keep body and soul together: bad luck, destiny, or, more usually, circumstances have a way of deflecting them from their path.

Chapter 10. The problem for women – and they do have a problem in Scorsese's America – is that they get suckered into believing in romantic love. It's illusory: impossible to attain, no matter who you are. Scorsese enhances our understanding of the way romance works against the best interests of women, at the same time gifting men with a means of protecting their prerogatives.

Man–woman relations are rarely harmonious affairs in Scorsese's work. In every film, there is a lesson on how women contrive to bring about their own unhappiness. Chapter 9 shows how different women respond to the ideal of romance in different ways. Whatever the response, Scorsese thinks romantic love is ruinous. His ethos has been called "anti-romance," a description I find wholly appropriate.

With his sour and, at times, rancid conception of romance, Scorsese has subverted Hollywood conventions and got away with it. But, there is an uncomfortable conservatism in his work and one that makes it seem that, for him, there is little use in trying to resist forces that seem elemental but are really cultural. Women can strive all they like to be free and auton-omous, but, in the end, the irresistible lure of romantic love will bring them into check. Women, no matter what they say or do, are looking for love. And this is their undoing.

Chapter 11. So much of Scorsese's films are about money, you could be forgiven for thinking that he worships Mammon. Or he could just be depicting a culture that honors it. One thing

Money confers a certain quality on its owners: it means they are successful.

that Scorsese is at pains to disclose is that the pursuit of money is not an entirely irrational one.

Money confers a certain quality on its owners: it means they are successful. The reverse of this is arguably more important: they're not losers. *The Color of Money* centers on the pursuit of the green stuff, but provides Scorsese with a framework in which he explores many of the themes that dominate his wider work.

The concluding chapter addresses these and brings together the three recurrent features that permeate Scorsese's compositions, giving his America structure, bearing, and orientation.

Does Scorsese *intend* to project a vision of America? Maybe not. But there is an incident that reminds us of the gulf between intentions and results and how, in a sense, the former matter far less than the latter. It concerns *The Last Waltz*, Scorsese's document of The Band's valedictory concert in San Francisco. Cinematographer Michael Chapman became involved in a dispute with Scorsese over how to light Robbie Robertson's number "The weight."

Chapman insisted it was a Protestant song and that, as a Catholic, Scorsese didn't understand the Gospel influences ("Go down, Miss Moses, there's nothing you can say. It's just old Luke, and Luke's waiting on the Judgment Day"). Scorsese wanted him to use the colors violet and yellow, suggesting a Catholic intonation in the song. Robertson had no say in the matter, but listened approvingly. "I liked everything they were saying because I had never thought of any of it . . . the song is about the guilt of relationships, not being able to give what's being asked of you," said Robertson (on pp. 115–16 of Mary Pat Kelly's *Martin Scorsese: A journey*).

It underlines the discrepancy between what artists and writers mean to express and what they actually do express, or how others respond to their expressions. Like Dylan, Robertson didn't recognize the meanings attributed to his work by others. Maybe I am about to attribute meanings that Scorsese won't recognize; though he might have got used to this over the years.

Take *New York, New York*, which even Scorsese himself admitted had problems and took a mauling from most critics. But not from David Thomson, who, in the *New York Times*, hailed it as "one of Mr. Scorsese's greatest achievements . . . his most penetrating study of the relations between men and women."

So, while this book is called *Martin Scorsese's America*, I anticipate that readers might object to my assumption that every film is part of an effort to advance a personal vision. After all, Scorsese himself has either scripted or co-scripted only a minority of the films he has directed. Following his own *Mean Streets* in 1973, he didn't write another screenplay until *GoodFellas* in 1990. Since then he has relied on other writers in all but a few films.

All films are a little like the great Frankenstein experiment: once the parts are stitched together and the voltage is turned up, they take on a life of their own and leave behind their creator, or creators – after all, there are scriptwriters involved, often more than one, and they, in turn, rely to some extent on source materials like novels or nonfiction books (I include a Filmography on pp. 269–72). Then there are editors who are responsible for the final cut that eventually makes it onto the screen, as well as countless other contributors to the end product. Any film is mediated not just by a director's own vision, but by countless other filters, the most purifying of which is commercialism.

So, why is it *Scorsese's* vision? Any vision, no matter how singular or even idiosyncratic it may be, is always a product of several forces, and not even a director as influential as Scorsese can control all of them. But, as director, he approves, rewrites, and often interpolates material to suit his own ends. It would be naïve to believe Scorsese would allow a film to bear his name and imprimatur without complete satisfaction that the end product faithfully recorded exactly the vision he wants others to experience and the words he wants others to hear.

Scorsese may not like the pontifical tirades directed

against Irish, Jews, or blacks, or the bile-spill of a war-damaged taxi driver, or the misogynist boasts of rock 'n' rollers. But he knows they are parts of America and his audience have to experience them. The words have what Raymond Williams, in his *Culture and Materialism*, called "an ambiguous relationship to naturalism" (p. 129). He meant that, film, like other art, often strives to be lifelike and historically and socially accurate; but it always conveys a *"reconstructed* environment." Scorsese puts the words, sentiments, and feelings in his films because his naturalistic style of representation commits him to giving a vivid picture with explicit detail.

Some of Scorsese's films are carefully nurtured and painstakingly developed, while the rest are projects initiated by others. *GoodFellas* is an example of the former, *Cape Fear* the latter. Some will argue in response that there can't be consistency in his work. I disagree: I hope to persuade the reader that there is a thematic continuity and an evenness of texture that allow us to investigate his work as a whole, an *oeuvre* in fact.

Naturally, no director can control how audiences will interpret, understand, or read a film. Scorsese occasionally explains what he was trying to convey and suggests the significance of particular scenes, characters, or events. But he can't make us *see* his vision. And yet, the impression remains: Scorsese seems to have been absorbed with ideas and thoughts that inhabit the mind and by an environment that encourages such ideas and thoughts and excites compulsive behaviors, preoccupations, passions, infatuations, fetishes, crazes, and phobias. His collective work implicates us in five generations of social history. And there *is* social history. It isn't a textbook history, or even a historical memoir, but there is an account of living, even if it is living at the margins of American life.

It is an account that combines brutality, corruption, religiosity, xenophobia, addiction, irrepressible strength, and incapacitating weakness. Scorsese has been our guide through a dark world of nineteenth-century crypto-fascism to a fetishistic twentieth century in which goods, fame, money, and power are held to have magical power.

"A grand, dark, American vision, a portrait of the facts beneath the headlines." MICHAEL WILMINGTON, *CHICAGO TRIBUNE*

As the title of this book suggests, my belief is that, taken collectively, Scorsese's films offer a model of American society – a society pockmarked by history and disfigured by contemporary flaws. Obviously, his work is that of a dramatist rather than an analyst, though there is no privileged way of envisioning America. Scorsese has "a grand, dark, American vision, a portrait of the facts beneath the headlines," as Michael Wilmington, of the *Chicago Tribune*, puts it.

Other writers have inferred from Scorsese's films that his endeavors are emblematic. "Scorsese is interested in characters who are representative either of a class or of a certain ideological grouping; he is concerned with their relationships to each other or to an antagonistic environment," discerns Robert Kolker in the 2000 edition of his *A Cinema of Loneliness* (p. 179). "Scorsese's films all involve antagonism, struggle, and constant movement" – characteristics of cultures in the throes of change, we might add.

Some of Scorsese's films offer metaphors, others reflections, still others morality plays. On occasion, he offers microcosms, miniature versions of larger places and events into which he thrusts human affairs that have relevance to nearly all of us. Some of his admirers may object to my dealing with him this way – as a social commentator rather than entertainer. After all, Scorsese works in the film industry, not education.

But entertainment and education are not necessarily in opposition, nor even separable. Many, many films are entertaining because they edify and enlighten, not by providing factual information or offering theoretical knowledge (though, of course, some do), but by provoking audiences into thinking about facets of life in new ways. Scorsese is far from alone in this type of endeavor, of course, though his range, consistence, and productivity tend to distinguish him.

If Scorsese can be approached as a social commentator, we should ask whether he is a good one. Writing for *Time*, Richard Schickel frowned on Scorsese's efforts: "*Mean Streets* first showed the conflict between Scorsese's natural gift for human observation and his attraction to social and psychological statements. Unfortunately, social comment does not come easily to him, and the strain shows" (p. 189 in Kelly's 1980 collection of reviews).

Over the course of this book, I'll seek to show that this relatively early (1976) verdict was rash. I believe Scorsese has assembled a corpus of work that illustrates how entertainment can be integrated with comment on society without showing signs of strain. In this sense, I agree with Bryan Palmer's verdict on *Gangs of New York*, in which "it is impossible not to engage with the politicised meanings of collective historical process, however unsettling they may be" (p. 321).

> **"I consider *GoodFellas*, with its encapsulation of a quarter-century of American life, and feel as if I'm observing a car wreck from the point of view of the passenger seat."** STUART KLAWANS, *THE NATION*

Scorsese's ability to produce this type of engagement in many other of his films rests on his way of bringing subjective states to the fore. As Raymond Durgnat stresses, in his article "Between God and the *GoodFellas*," "he [Scorsese] discerns *experiences*, abstracted from reality, yet heightened, and woven into a stylized yet illuminating logic" (p. 24).

Events and processes, whether an undercover sting in Boston, an impossibly extravagant aircraft project in Tinseltown, or a paramedic's twisted descent into Hades, are dependent on what goes on in the minds of men – and all but a couple of Scorsese's principal characters are men – specifically on values, motivations, and knowledge.

Ideas, for Scorsese, do not spring fully formed from the fertile imagination: they have origins in everyday encounters, in surroundings, contexts, and circumstances; in short, society. Perhaps this is what Parker has in mind: it certainly distinguishes Scorsese as a sociologist among directors. Never

When Frank Costello expresses his hope, "I don't want to be a product of my environment. I want my environment to be a product of me," he misunderstands the extent to which he has been affected by living in contemporary America. (© Kobal)

content to examine the progression of an idea through a plot or series of plots, Scorsese tries to suggest connections, some of which he makes, others of which he leaves like orphaned children, as we will see in the chapters to follow. But he always tries to humanize society and socialize humans. So, when, Frank Costello, in *The Departed*, expresses his hope, "I don't want to be a product of my environment. I want my environment to be a product of me," he misunderstands his own predicament. He already is inescapably a product of his environment; and, while he apparently doesn't realize it, he's helping build that environment – and contributing to its destruction.

Clearly, abstracting subjects and themes from an artist's work is artificial: in the flow of Scorsese's films, the themes collide and flow over each other. My effort has been not to dismantle the pictures, but to represent them in a different and illuminating way. This is an alternative approach to examining his films individually, though one of Scorsese's films is so densely packed with clues about his thinking it deserves special attention.

"It is as if Scorsese knew reality is never objective because there is always a subject experiencing it," suggests Maurizio Viano, in his 1991 review of *GoodFellas*. "Experience, moreover, is never a passive reception of stimuli but an activity – an activity that Scorsese mirrors" (p. 48).

Stuart Klawans, of *The Nation*, makes a related point about the same film, though using more gruesome imagery: "I consider *GoodFellas*, with its encapsulation of a quarter-century of American life, and feel as if I'm observing a car wreck from the point of view of the passenger seat" (p. 539).

GoodFellas approaches a distillation: it's close to an "essence of Scorsese's America" and, as such, commands more consideration than any other film, particularly in Chapter 2, but elsewhere in the text as well. Similarly *Cape Fear* occupies most of the attention in Chapter 7. But there's no film-per-chapter organization. I'm interested in the overall vision and the thematic approach I've taken means that, unlike other books on Scorsese, I don't cover the films one-at-a-time.

There are several other books that have analyzed Scorsese in this film-by-film manner, and the reader will find many of them quoted in the text and fully referenced in the Bibliography. Scorsese has been anatomized in other ways too. For example, there are philosophical musings, psychoanalytic dissections, ethnic-theological investigations to complement the many in-depth penetrations of his films. Again, the reader will find these in the Bibliography.

There's much to learn and pleasure to be gained from examining the relationships between Scorsese's films and the many, many others that have influenced, if not inspired, them. Several books have **Is Scorsese a conservative commentator or a commentator on a conservative society?** traced connections between, for example, the red-imbued deserts of King Vidor's 1946 *Duel in the Sun*, and the prologue sequence in *Alice Doesn't Live Here Anymore*; or the set-piece ballet that punctuates the drama of Michael Powell and Emeric Pressburger's 1948 *The Red Shoes* and the "Happy Endings" Broadway production that didn't make the final edit of *New York, New York* on its initial release.

Every Scorsese film, like every other film, and, indeed, every other work of art, is a product of intertextuality: in terms of style and structure, arts draw on themselves; nothing stands alone, not even the works of astounding originality. So, while I'm not ignoring the cinematic influences, I'm more interested in how social influences play in Scorsese's film. My purpose is not to evaluate Scorsese's debt to other filmmakers, vivisect his texts, inspect his secular Catholicism, explore his psychology, or even examine the contexts in which his films were made. In this book, Scorsese the social commentator will occupy center stage.

Scorsese's early directorial career coincided with the civil rights movement, the women's movement, and America's nomination of itself to the position of global peacekeeper. His work reflects these changes, though perhaps not in a way that prompts challenge. Black people are, for the most part, dealt with as disposable henchmen or peripheral acquaintances in his dramas. His documentary *No Direction Home* offers a different view, as we will discover in Chapter 5.

Even when women attempt to shape their own destinies, they are stymied by their obsessive pursuit of romance. The stubborn reality is that women's destinies are ultimately in the control of men. American values are disfigured, warped, and bent to suit the interests of specific groups, but their propriety is never questioned. So the vision is credible in the sense that it is believable, plausible, and has the ring of truth. But a question remains. Over the course of the next ten chapters, we will decide whether Scorsese is a conservative commentator or a commentator on a conservative society.

Before readers rush to Scorsese's film scripts and challenge my quotations, I should point out that I have extracted dialogue from the films themselves, not the scripts. In some films, *The Age of Innocence* for example (from which I have abstracted the epigraph that opens this chapter), the dialogue sticks closely to the script. In others, such as *Raging Bull*, practically every line of Paul Schrader and Mardik Martin's script is changed to accommodate Scorsese's keenness to use naturalistic improvisation.

Inferring Scorsese's vision of America from the raw material of his films is like trying to assemble a toy with a mixture of Lego and Megablok pieces. The interlocking bricks are compatible, but they don't share the same provenance. And, there are even a couple of errant bricks that don't fit at all. *The Last Temptation of Christ*, Scorsese's treatment of Nikos Kazantzakis' novel, and *Kundun*, his chronicle of the early life of Tenpin Gyatso, the 14th Dalai Lama, don't fit. Each focuses on the human rather than spiritual travails of figures that are central to major world religions and, while they may bear stylistic comparison with other Scorsese films, neither sheds light on its director's conception of America. As such, I've chosen not to include them in my analysis.

2

DREAM GONE TOXIC

Is it not a very disgraceful circumstance that such a man as So-and-so should be acquiring a large property by the most infamous and odious means, and notwithstanding all the crimes of which he has been guilty, should be tolerated and abetted by your Citizens? He is a public nuisance, is he not?

Yes, sir.

A convicted liar?

Yes, sir.

He has been kicked and cuffed, and caned?

Yes, sir.

And he is utterly dishonorable, debased and profligate?

Yes, sir.

In the name of wonder, then, what is his merit?

Well, sir, he is a smart man.

A GoodFella? Charles Dickens didn't use the term, of course, in this conversation extracted from his *American Notes for*

Circulation, a record of his tour of America in 1842, but the similarities are there.

It was, as Robert K. Merton later observed, a "caricature of conflicting cultural values." Americans were, and still are, encouraged to be successful: incentives for success are everywhere. They shout at us from television commercials, jump out of magazines, scream through every media. They take the form of advertising for cars, jewelry, homes, and the countless other material goods that tantalize people. Symbols of success are abundant – for those who have the money to buy them. Or, for those who have the resourcefulness, enterprise, ingenuity, and nerve to acquire them by what Dickens called "odious means."

GoodFellas, more than any Scorsese film, is about living the American Dream. True, the Dream is present in the director's other work, most conspicuously *The Color of Money*, in which pool players' striving toward excellence becomes equated with, as the title suggests, the pursuit of greenbacks. Rupert Pupkin's motto, "Better to be king for a day than a schmuck for a lifetime," reflects the remorseless success-at-any-cost striving that drove his ultimately successful quest in *The King of Comedy*. The crooked progress of characters in films such as *Mean Streets* and *Casino* is also motivated and shaped by the Dream.

Even *The Last Waltz*, the core of which is The Band's farewell concert, tells a backstory of a troupe of aspiring Canadian musicians who move south and drag themselves from pennilessness (they tell of having to steal food from stores) to a premier rock band over sixteen years. It's practically impossible to find a Scorsese film where the Dream doesn't have a presence, usually a perverse presence.

But, think of *GoodFellas* and you think of what Kathleen Murphy calls "the American Dream gone toxic." The products of the Dream in this film are not at all like Horatio Alger's "Ragged Dick," who hauled himself out of poverty

Karen and Henry Hill are addicted to the good life, the constituent parts of which are a cornucopia of material goods, freedom from work, the admiration of others and an endless supply of any stimulant they want. They live the American Dream. (© Kobal)

with honest hard work and perseverance: most are like Henry Hill, who, as he tells the audience, only ever wanted to be a gangster and, when he became one, just wanted more of, well, everything money could buy.

The first part of Hill's aspiration is not shared by all of course, though the second might be. "The things Henry covets are nothing but the things which most men are after," notes Maurizio Viano in his 1991 review (p. 47).

Across the street from his home in a blue-collar neighborhood of New York, Hill, whose father is Irish and mother Sicilian, watches a taxi stand that functions as a front for a mafia gang. Hill is the kind of character who might have strayed out of any other Scorsese movie set in the Italian-American neighborhoods of the postwar period – the difference in this case being that Hill's story is based on a real-life memoir, *Wiseguy: Life in a mafia family*, as recounted by Nicholas Pileggi. In common with the people we see in *Mean Streets* and *Raging Bull*, Hill grows up without any of life's more obvious advantages and becomes enthralled by the people he sees enjoying what he considers the good life. Gleaming Cadillacs, mohair suits, and rolls of money as big as fists get his attention.

Tantalized, the young Hill senses a challenge as he watches the gauche display of success. The song "Rags to riches" soundtracks his early musings: "Must I forever be a beggar, whose golden dreams will not come true? Or will I go from rags to riches?" sings Tony Bennett.

Hill is enthralled by the people he sees enjoying what he considers the good life. Gleaming Cadillacs, mohair suits, and rolls of money as big as fists get his attention.

In 1955, when Hill absents himself from school in order to run errands for the mob, the school sends notification to his father, who punishes him. Hill learns an early salutary lesson when his unofficial employers forcibly instruct the mailman not to deliver any more letters from the school. Fearing for his life, the postal worker obeys and the problem is painlessly, effortlessly, but comprehensively removed. Fear can be a powerful friend.

Hill's passion is at first for the trappings of success that seem to be so easily available to gangsters. The luxuries he suspects his parents want but can never afford appear to be there for gangsters' taking. But, soon, it is the humble submission of others that convinces him: *everyone* yields to gangsters, even the forces of law and order, which, he soon realizes, are infinitely corruptible. As he later reminisces, "We paid off cops. We paid off lawyers. We paid off judges."

Once he appreciates that everyone and everything has a price, Hill's career path is clear. As John Simon puts it, in his 1991 article "The mob and the family," "He yearns to become a gangster, the way other kids want to be firemen or auto racers."

Hill wants the same ends as anyone else; his chosen means, as he sees them, are just a more efficient way of reaching them. Viano sees legal and illegal means as straightforward options in some environments; some people choose one, Hill chose the other: "Believers in the dream cannot criticize the wise guy for what he does, because after all he is just refusing to play straight in a game which is certainly not known for its fairness" (p. 47).

Hill continues his alternative education, learning at the feet of mob masters, like Paulie Cicero, the outfit's boss, and the adroit thief Jimmy Conway, who impresses with his sharp suits and generous tips. Cicero and Conway become surrogate heads of an extended family that includes relatives with names such as Freddy No Nose, Pete the Killer, and Johnny Roastbeef. The benefits of being in the family are abundant and immediate. No sooner has Hill been accepted than he reaps the rewards of money, glamour, and status. "We were treated like movie stars – with muscle," laughs Hill. "We had it *all*."

Scorsese's famous Steadicam shot tracking Hill as he enters the Copacabana nightclub encapsulates this. Accompanied by his overawed date, Hill circumvents the line-up at the club's entrance by strolling through the fire exit, across the kitchen, and into the bar area, peeling off $20 bills to respectful flunkies as he homes in on his favorite spot near the stage, which is cleared especially for him. As he moves, hands leap out begging to be shaken and a bottle of champagne arrives at his table courtesy of another guest. Hill greets his friends as a monarch might deign to acknowledge obsequious subjects. The method is as simple as that employed by every figure of influence from Genghis Khan to George W. Bush, Paul

Getty to Rupert Murdoch: make people either respect you, or be scared of you. It doesn't matter to Hill that, in his case, it's probably the latter; it looks like, feels like, and has much the same effect as the former. So, it's a reliable measure of success. "For us to live any other way was nuts. To us, those goody-good people who worked shitty jobs for bum pay-checks, who took the subway to work every day and worried about their bills were dead. They were suckers. They had no balls. If we wanted something, we just took it."

Hill's education is often bloody. He learns that to maintain status, the occasional demonstration is necessary. The erratic and irascible Tommy De Vito is exemplary: he is uproariously entertaining one second, barbarically, pitilessly, sadistically treacherous the next. When a waiter who is serving him drinks during a card game fails to execute his orders quickly enough, De Vito shoots him in the foot, then resumes the game. The same waiter, bandaged and limping, later summons up enough courage to answer back, an affront De Vito can't permit in the company of friends. This time he shoots the waiter dead.

Even Hill himself is almost caught out by De Vito's sudden eruptions, which seem spontaneous, but conceal cunning. In a memorable scene, De Vito charms the gang with one of his signature stories. Amid the laughter, Hill innocently acknowledges, "You're a funny guy." Unexpectedly, De Vito snaps back, "Whad'ya mean, funny? Funny *how?*" There follows a tense sequence in which the disconcerted Hill tries to explain that he meant to pay a compliment. "Funny like a clown? I amuse you. I'm here to fucking amuse you? What the fuck is so funny about me?" asks De Vito and, for a while, internecine bloodshed looms. Hill, either through daring or, more probably, an astute reading of the code, disarms his taunter with, "Get the fuck outta here." The tension subsides and there is a chorus of laughter. Yet the abiding impression is that it could have gone either way and De Vito has made his point: he is like Semtex – pliable, but explosive. For an encore, he playfully smashes a bottle over the head of a member of staff who advises him that the bar tab has reached $7,000.

Another eruption at a bar ends with De Vito, abetted by Conway, kicking unconscious and, later, killing a "made man," a status conferred on those who have scaled the internal hierarchy of the mob and are effectively untouchable. For this heinous failure to respect mafia codes, De Vito is later "whacked," the fatal shot administered in such a way to mutilate his face, denying his mother the chance to see his body in an open casket at his funeral.

The spell that brought Hill his charmed life appears to break when he, along with his confederates, is imprisoned for four years after a routine debt collection in Tampa, Florida, goes wrong. By this time, Hill has enough business sense to turn circumstances to his advantage and prosecutes lucrative drug dealing in prison. At the time, drugs were taboo to the mob: profiting from dealing or couriering was against mob codes. On his release, Hill is told to desist. Perhaps sensing he is invulnerable, Hill continues what becomes a remunerative sideline and, in the process, acquires a cocaine habit, once more pointing out the addictive properties of not just the good life, but all its appurtenances.

This indulgence is echoed in the behavior of several gang members after a spectacularly successful $6 million heist from a Lufthansa cargo terminal at JFK airport – "the ultimate score." Disregarding Conway's warning not to spend their cuts extravagantly, they splash out on cars, clothes, and jewelry, as if advertising their ill-gotten gains. Conway, played by De Niro, arranges fratricidal retribution for their defiance. Like a Borgia, he orders the deaths of his collaborators: one is knifed behind the wheel of his car, another skewered

on a meat hook and frozen solid in the back of a refriger-
ated delivery truck. (The 1978 JFK robbery is the subject
of another film, Robert Markowitz's *The Big Heist*, 2001, in
which Conway, or Jimmy Burke as he really was, is played by
Donald Sutherland.)

There is a thin line between conspicuous consumption
and extravagantly showy exhibitions of success, the latter
being a weakness. Conway's anger resembles that of Eddie
Felson in *The Color of Money* when his protégé flashily show-
cases his pool skills. "That wasn't pool," growls Felson. "It
was a circus." The reasoning is similar: exhibit success, but
don't let others know exactly how much you've got, whether
it's money or skill. Dispense it in a way that suits your own
purposes.

Hill is eventually expelled by Cicero after being arrested
on a drugs offense. His
efforts to calibrate dealing
with his "day job" and
domestic duties are com-
promised by a progressive
dependence on his own
merchandise. Scorsese
condenses this into one
long "Aftermath" in which
Hill multitasks feverishly, cooking ziti while organizing the
reception of a consignment of drugs, trying to sell guns, and
availing himself of his drug of choice, all the time panicking
over a hovering helicopter he suspects is tailing him.

> "A sacrificial crisis, as the last vestiges of social order and decency are obliterated in a flood of undifferentiating violence." ROBERT CASILLO ON *GOODFELLAS*

Early in the film, Conway tells Hill that one of life's
important lessons is to keep his mouth shut when questioned
by the police. After his expulsion, Hill switches to survival
mode and volunteers information in exchange for entry into
the federal witness protection program. In other words,
he is given a new identity and a fresh start as what he calls

"an average nobody, a schnook." He reflects on how much he misses being a crewmember. "It was a license to steal, a license to do anything," he laments. "The hardest thing for me was leaving the life."

And so concludes Hill's story, which plays, as *The New York Times*' Susan Linfield puts it, "like an almost madcap satire of capitalist accumulation."

While Scorsese changed names of the supporting players from Pileggi's *Wiseguy*, their real-life counterparts are identifiable (he also changed the title to avoid confusion with Brian De Palma's 1986 movie *Wise Guys*). Although the film discloses only the early phases of its collapse in 1980, the entire order of the mob family collapsed in subsequent years. "What *GoodFellas* depicts," says Robert Casillo in his *Gangster Priest*, "is a sacrificial crisis, as the last vestiges of social order and decency are obliterated." Further, "A major reason for this collapse is the prevalence of mimetic desire and its ensuing rivalries, which lead to envious hostility and retaliation" (p. 301).

How pervasive is "mimetic desire"? If Casillo means jealousy, envy, and an aspirational longing for the lifestyles and trappings of others, then it's by no means confined to the mob. Perhaps its more prevalent now than in 1980 when the film closes. The social consequences have not been so detrimental; in fact, consumer culture is predicated on our self-replenishing demands for the goods and products we see on the tv and other media and for the status enjoyed by those who dominate the headlines.

In Hill's closed culture, wanting more than he was due was a virtue that morphed into a vice. When he brags, "I didn't have to wait in line for bread at the bakery," he describes a minor privilege with major implications. As Scorsese himself told *Rolling Stone*'s Anthony DeCurtis in 1990: "It's the American way – getting treated special. It's really a film about that. It's a film about getting to a position where you don't have to wait on line to get served in a store."

When first urged to explain what he does for a living, Hill tells then girlfriend Karen he is in construction. She suspects he is lying, but her attraction to the glamorous, high-maintenance lifestyle he enjoys overpowers any reservations. Scorsese lets her explain herself through a passage in the narration. Karen recalls the frisson of excitement when handed a blood-smeared gun Hill has used to pistol-whip one of her neighbors. Once married to Henry, Karen becomes accustomed to the habitual extortion, theft, and bribery, and confesses that, "None of it seemed like crime . . . it seemed like Henry was enterprising." When police visit with a search warrant, she offers them coffee and resumes watching tv in the luxury of her expensively furnished home: "It got to be normal."

Money conquers all for Karen. She endures tiresome rituals with other gangsters' wives and the dissatisfaction of having to sacrifice her own career in exchange for a way of life. "I want to go shopping," she announces one morning, to which Hill replies, "How much do you need?" Instead of giving a figure, she gestures by shaping her thumb and index finger into opened pincers. She measures money not by amount, but by the width of the wad. This is, for her, the good life.

Once inured in the lifestyle, Karen finds it hard to do without. "I still found him attractive," she explains, somewhat meekly, in her narrative after discovering Hill has been a regular visitor at an apartment he has bought for a mistress. Even after confronting the mistress and Hill, she tolerates the arrangement, presumably in exchange for the material comforts. She remains slavishly loyal to Hill, smuggling in

drugs during his incarceration. The loyalty is not recipro-
cated: on his release, he has a coke-infused relationship with
his former mistress's best friend, Sandy.

Karen, no less than Henry, is addicted to "the life." The
constituent parts of this life are a cornucopia of material goods,
freedom from work, the admiration of others and an endless supply of any stimulant she wants. While the viewer sees only Henry Hill, picking up the morning newspaper and reluctantly adjusting to the mundane life, one guesses Karen is suffering withdrawal symptoms just as

> **Karen is addicted to "the life," the constituent parts of which are a cornucopia of material goods, freedom from work, the admiration of others, and an endless supply of any stimulant she wants.**

badly. She too yearns for what George P. Castellitto, in his
"Imagism and Martin Scorsese," calls "the excitement of the
insubstantial" (p. 26).

In 1938, Robert K. Merton, whom I quoted earlier, offered
one of the most penetrating analyses of America's obsession
with money and the success it confers, in his essay "Social
structure and anomie." Reflecting on a society emerging
groggily from the Great Depression, Merton noticed how
"the goal of monetary success is entrenched in American
culture," which was to say "that Americans are bombarded
on every side by precepts which affirm the right or, often,
the duty of retaining the goal even in the face of repeated
frustration" (p. 253).

It became everyone's bounden duty to be successful: "The
American Dream can be realized if one but has the requisite abilities," wrote Merton (p. 253). Those abilities have
to be aboveboard. Americans of the mid-twentieth century
were brought up in a culture that valued material success:

people learned to search for it and, once they'd gained it, display it – conspicuously, so that everyone could see evidence that they'd made it good. Good clothes, cars, electrical appliances: these were all commodities that were relatively recent arrivals in the 1930s marketplace and, by the 1950s, ones that people wanted, perhaps craved.

People valued their ability to consume and they were encouraged through various media, such as schools and particularly advertising, to maximize this ability – within certain boundaries. Merton's view was that the boundaries defined the legitimate means through which people could achieve their goals. There are right ways and wrong ways to achieve them. "American culture [places] great emphasis upon certain success-goals . . . without equivalent emphasis upon institutional means," wrote Merton (p. 252).

When people strove for material goods but lacked the means to get them, they often "innovated," as Merton puts it. *GoodFellas* turned the innovative adaptation into an organized program, a proper business enterprise. Hill sees perfect rationality in revealing that, whenever he and his colleagues wanted something, "we just took it."

In *GoodFellas* there is innovation within innovation, so to speak. Hill and the others are members of a subculture in which there are codes, or conventions, unwritten rules that prescribe a certain morality. But, as Merton pointed out, "in the American Dream there is no final stopping point . . . 'just a bit more' continues to operate" (p. 252). The three principals become "unable to take direction and overly given to the kind of dangerous improvisation that can derail a shoot," observes Kathleen Murphy in her 1998 article "Made men." De Vito's bar-room killing of a *capo* is a serious violation of the mob's code and it's this rather than the felony itself that brings him down. Conway cannibalizes his own crew as his mistrust of confederates approaches paranoia. Hill's

boundless rapacity prompts him to disregard explicit warn-
ings about dealing in dope.

We've all heard the tragic stories of people turning to
crime in desperation when they run out of money to pay the
bills, keep up the monthly payments, or perhaps just put food
on the table. They turn to theft, burglary, even armed robbery in the struggle to make ends meet and shield them from
the abjection of having their pecuniary failures made public.
This is not the case with Hill. He never turned to crime
out of a despairing sense of hopelessness; for him, it was a
rational business decision that led to an irrational greed.

Or was it irrational? After all, the logical extension of
Merton's argument in the 1930s is that we all pursue the
American Dream, and, whether by fair means or foul, we all,
to some extent bear responsibility for our own success. By
the 1960s, when Hill was accepted as a wiseguy, the advertising industry was in its ascendancy, its center Madison Avenue
becoming something of a symbol of modern America. The consumer society written of in the late 1950s by J.K. Galbraith in
his *The Affluent Society* and Vance Packard in *The Status Seekers*
was one in which traditional values, such as abstinence, pru-
dence, and frugality, were replaced by the ethic of well-being.

The narcissistic impulse to pay close attention to one's own
physical self was complemented by an endless supply of commodities that would, in some way, enhance, enrich, or just
improve experience. But, there was more to the consumption
than buying, using, and displaying products: there was always
a need to want more. As Christopher Lasch pointed out in his
The Culture of Narcissism, the biggest and most valuable item
ever bought was "consumption as a way of life" (p. 72).

But, it's a way of life that gradually destroys or at least
damages itself. In his smart 1999 article "Descartes goes
Hollywood," Stephen T. Asma compares *GoodFellas* with
Plato's *Republic*. The latter "builds up a narrative of how one

becomes an unjust person, showing how and why people sell their soul submitting to both political tyranny and the psychological tyranny of their own cravings" (p. B7).

In both the film and the Greek philosopher's disquisition, the life of a scoundrel is revealed to be not only attractive but exhilarating; the material benefits are liable to cause a dangerous dependency. "After parading the intoxicating pleasures and almost limitless powers of such a criminal life, both *The Republic* and *GoodFellas* reverse the picture to reveal the inner slavery beneath the flashy appearances," detects Asma.

GoodFellas illustrates Plato's two central arguments, according to Asma: "The unjust person lacks psychological peace, and no friendship exist for such people." Like Plato, Scorsese avoids introducing divine retribution, and, while Hill is eventually arrested and forced to turn evidence against his fellow gangsters, the forces of law and order are not responsible for his downfall. The more insidious menaces were indigenous. In this respect, *GoodFellas*, like *The Godfather*, effectively portrays a philosophical issue. "Those movies showed us the exhilaration, the brutality, occasionally the humour, of men who are a law unto themselves, but they were always shadowed by an awareness of the moral corrosion within," writes Anthony Quinn in his 2007 review "Heroin chic? Just say no" (p. 7).

Asma is not the only writer to draw comparisons between *GoodFellas* and Plato's masterwork. In his "*GoodFellas*, Gyges, and the good life," Dean A. Kowalski explores whether Hill and his associates really did live the "good life." Certainly Hill's own testimonies suggest that, for at least a while, he did; though Kowalski argues that this is a narrow conception. Kowalski notes that what Hill wanted most was "*appearing* to be a good person without actually being a good person" (p. 50).

Philosophers, especially Platonic scholars, have a tendency

to visualize forms, these being unchanging entities or states. The good life that Hill and company chased and – if his and Scorsese's version of events is to be accepted – found was not an abstract, universal form, but a series of expectations that were under constant revision. Once Hill had a foot in the American version of the good life, he found himself on an escalator, an endlessly circulating belt of steps driven by the motor of demand.

At thirteen, Hill was making more money than most of the adults in his neighborhoods. He could buy clothes, cars, jewelry, guns, practically anything. And the appetite for wanting more was never satiated. On the contrary, it replenished itself. It was a ferociously acquisitive and constantly moving good life, quite different from Plato's moral good life, which was fixed and permanent; much more in keeping with robust postwar American ambitiousness.

> **"In the American Dream there is no final stopping point."**
> ROBERT K. MERTON

But, for Hill and company, it was also a good life that promoted an ethic of hedonism and possession, which usurped the values of thrift, hard work, and self-denial. Increasingly large doses of externally provided stimulation and idolatry were always available.

There was neither room nor time for reflecting on the morality of what the mob was doing: at no time in the movie does Hill hint at a troubled conscience. He hears no inner voice whispering, "This is wrong," as he assists in beatings or murders. He laughs out loud when Conway throttles a remiss debtor and when De Vito attacks an innocent bar worker. He doesn't think twice about keeping his wife and mistresses like well-fed cattle for his own personal use and periodic abuse. The only priority is Henry Hill.

Progressively, Hill disregards what Julie Salamon in *The Wall Street Journal* calls "the moral compass that makes perfect sense within their [the crewmembers'] universe and to no one at all anywhere else" and relies on his personal lodestone for guidance – a self-justifying practice shared by many other Scorsese characters, as we will see. The family that cared and provided for him during his early years with the mob is eventually abandoned as he pursues his own entrepreneurial ventures, and, in his final act of treachery, he commits the most iniquitous of sins when he rats on his crew.

The only morality informing Hill's mercantile self-improvement is that contained in the proverb, "full speed ahead and the devil take the hindmost." While his early education was to keep his mouth shut, he learned a more valuable lesson: look after your own interests rather than those of others. This is presumably what Murphy has in mind by "the American Dream gone toxic," though it could be argued that Hill's was an excessive purification of the Dream rather than a contamination of it.

"Where *The Godfather* examined the pyramid of power from the viewpoint of the pharaohs for whom it is intended, *GoodFellas* is down with the slaves who tote the bricks, picking up their own lavish rewards while they are so doing." The comparison is that of Tom Milne, writing in 1990 (and presumably forgetting that slaves' rewards were never lavish). "While *The Godfather* tried to blueprint the pyramid systematically erected out of carefully sculptured blocks of honour and respect, *GoodFellas* sets out to explore the profit motive that makes those qualities so eminently desirable" (p. 356).

For Scorsese, America is not the land of the pharaohs but a place where the pursuit of wealth, freedom, and liberty often takes a less uplifting form than it's supposed to.

GoodFellas is but one of a number of Scorsese's films based on innovative routes to profitability. *Italianamerican*, his early documentary featuring his parents reminiscing about life in New York's Little Italy in the 1950s, suggests how culturally diverse groups disregarded differences in the face of a common objective – to climb the ladder of meritocracy in the new land.

The reminders of American affluence bounce back in 1964's *It's Not Just You, Murray!*, in which a petty crook boasts of his expensive car and clothes, all made possible by opportunistic enterprise, work, and the help of a good friend (who is also having an affair with his wife). "Do you see this tie? Fifty bucks. Do you see these shoes? Seventy-five bucks," Murray starts to catalog his possessions, ultimately pronouncing, "We are very happy."

But it was in *Mean Streets* where Scorsese first developed his idea that, for some ambitious rogues, innovation was not just an option, but the only option. "*Mean Streets* dealt with the American Dream, according to which everybody thinks they can get rich quick, and if they can't do it by legal means, then they'll do it by illegal ones," reflects Scorsese, offering clues about the thought processes of his central characters: "These guys' idea of making money, maybe a million or two, is by stealing, beating or cheating someone out of it. It's much sweeter, much better than actually earning it" (quoted in Thompson and Christie, p. 47).

The same thought goes through the mind of Eddie Felson, in *The Color of Money*: "Money won is twice as sweet as money earned," he reminds his trainee pool hustler, Vincent Lauria. The logic guides what Scorsese calls a "disruption of values," but one curiously still emblematic of America.

The men in *Mean Streets* are all enterprising: they're convinced that initiative, self-reliance, and responsibility will compensate for the moral flaws in their approach to life. But, in Milne's terms, they are brick-bearing slaves and, as such, a shared experience of toiling holds them together. Well, almost: the exception is the freewheeling Johnny Boy, who has no sense of obligation to his Italian-American brothers, no work ethic, and whose idea of initiative is to borrow money from usurers without paying them back. His fecklessness undermines his close friend Charlie, for whom a glittering prize awaits.

Charlie's uncle, a local mob boss, promises him a restaurant. But he is counting the days anxiously till he takes over. Johnny Boy owes $3,000 to Michael, a loan shark, who is also a friend of Charlie's. Michael warns Charlie about the gruesome fate that awaits reneging debtors and Charlie passes on the warning to Johnny Boy, who advises his only chance of repaying the debt is for Charlie to ask his uncle for a loan. This would ruin Charlie's credibility with his uncle, who already considers hotheaded Johnny Boy a "half-crazy" menace. "Honorable men go with honorable men," his uncle advises.

Charlie's situation is further complicated by his affair with Charlie's cousin Teresa, who has epilepsy, a neurological disorder interpreted by Charlie's uncle as "sick in the head." Charlie's ambitions overpower his emotions and he tells Teresa they have to part. But the link of kinship with Johnny Boy is tougher to break and he contrives a meeting at which his friend can structure a repayments schedule with Michael. Being impervious to rational planning, Johnny Boy just spits insults, calling Michael a jerk-off for being gullible enough to loan him the money in the first place.

Scorsese calls the film "an anthropological or sociological tract," though the yarn of dangerous companionship in Little Italy can also be read as a parable: even among rulebreakers, there are rules and those who ignore them perish. Johnny Boy tries to flee to Brooklyn, but is tracked down

and shot while Michael watches, his eyes filled with vengeance mixed with regret.

There's another aspect to the parable and one that's
repeated in *GoodFellas*. "It's business, it's work, it's organization," Charlie hears from his friends. He knows that, if he's
going to succeed, he has to be selfish, look out for himself,
and put his own interests before others'. Individualism is not
always an easy mode of conduct in a neighborhood that thrives
off collective enterprise, as Henry Hill divined. This is a theme
that also recurs in later Scorsese works, particularly *Casino* and
The Departed, which we will move to in Chapter 3. It's also
something of a motif of America from the 1960s: the organization, whether criminal or legitimate, allowed little or no room
for mavericks who refused to conform, and dealt severely with
renegades who threatened its structure or functions. Somehow
individuals have to be brought into harmony with the system.

In his 1990 article "Reign of terror," Brian D. Johnson
writes, "Scorsese mirrors the larger evolution of American culture" (p. 55). In all the films covered in this chapter,
Scorsese reaffirms central American values, especially
free enterprise, but also the nuclear family, patriotism,
and libertarianism, and indicates how they have

> **Scorsese's men grow up in a milieu that encourages enterprise but rarely provides the raw material to commission it.**

been adapted to suit particular circumstances. Some might say
they're distorted, though the films suggest otherwise.

Mean Streets, like *GoodFellas*, is a study of innovative free
spirits, who recognize the rules, obey them when it suits them,
but don't allow them to get in their way. Figures like Hill
and Charlie could have been pulled straight out of Merton's
study. To repeat Merton's statement above: "American culture [places] great emphasis upon certain success-goals . . .

without equivalent emphasis upon institutional means." The success-goals, even then, were "wealth and power."

Scorsese's men grow up in a milieu that encourages enterprise but rarely provides the raw material to commission it. Initiative and resourcefulness are in abundance; education, training, and capital are not. These men's pursuit of the American Dream is an inventive if imperfect adaptation; as Merton described it, "they abandon institutional means while retaining the success-aspiration" (p. 261).

Gangsters are cut from the same cloth as ordinary citizens: they want money and are looking for the most reasonable ways of getting it. Violence is not one of those ways; or, if it is, it has severe limitations. As Hill explains to Karen when she expresses concern about his endeavors, "Nobody goes to jail unless they want to, unless they make themselves get caught. They don't have things organized. I know what I'm doing: I got things organized with these guys. You know who goes to jail? Nigga stick-up men. That's who. You know why they get caught? Because they fall asleep in the getaway car."

By contrast, Hill sees his own enterprise as a calculated exercise in which every risk has been assessed and minimized. In this context, violence is like a free radical – highly reactive, short-lived, and with unpredictable consequences. The main task is to make money; killing or hurting people is an unwanted, but regrettably necessary, distraction.

In *GoodFellas*, violence is, for the most part, normalized, that is, part of a normal condition or state. It's in the professional activity of being a gangster. "It was business," Hill reminds the audience, just as Charlie had been reminded in *Mean Streets*. The crew approaches violence and death as football players might approach torn tendons, or a bank teller's paper cuts – inconveniences, but part of the job.

So when Tommy De Vito kills waiters or made men out of other, non-business, motives, he elicits different responses, depending on the position in the mob hierarchy. Those in upper echelons condemn the excessive violence and instigate quasi-judicial procedures. De Vito's fellow crewmembers are upset, though only by the mess he creates by leaving blood-drenched dead bodies. They have become desensitized to the suffering of death. In a sense, so has the audience.

"*GoodFellas* is like a history of postwar American consumer culture, the evolution of culture style," Scorsese explained to Gavin Smith in 1998. "There's a kind of innocent mischief and charm to the worldliness. But then at a certain point it becomes corrupt" (p. 69).

At what point? When the film begins in the 1950s, the innocent mischief involves the physical intimidation of a harmless postal worker and a man's being shot in the arm (the young Hill is reprimanded for using clean aprons as impromptu bandages when he assists him). In the same period, Jimmy Conway is introduced respectfully as some-one who was "locked up at eleven, doing hits for the mob at sixteen." In his narrative, Hill seems to concur with Scorsese when he reflects, "It was a glorious time."

Later, things get more serious: some killings are willful and planned, while others are just impulsive. The former are what psychologists call instrumental: they serve as a means in pursuing a goal. Killing, in this sense, rarely poses a moral problem; its consequences are what matters. Clearing up, hiding evidence, avoiding retribution: these are the issues that concentrate the mind of the wiseguys, not the many acts of habitual violence they either observe or instigate. Scorsese himself, when talking to Smith, is oddly approving: "The morality – you know, there's none, there's none. Completely amoral. It's just wonderful" (p. 69).

Setting aside Scorsese's own evaluation, we can understand

his reasoning. In the 1950s and 1960s, perhaps before drug dealing became a mainstay of organized crime, a "moral code" as he calls it governed the behavior of gangsters. So, the subculture depicted in *GoodFellas* is perhaps not "amoral," if by this we assume a lack of principles, standards, or scruples; all these exist, though in an exaggerated or distorted shape.

Whether or not De Vito is a spleenful sadist, an out-and-out psychopath, or a product of an abusive background is not a question we can answer. But we are sure "he kills for reasons which are well beyond the mafia systemic violence," as Arthur Gilbert puts it in his 2004 paper "Godfathers, GoodFellas, and Reservoir Dogs." "When he is murdered by the mafia it is because in the world of mafia violence there is a vast difference between on the job killing and random and gratuitous violence" (p. 11).

Scorsese rarely acts like a traffic cop, pointing us to the right or wrong place, ethically: if we find ourselves at crossroads, we make the decisions about which way to go. Anyway, *GoodFellas'* traffic moves at such a lick that we don't have much time to reflect whether the violence is condonable. It just happens. And maybe that is the point: violence, whether systemic or random, to use Gilbert's distinction, just happens in America. It always has.

There is a tiny moment in the film that serves to establish a link, however tenuous, between the stylized violence on the screen and the kind most of us encounter, perhaps in an incidental way. De Vito is invited to an initiation to "make" him – advance him into the mafia inner circle of *Uomini D'onore*. When Conway calls from a payphone to congratulate him, he hears that there has been a problem, meaning that the invitation was a subterfuge: De Vito has been whacked for his earlier infringement of mob code.

Conway, in an uncharacteristic release of strong emotion, repeatedly slams the handset into the box. It's a short eruption and it quickly subsides as Hill rushes to console him. Remember Hill's introductory remarks about Conway: "Hits never bothered Jimmy." He'd been killing for money since he was sixteen; yet he's still capable of the kind of uncontrolled rushes of aggression that most of us have felt surging inside us at some time. And, even if we haven't taken it out on a phonebox, few of us have not witnessed remnants of others' rages, perhaps in the form of wrecked payphones.

It's these familiar moments rather than the Grand Guignol scenes that prompt Ian Christie, in his 2006 article "Scorsese: Faith under pressure," to wonder, "is it in our nature to be compassionate, or to deal with problems by violence?" While Christie doesn't provide an answer, his assumption is that Scorsese's films provide one. But, is it an accurate assumption?

In *GoodFellas*, no less than his other ventures into gang territory, Scorsese is at pains to show that rationality and irrationality are companions. For every sensible, well-executed, profit-oriented maneuver, there is an accompanying piece of illogical foolishness. A history-making heist that works like a $100,000

Hill learned early on that fear of violence is the potent emotional response that successful gangsters engender in others.

TAGHeuer chronograph is followed by a senseless splurge that effectively advertises the perpetrators. An evening out that starts promisingly disintegrates into an exchange of insults and, later, ends with a killing that subverts moral codes and leads to an execution.

Violence is unwelcome; its function is as a final payload. As Scorsese explained to Susan Linfield of *The New York Times*, "The violence is not the main thing – it's just a way to consolidate power to get the money." In other words, as

Hill learned early on in his socialization, fear of violence is the potent emotional response that successful gangsters engender in others. Fear or respect: it didn't make much difference. What *is* important is the perception that, if necessary, violence can and will be used. This is entirely rational. The actual use of violence is not. Not in the gangster milieu, not in any other.

Raymond Durgnat ends his 1991 "The gangster file" review with a puzzling question: "How far does gangster amorality/violence/greed require some Ingredient X, or some special, somehow defective, character structure; or how far is callous amorality normal, natural, rational and sane?" (p. 96). Put simply: is what the wise guys do normal?

Scorsese's audiences become guilt-free voyeurs. It's as if Scorsese is selling them a tour into parts of America that are off-limits in the usual course of things. "Come with me to the mean streets of America, where the usual rules don't apply. You can see how these fascinating Italian Americans live out their daily lives in a gripping culture of crime, corruption and all-round wickedness. And, when you've finished watching the film, you can return to the safety of your urban dwellings, content in the knowledge that these kinds of characters will never bother you." Though perhaps with the disturbing suspicion that, as Stanley Kauffmann puts it in his 1990 review "Blood money," "there's a touch of the awestruck Henry Hill in all of us."

But there is a different sales pitch: "Welcome to America. Not the one you might recognize, but America nonetheless. This is a world that you might not like, but it will fascinate you just the same. After the film, you'll go home to a very different world. But with an unsettling reminder: this is still America. This vicious culture of unrestrained avarice, prolific killing and promiscuous brutality is just as much part of this country as any other. In fact, it's like one of those Hall

of Mirrors at the fairground that distorts images into shock-
ing, sometimes horrific resemblances. They don't really look
like us, but we know they're our likeness."

GoodFellas runs from the mid-1950s to 1980. It was a period in
history when the civil rights movement surfaced and prompted
the desegregation of American society, though the world of
Hill et al. is conspicuously segregated. In fact, the only African
American crewmember is Stacks Edwards, played by Samuel
L. Jackson, who becomes expendable and is executed by De
Vito in his own apartment. Edwards' insignificance is empha-
sized when De Vito jokes about making coffee "to go" in the
immediate aftermath of the briskly efficient killing.

The period also witnessed significant changes in the legal
and social status of women. Greater availability of contracep-
tion and abortion released
women to explore possi-
bilities undreamed of as
recently as the 1960s,
though there is no sug-
gestion of this in the film.
The women never express
any desire other than to be kept: they are housewives in the
proper sense of the word – their occupation is caring for their
families, managing household affairs, and doing household
chores.

"The film is about a world willed into being by obsessive desire."
LESLEY STERN ON *GOODFELLAS*

For this they are rewarded with any material comfort
they want and an inexhaustible supply of money. This is
made clear to Hill when, after an awkward first date, he
stands Karen up and asks to make amends by going out with
her again. "It'll cost you," she warns him. Eventually, she
becomes a tragic figure, a cocooned wife of a philanderer,
who remains steadfast and even risks her own freedom by

assisting his prison trafficking operations. (In reality, Hill and his wife later divorced.)

Amid these changes, the United States has continued its all-conquering quest for economic leadership. We find this theme miniaturized in *GoodFellas*. In Scorsese's vision, Middle America is malicious, avaricious, and insatiable in its search for life's most obvious form of enrichment. As Lesley Stern, writes in her *The Scorsese Connection*, "The film is about a world willed into being by obsessive desire, it's about the reality of fantasy" (p. 9).

The film was released in 1990 at the start of a decade of cultural change. Among the decade's early highlights were the first Gulf War, the first military conflict to be covered "live" by television (in this case, CNN), and the Mike Tyson rape trial of 1992, which was the first great *cause célèbre* of the 1990s. It was followed and even overshadowed by the O.J. Simpson trial. Within months of the film's release, the video of four white LAPD officers beating African American Rodney King assumed iconic status. A year later, in 1992, the acquittal of the police officers provoked riots in several major American cities. In a sense, these events served as reminders that the kind of violence and aggression Scorsese had depicted were more endemic than even his film suggested. In fact, the film might be accused of understatement.

Unlike *The Godfather*, to which it has often been compared, *GoodFellas* did not give rise to a series of sequels. At least, not officially: five years after its release, Scorsese's *Casino* was received as a functional equivalent of "GoodFellas II." Again, De Niro and Pesci took lead roles and stayed close to their original characters; for all the similarities, however, the film offered a rather different scope on crime in America, as we will see in the next chapter.

Perhaps the closest dramatic equivalent to *GoodFellas* was the HBO television series "The Sopranos," which started in 1999 and which was described by *The Washington Post*'s Ann Hornaday as "a direct descendant." (I'll return to "The Sopranos" in the Conclusion.) Like Scorsese, its creator David Chase scoured away the surface mythical or heroic elements of the classic mafia stories, revealing the humdrum life of a mafia boss in therapy. The links with *GoodFellas* were deliberately forged. Lorraine Bracco, who played Karen in *GoodFellas*, appeared in "The Sopranos" as a psychotherapist. Michael Imperioli, who was Spider, the hapless waiter who was shot in the foot then killed by De Vito, returned, this time as a Hill-type Mafioso understudy. Indeed, as Deborah L. Jaramillo points out in her 2002 article "The family racket," in one episode Imperioli "shoots a bakery clerk's foot, clearly referencing his own character's fate in *GoodFellas*" (p. 69).

In *GoodFellas*, Scorsese plants the lawbreaking seed deep in the American earth: the characters grow from the same soil as the financiers of Oliver Stone's *Wall Street* (1987), the politicians of Tim Robbins' *Bob Roberts* (1992), and the industrial workers of Paul Schrader's *Blue Collar* (1978), none of them disaffected social outcasts, all quite normal. And all, in their own ways, both products and representatives of America.

3

WHOSE LAW? WHAT ORDER?

When I was your age, they'd say: you become cops, or crimi-nals. What I'm saying is this: when you're facing a loaded gun, what's the difference?

Frank Costello poses this as a sort of moral conundrum, though the answer seems obvious: it depends who *you* are.

So when Colin Sullivan stares at a gun, he frantically tells his assailant, "Only one of us is a cop here, Bill . . . no one knows who you fucking are. I'm a sergeant in the Massachusetts State Police. Who the fuck are you? I arrest you." Billy Costigan, who holds the gun, is unmoved. "You arrest me, uh?" he mocks as he secures handcuffs on Sullivan. Costigan has tricked him into a meeting on the roof of an empty building in downtown Boston; there are no wit-nesses. "Go ahead, shoot a cop," invites Sullivan. "See what happens."

Sullivan tries to disabuse Costigan of ideas that he is a vil-lain masquerading as a hero. He can see why Costigan thinks he's mixed-up with known criminals and insists Boston's organized crime boss Frank Costello was his informant not confederate. "He was a rat . . . he was working *for me*." The unexpected arrival of a gun-carrying police officer brings some relief to Sullivan. "Drop your weapon and step away from Sergeant Sullivan!" orders Trooper Brown, pointing his gun at Costigan.

Costigan reminds Brown, "You know who I am. . . . He's Costello's rat, alright?" Brown doesn't know whom to believe. Can his sergeant really be the crime boss's informant? Or is his trusted friend and former police colleague desperately trying to buy time? So he repeats his instruction to drop the weapon, whereupon Costigan hauls his captive to the elevator, being careful not to provoke Brown into shooting.

Unbeknown to either, another cop, named Barrigan, is waiting below and, as the arriving elevator's doors part, he squeezes off a shot into Costigan's head. "You think you were the only one he [Costello] had on the inside?" Barrigan inquires rhetorically before attaching the rider, "Costello was going to sell us to the FBI. It's you and me now, you understand? We gotta take care of each other." Sullivan picks up Costigan's gun, wipes it off and, as Barrigan turns away, clinically shoots him in the head.

Sullivan was telling the truth: he *is* a cop. Costigan's suspicions were also true: he *was* an informant for Costello. "Was" because he killed Costello, his former boss. Costigan was also a law enforcement officer, though he was attached to an elite Special Investigations Unit (SIU), and had been working deep undercover, having spent time in prison before insinuating himself into Costello's organization. Only the two officers who mandated his duty know he was actually a police officer. "We're the only two people on the face of this earth who know you're a cop," he was reminded.

After his death, this is revealed and he receives an honorable burial, with an ironic recommendation from Costello – his killer – that he is awarded the Medal of Merit. The priest's graveside oratory closes with, "May his soul and the souls of all the faithful departed through the mercy of God rest in peace." Hence the title of Scorsese's film.

In *The Departed*, Scorsese suggests that good and bad alike all meet their maker sooner rather than later. It's how they coexist until that point that demands examination. The final scene sees a self-satisfied Sullivan arriving home at his lavish Beacon Hill condominium with a view of the Boston State House's golden dome ("If you move in, you're upper-class by Tuesday," the real estate agent tells him).

Whose law? What order? These are the questions that Scorsese has asked many times.

An SIU agent is waiting for him and shoots him in the head. This appears to be no more than his just deserts for a life of duplicity-within-duplicities. He has deceived the police, his partner, who is carrying his child, Costello, who has groomed and taken care of him since he was a boy ("You wanna earn a little extra money? You come on by") and for whom he has infiltrated the police force, and the public whom he ostensibly serves. He is, after all, charged with the responsibility of upholding law and order.

Costigan is a more straightforward case: working-class family from the Irish district of South Boston, his father a man of rectitude who resisted Costello's attempts to draw him into crime, uncle a less righteous character who involved himself with Costello, but who becomes retroactively useful as a reference when worming his way into the underworld. Costigan positions himself on the side of the law, though, while undercover, he's not averse to participating in crime, or to harming those who threaten to expose him.

This is a place "Where every cop is a criminal," as Brian D. Johnson puts it in the title of his 2006 review. The line is from the Rolling Stones' 1968 track "Sympathy for the devil" and it's followed by "and all the sinners saints." The couplet captures Scorsese's vision of law and order in America. As Scorsese puts it himself in the documentary *Stranger Than Fiction* (directed by Barbara Toennies and Gidion Phillips, 2007), "In terms of black and white, there isn't any – it's *all gray*."

Or, to put it another way, birds of a feather do not flock together: hawks fly with doves and doves mix with hawks – and, to paraphrase Costello's righthand man, Archie French, rats are everywhere. The term "rat" has had a special resonance in American crime drama ever since James Cagney's fabled "You dirty rat" (fabled because his actual words in Roy Del Ruth's 1931 film *Blonde Crazy* were, "That dirty, double-crossing rat"). There is a tradition of films concerned with the interpenetration of criminals and crimefighters, law-breakers and law enforcers.

Whose law? What order? These are the questions that Scorsese has asked many times, starting perhaps with his 1964 New York University project *It's Not Just You, Murray!*, which tells of a petty criminal whose rise is abetted by a friend, who is also ripping him off and sleeping with his wife. In this and several subsequent films, including *Mean Streets* and *GoodFellas*, Scorsese approaches crime as economic activity. Organized crime is like many other American industries: its laws are those of supply and demand.

The Departed was adapted from Hong Kong-based *Infernal Affairs*, directed by Andrew Lau Wai and Alan Mak in 2002, which engendered both a prequel and a sequel. Scorsese's film is a stand-alone, though it invites elaboration, particularly about Frank Costello, who exudes sometimes the bonhomie of a friendly neighborhood philosopher ("In this country, it doesn't add inches to your dick to get a life sentence"), and sometimes the venom of a scorpion ("One of us has to die; with me it tends to be the other guy").

There is little surprise when it's revealed that he has been an FBI stool pigeon all along. If indeed, he has: the plot is so full of subterfuge, misinformation, and *dis*information that it's possible that Costello is just being maligned – or commended, depending on your perspective. What we do know for sure is that the Costello character bears a pronounced resemblance to a real person who, if alive, is still on the lam.

James "Whitey" Bulger was a member of a criminal outfit that controlled gambling and protection rackets in Boston. At some point in the early 1970s, he brokered a deal with the FBI, the terms of which provided him with a degree of immunity in exchange for key information on criminal activity. In the terms used habitually in *The Departed*, he was a rat. This allowed him to eliminate rival gang members and expand into loan sharking, gambling, and robbery with impunity.

In the 1980s, when drugs were a highly profitable line of business, he diversified into cocaine and marijuana trafficking, but not heroin. There might have been ethical or practical considerations behind this decision, but, either way, those who ignored it were usually punished. Bulger was forced to flee his empire in 1994 after the Drugs Enforcement Administration, the Massachusetts State Police, and the Boston Police Department combined in a joint task force to investigate his gambling operations. The FBI was specifically excluded, thus depriving Bulger of his key intelligence and protection. Whether or not Bulger ever planted a "mole" inside the Boston or Massachusetts State Police organizations is not documented.

Maybe Scorsese, or his writer William Monahan, didn't consciously model Costello on Bulger. But there are obvious parallels and one significant divergence. In the film, Costigan reckons, "Costello recorded everything. He put all the tapes in a little box and kept it with his lawyer. That was his insurance." Presumably, Bulger didn't take this precaution – which is why he is currently on the FBI's "Most Wanted" register (along with Osama Bin Laden).

The film is rather like a Rorschach test, in which a symmetrical inkblot is presented to someone, who is then asked to describe what the pattern resembles or suggests. The characters not the audiences are asked for their descriptions. So, where Sullivan, played by Matt Damon, sees a corrupt and endlessly compromised police in which straight and crooked cops watch each other's backs, but would kill each other if their own survival depended on it, Costigan sees a basically wholesome institution which has been forced to sacrifice a few good men

In Scorsese's America, no one can get through a working day without intersecting with some form of criminal activity.

in order to get results. Despite this, Costigan is not ingenuous: he loathes some of his peers and thinks they are delivering him to slaughter by insisting he remains undercover. "When you gonna take Costello, eh?" he asks a year after infiltrating the gang. "What's wrong with taking him on one of the million felonies that either you've seen him or I've seen him do. . . . The guy fucking murdered somebody and you don't fucking take him. What are you waiting for?"

The answer of his superior officer is not at all convincing: "We're building a case; it takes time." In the meantime, Costigan, played by Leonardo DiCaprio, is not just a witness to, but a perpetrator of, serious crimes, some involving killing. The ends may justify the means. Yet, for Costigan, those means are only marginally, if at all, better than the ends he seeks. When Costello does meet his end, it's at the hands of the very person he'd entrusted as his man on the inside – Sullivan, who also murders fellow police officers before joining them in the vestibule of the departed.

Crime is everywhere: in Scorsese's America, no one can get through a working day without intersecting with some form of criminal activity. The operations or ownership of trucking companies, shippers and freighters and construction firms have all been influenced by organized crime. So shopping for food, or clothes, or even just living in a home might implicate someone with organized crime, albeit unknowingly. You don't have to patronize prostitutes, bet on numbers, or borrow from loansharks to be involved. It's practically impossible not to be.

It's an anodyne observation: crime is normal. It certainly is in Scorsese's America. Is this a problem? It depends. To be sure, the likes of Costello, Henry Hill, Murray, and the other out-and-out rule-breakers in Scorsese's lens are problems to law enforcement agencies. But from their point of view, law enforcement agents are the problem.

In *GoodFellas* and his earlier ventures, Scorsese examined the rites of passage into a criminal career and the day-to-day activities of life in the mob. Films such as *Who's That Knocking at My Door?* and *Mean Streets* inspected minor gangsters, wannabes, or hangers-on itching to crack the big time. In these films, cops were usually paid off. *The Departed* presents a rather different image of a society in which law and order didn't just coexist with crime; they have a mutually beneficial relationship and interact in a close association. Typically, the relationship is of advantage to both.

When Paulie Cicero in *GoodFellas* recounts how he and his accomplices "offered protection for people who can't go to the cops," and Henry Hill explains that, to ensure their own protection, "We paid off cops, we paid off lawyers, we paid off judges. Everybody had their hands out. Everything was for the taking," they refer to relatively primitive arrangements. Organized crime in America now has more systemic provisions. The conditions under which these provisions arose and prospered are those of scarcity: where there is demand, but no legal supply.

Prohibition was the template. When, in 1920, the US federal government decreed that alcohol was illicit, it effectively commissioned the growth and prosperity of organized crime. Millions wanted the scarce commodity and underworld racketeers responded by producing and distributing bootleg liquor. In the previous fifty years, migrants had been disembarking at American ports at a rate of over a quarter-of-a-million per year, most crystallizing into ethnic groups. Established groups, such as Irish and Jewish, were joined by "new immigrants" from central and southern Europe, each developing their own criminal subcultures. Italians had been distilling their own liquor and were well placed to capitalize on the market opened up by Prohibition. But, to capitalize effectively, they needed to get organized, and this meant improving the efficiency of production and transportation, which, in turn, meant securing the cooperation of law enforcement officials.

By the end of Prohibition in 1933, organized crime was well established and Italian crime syndicates had become synonymous with the mafia. This notorious organization has origins in Sicily and, while some argue its deep roots lie in a secret society of the ninth century, its surge to prominence in the US is traceable to its success in mobilizing disparate gangs into a structured hierarchy of "families," each with quasi-military ranks. The repeal of Prohibition, far from ending the mafia's operations, forced it to consider how it could diversify into ostensibly legitimate businesses, which could serve either as fronts for other ventures or as investment vehicles for laundering money appropriated illicitly.

The provision of in-demand but forbidden services and commodities was still a principal venture. Gambling and usury were the main components of what was, by the 1940s, an enterprise not unlike legitimate forms of commerce and industry. This was confirmed officially in 1950–1 when the findings of Senator Estes Kefauver's commission on organized crime in interstate commerce were heard on "live" television. Kefauver concluded there was "a nationwide crime syndicate."

Unlike other forms of crime, the mafia was pervasive: its influence was spread throughout American society. Because its reach had extended deeply into legal businesses, particularly labor-intensive businesses such as construction, trucking, and manufacturing, the mafia had begun to associate with organized labor, including the Teamsters, one of the nation's largest unions.

From 1957, Jimmy Hoffa was President of the Teamsters. After ten years of dubious business transactions, often with members of organized crime families, Hoffa was convicted of fraud, looting pension funds, and attempting to bribe a federal court judge. President Richard Nixon commuted his sentence; he was released in 1971 and disappeared mysteriously in 1975, rumored to have been the victim of a mob hit (and subject of a 1992 movie directed by Danny De Vito, *Hoffa*, in which he is played by Jack Nicholson, who also plays Frank Costello in *The Departed*).

Having ties with organized labor was crucial to the mafia's expansion into legitimate business. So, in 1946, when Benjamin "Bugsy" Siegel built what was then a breathtakingly extravagant and ostentatious casino known as The Flamingo in Las Vegas, Nevada – the only state that permitted legal gambling – he needed the cooperation of the unions. By the time of Frank "Lefty" Rosenthal's appearance in Vegas in the early 1970s, The Strip was aglow with monstrously illuminated Towers of Babel. And the moral landscape was as flat as the Nevada desert.

Rosenthal was closely involved with the mafia, though, as a Jew, he could never be a made man. He was a skilled sports handicapper and made a decent living in his native Chicago before the mob asked him to move to Vegas, where he would effectively run several casinos on its behalf. Officially, he didn't hold the requisite gaming license that would enable him to run a casino, but it was widely known that he made the operational decisions. For a while, he even hosted a local television talk show. Such was his reputation that guests such as Frank Sinatra joined him on the show. The mob took a dim view of this kind of exhibitionism and Rosenthal would have realized that he was inviting censure.

Like Whitey Bulger, Lefty Rosenthal was perfect raw material for Scorsese: a real-life character with something of a mythology surrounding him; a man with a less than impeccable record, but who was uncannily adept at evading his enemies. Rosenthal narrowly escaped death when his car exploded as he turned its ignition. Presciently, he had a bomb-proof metal plate under the driver's side seat. Eventually, he was banished from Vegas, whereupon he resumed sports betting for a living at first in San Diego, California, then in Boca Raton, Florida. He died in 2008, aged 79.

Rosenthal's outwardly glamorous life in Vegas concealed a hellish private life. He and his wife had a turbulent marriage and, when they divorced, she absconded with a chunk of his money. She died aged 46 from a suspected overdose of Valium, cocaine, and whiskey.

Rosenthal is a central figure of Nicholas Pileggi's book *Casino: Love and honor in Las Vegas*, which is the source of Scorsese's film *Casino*. In the latter, Rosenthal becomes Sam "Ace"

"I got a hundred million a year going through the place," says a self-satisfied Sam Rothstein, whose plan is to launder ill-gotten gains into legitimate operations. For Rothstein, the line between legal and illegal activity is indistinct. (© Kobal)

Rothstein, whose background is identical to Rosenthal's, except that he hails from Kansas City rather than Chicago, both Midwestern cities, of course. The idea is that the Vegas casinos appear to be owned and run by locals, though in reality, they are controlled by the mob in the Midwest. (As well as authoring *Casino*, Pileggi, with Scorsese, co-wrote the screenplay of *GoodFellas*.)

The film shows the smooth functioning of an elegant scheme, suitcases heaving with millions of dollars carried effortlessly from the casinos, onto planes and into offices incongruously situated behind a Kansas City fruit produce store. It is, to borrow a phrase used by *Maclean's* Brian D. Johnson in 2006, "legalized robbery."

The beauty of the system – and it seems fair to call it a "system" – was that the Tangiers casino, which is really run by Rothstein, appears to be in the control of Philip Green, a corporate type with an unblemished record, whose face has been on the cover of *Business Week* magazine and who has even played golf with the President.

Green doesn't realize that the union is tied up with the Midwest mob. He is strictly a front man for a lucrative mafia collaboration with the Teamsters. Green never sees, less still meets, the crime bosses, or *capos*, who stayed in the safety of the Midwest, happy to take receipt of suitcases full of cash, this being the result of a regular skim from the counting rooms of the casinos. "These are the guys who secretly controlled Las Vegas," the voiceover tells us, "because they controlled the Teamsters' Union, and that's where you had to go if you wanted to borrow money to buy a casino."

> **"Anywhere else in the country, I was a bookie, a gambler, always looking over my shoulder, hassled by cops, day and night. But here, I'm 'Mr. Sam Rothstein.'"** SAM ROTHSTEIN IN *CASINO*

As in *The Departed*, there is a kind of interface, an area where two systems, or organizations, meet and interact; there is a common boundary between crime and lawfulness but it's a permeable one. Upright citizens receive illegally obtained money, which has its source in the hard-earned cash of blue-collar workers, while professional criminals dispense money to union leaders, lawyers, politicians, agents of law enforcement, and other irreproachable types. When Rothstein calls Vegas "kickback city," he means that everybody, from the politicians to valet parkers, expects cash inducements.

He's happy to pay out small and, occasionally, substantial sums; he looks on these bribes as his way out of one part of America and his entry to another. "Anywhere else in the country, I was a bookie, a gambler, always looking over my shoulder, hassled by cops, day and night. But here, I'm 'Mr. Sam Rothstein.' I'm not only legitimate, but running a casino."

As one expects from a Scorsese film, there is a tale of lust, greed, and wantonness with the kind of innovation-within-innovation that propelled the action of *GoodFellas*. Once more Joe Pesci's character brings the irrationality that threatens to disrupt the ordered scheme established and maintained by Rothstein, played by De Niro. Pesci's Nicky Santoro is, for intents and purposes, a clone of *GoodFellas'* Tommy De Vito. He comes from the same neighborhood as Rothstein, has the same mob connections, and shares the same passion for making money. But he sneers at the way Rothstein has shed his old values in his search for respectability. For Santoro, Vegas is a cornucopia guarded by saps. Bankers, politicians, corporate heads – none of them are a match for Santoro. So, when he menaces a bank manager and Rothstein, dismayed, asks him, "Where's your head?" Santoro reacts explosively, "Where's my head? Where's *your* fucking balls?"

Rational explanations cut no ice. "I'm responsible for thousands of people. I got a hundred million [dollars] a year going through the place. It's all over." Santoro doesn't grasp Rothstein's plan, which is to launder ill-gotten gains into legitimate operations; or, perhaps he grasps it, but can't stomach the idea of going completely legit. "Because Nicky enjoyed being a gangster, and he didn't give a damn who knew it," explains Rothstein.

Santoro remains incredulous. "A million times I wanted to yell in his fucking ear: 'This is Las Vegas! We're supposed to be out here robbing, you dumb fucking Hebe.'" (Santoro and others habitually use this and other anti-Semitic epithets in reference to Rothstein.) Rothstein, having established, or nearly established, himself as a burgher of Lotusland, wants distance between himself and his friend from the old neighborhood, "I don't wanna be involved in anything you're talking about."

Rothstein senses he is within grasping distance of legitimacy. He is far from the underworld in which Santoro revels. Even when Santoro reminds him that he sanctioned a violent attack on someone he disliked, Rothstein remains unimpressed. This was a momentary loss of control in an otherwise highly organized, seventeen-hour working-day routine based on managerial rather than mob principles.

Predictably, the conflict becomes internecine and both men are damaged. Santoro's self-serving enterprise involves assembling his own crew specializing in extortion and theft. Rothstein loses favor with the Kansas City bosses when the suitcases of skim get lighter. There is a comic moment when it dawns on the *capos* and one fulminates, "Wait a minute! You mean to tell me that the money we're robbing is being robbed? That somebody's robbing from us? We go through all this fucking trouble, and somebody's robbing us? . . . What's the point of skimming if we're being skimmed? Defeats the whole purpose of what we're doing out there."

Eventually the system is brought down by the very thing that brought it into being. As Rothstein remarks when grudgingly admiring a winning gambler who becomes a little too avaricious, "They're all greedy." And, in Vegas, greed is vulnerability.

There's regret in Rothstein's voice as he explains the decline of an order and the rise of another. His allusions to the Egyptian empire are embellished with images of the Luxor, a casino built in a thirty-storey faux pyramid with a life-size sphinx with moving eyes as sentry. Like the Egyptians who reigned 4,000 years ago and whose civilization produced mathematically precise architecture, medicine, and hieroglyphics, Vegas' rulers were brought down by aggressive conquerors. In ancient Egypt, the nemesis was Assyrians; in Vegas, as Rothstein points out, "corporations took it all over."

"*Casino* depicts the decline of the mob through internal disloyalties and inability to compete at the corporate level," concludes Robert Casillo in his *Gangster Priest*. "It [the mob] appears as a casualty of modernization" (p. 341).

In the film, Rothstein reflects similarly, "After the Teamsters got knocked out of the box, the corporations tore down practically every one of those old casinos." Scorsese's signature fin-de-siècle atmosphere surrounds the closing scenes of controlled explosions, tumbling casinos, and families herding into a sanitized environment full of slots that Rothstein likens to "Disneyland."

The corporate interests had their own sources of finance in the stock market in high-yielding, high-risk investments issued by companies seeking to raise capital quickly. "Where did the money come from to rebuild the pyramids?" asks Rothstein rhetorically – "Junk bonds." Whether there is a purpose in the elision is not clear, but he makes no reference to the end of criminality in Vegas. Perhaps the insinuation is that one form was replaced by another.

"It's *all gray*." Scorsese's stage whisper serves as a useful reminder when interpreting his conceptions of criminal justice. In Scorsese's society everything has blurred into half-tone: black vs. white, good vs. evil, and right vs. wrong are all meaningless divisions. Upright citizens are crooked and cops are criminals. Even the agents of honest labor are implicated in diabolical dealings. Scorsese's point was supported in 1988 when federal government prosecutors launched an anti-corruption initiative by filing racketeering charges against the International Brotherhood of Teamsters (IBT), to give the union its full name. The Justice Department was in no doubt: "The IBT leadership has made a devil's pact with La Cosa Nostra." (*La Cosa Nostra* is Italian for "this thing of ours" or "our affair" and refers to the American manifestation of the mafia.)

The quotation is from a detailed analysis for *CQ Researcher* by Richard L. Worsnop in 1992. His assessment of the impact of the law enforcement campaign offers a way of gauging whether the decay Scorsese depicts is such a feature of American society and, as such, is worth considering.

At the time of Worsnop's report, 51-year-old John Gotti was on trial for murder and several other charges relating to dishonest and fraudulent business dealings. The accused, who later became the subject of a 1996 Robert Harmon film, *Gotti*, was something of a harbinger for celebrity culture (which we'll consider in Chapter 6). He attracted and reveled in the kind of media attention typically reserved for Hollywood's A-list, primo rock stars, or supermodels. Like *Casino*'s Rothstein, Gotti appeared to believe that the media could function as a protective canopy: celebrities seem to get away with saying and doing the kind of things others would like to say and do, but don't for fear of prosecution.

The ostentatious Gotti claimed to make his living selling plumbing supplies, though it was widely known he headed the powerful Gambino family. In their book on Gotti, *Mobster*, John Cummings and Ernest Volkman catalog some of the activities of the Gambino family: "Narcotics, extortion, illegal gambling, pornography, union racketeering, robbery, business swindles, hijacking, auto theft, loan-sharking, and murder" (p. 6).

One might naively assume that a character specializing in these and several more equally disreputable activities might generally be regarded as despicable, detestable, odious, and worthy of only contempt. The fact that Gotti was something of a celebrity and that, as Cummings and Volkman put it, "his story represents a perverse American success story" owes something to the manner in which cinema and its audiences have responded to gangsters.

The mafia has been in the popular imagination for many years, of course. Scorsese himself has cited among his influences Howard Hawks' 1932 *Scarface*, the first of several films based on Al Capone's criminal domination in Chicago in the 1920s. (Capone was imprisoned in 1931 for income tax evasion.) In his 1995 *A Personal Journey with Martin Scorsese through American Movies*, Scorsese suggests that the recklessness and delinquency created by Prohibition was perfect raw material for filmmakers: "That world was almost attractive because of its irresponsibility."

More seminal, at least for Scorsese, was Raoul Walsh's *The Roaring Twenties* from 1939: this followed the lives of three World War I infantrymen who return to a nation beset by high unemployment and find crime a serviceable career option. "A twisted Horatio Alger story" is how Scorsese describes it, acknowledging its direct influence on both *It's Not Just You, Murray!* and, twenty-six years later, *GoodFellas*.

Walsh's film made the gangster into a plucky, but tragic figure. The famous line "He used to be a big shot" is uttered pitifully by Gladys George as she holds the dead body of James Cagney in what Scorsese calls a *Pietà*-type image (i.e. in which the Virgin Mary holds the body of Jesus Christ).

There's nothing new in turning outlaws into folk heroes. Americans might have refined the process with films such as Henry King's 1939 *Jesse James* and Arthur Penn's 1958 *The Left-Handed Gun* as well as multiple others on Capone, Siegel, Gotti, et al., but the British have lionized the semi-legendary medieval bandit Robin Hood and the notorious eighteenth-century highway robber Dick Turpin, the former of whom got the Hollywood treatment, starting in 1922 with Allan Dwan's *Robin Hood* (with Douglas Fairbanks as the twelfth-century outlaw). Unlike these characters, the gangster occupies a unique position in American folklore.

Whereas the likes of Jesse James and Robin Hood, or at least the idealized images based on them, struck chords by virtue of their distinct approaches to the redistribution of wealth (James stole from banks and those with money enough to travel by railroad; Hood putatively robbed the rich and gave to the poor), Capone and other prominent gangsters offered a motif for a nation born on the idea of new beginnings and second chances. As I suggested in the previous chapter, the decision to turn to crime is one born out of the desire to be successful in a land where success is a *sine qua non* – an indispensable condition. As *The Departed*'s Costello's underboss Archie French proclaims, "This is America. If you don't make money, you're a douche bag."

Worsnop, like many other writers, senses that "ordinary citizens continue to find the exploits of old-time gangsters fascinating," and, in addition to Capone, suggests that Siegel and Sam Giancana, who was linked to John F. Kennedy and Marilyn Monroe among others, possessed auras. But, by the 1980s, Gotti was an odd presence: most *capos* avoided attention or publicity, opting for the anonymity of a regular business-man. *Casino*'s Rothstein and the real-life Rosenthal on whom he is based were parts of a dying breed of flamboyant types who enjoyed engaging with the media and exhibiting their success through their clothes, cars, and other possessions. Rothstein points out in the film how his end coincided with the coming of big legitimate corporations. Organized crime had to adapt or perish. Some say it began to perish.

"The American Mafia on its last legs?" asked Worsnop, marshaling evidence in his answer. After decades of seeming invincibility, federal and state prosecutors, often working together, enforced a new generation of anti-racketeering laws, the main one of which was known as Rico (for Racketeer Influenced and Corrupt Organizations Act, 1970). The crucial relationship between organized crime and the labor unions was dealt a blow in 1989 when the Teamsters agreed to hold secret ballots to elect senior officials and, in 1991, the union president publicly waved "goodbye to the mafia."

In the Nevada gambling industry, the mob's grip was loosened by legislation which opened up the state to the likes of Bally's, Hilton, and MGM. Rothstein's observations at the end of *Casino* presage actual changes in the industry, which became much more service-oriented. In the film, there isn't a slot to be seen.

In 1992, the academic publication *Journal of Contemporary Criminal Justice* was moved to make an editorial pronouncement on "the considerable controversy" over organized crime. Rejecting notions of a unified national syndicate (which was how Kefauver had described it in the 1950s), Gennaro F. Vito, on behalf of the journal, concluded, "Instead, crime bodies are independent, local entities often centered in major cities with no formal national ties. Rather it [organized crime] follows an informal, loosely structured, open system. Structure is largely determined by function, not rational bureaucratic action" (p. iii).

The idea of an indestructible America-wide crime conglomerate has been an appealing one for filmmakers and, in the 1970s, the first two *Godfather* films no doubt helped persuade the public that such an entity existed. Maybe it did then. But, by the early 1990s, evidence of a national set-up was scarce and the "loosely structured" open model suggested by Vito was more congruent with the reality of organized crime. Gotti had been called "the godfather" many times, but evidence of his influence suggested it was a good deal more limited than that of the fictional Don Corleone.

While it's reasonable to suppose that Gotti's undisguised belief in his invulnerability contributed to his own demise, it's also fair to say that he might have survived in a previous era. Gotti was imprisoned for life in 1992 and died with cancer ten years later. Much of the case against him was compiled with data from surveillance technologies: wiretapping telephone conversations, private discussions, even street chat were recorded. Methods were relatively primitive in the *Casino* period, though Rothstein and Santoro talk in code, or use their wives as proxies or sometimes meet secretly in the desert to ensure their conversations are not bugged.

By the time of *The Departed* cellphones had made private communication easier and less detectable, though not completely impossible to trace. Text messages are used to convey instructions from undercover agents to the police, and from infiltrators to organized crime, and vice versa in the knowledge that these are unlikely to be intercepted.

The Gotti trial featured evidence recorded through electronic surveillance, though the testimony of Sammy Gravano, a Gambino family *consigliere*, or advisor, was also damning. Gravano's was one of a series of defections, like that of Henry Hill of *GoodFellas*. Worsnop plausibly suggests that the same kind of narcissism that has bred the "me generation" has affected the previously cohesive mob. When, early in *GoodFellas*, Jimmy Conway warns Hill never to talk to police, it is intended to function as a prudent guide for future action. The collectivity always took precedence over the individual. As that value changed, so did the solidarity of the mafia.

Hill fled to the relative security of a government protection program, and this became a haven of many more turncoats. The indications were that the previously dense, impenetrable network of alliances had been breached. The hegemony of the mafia has been threatened by the arrival of new criminal organizations in America. The so-called Russian mafia has been prominent among these, though the Triads from China, the Japanese Yakuza, the Yardies of Jamaica, and Colombia's Medellín drugs cartels have all encroached on territory traditionally owned by the mob.

Against this background, *GoodFellas* and *Casino* seem like historical documents charting a bygone age. *The Departed* shows a kind of response to the breakup of the old order. Bribing police officers and any number of other officials is no longer enough: intelligence, knowledge, information have taken on added value. Hence Costello has his confederate leaking out police information and the police have an undercover man feeding back information on Costello.

There is arbitrariness about whether to choose a righteous or sinful path – at least in areas like south Boston or Kansas City's Northland, where there are no career paths signed "legitimacy" or "prison." People gravitate toward whichever territory offers them the best prospects. Frank Costello's opening stanza in *The Departed*, cited in the introduction, includes a revealing though unattainable aspiration, "I don't want to be a product of my environment. I want my environment to be a product of me."

True, the environment is what surrounds us, the conditions we live under, the backdrop against which we experience the world. But it's also inside us: it influences our values, motivations, ambitions, hopes, and projects. Costello's project to become and remain the kingpin of organized crime in Boston and beyond is, of course, an attempt to rearrange the landscape of the city in a way that accommodates his interests. So, in a sense, the environment and he are inseparable: it influences him and he, in turn, influences it.

Both *The Departed* and *Casino* are about environments that commission egoism and law breaking. Scorsese's earlier efforts, most notably *Mean Streets* and *Who's That Knocking at My Door?*, showed the mob as what Maurizio Viano, in his review of *GoodFellas*, calls "a menacing horizon, a limit which forced the characters to some kind of adjustment" (p. 44). And *GoodFellas* documented precisely that adjustment. Yet the likes of Sam Rothstein and Frank Costello are not so much adjusting or making an accommodation, as building architecture capable of housing both criminal activity and legalized robbery, on the one hand, and their personal ambitions, on the other.

Scorsese's neighborhoods are as likely to produce corrupt cops as kind-hearted villains. Each have a clear understanding of the moral neutrality, or *grayness*, of the territory they share. "There is no one more full of shit than a cop . . . except for a cop on tv," observes Billy Costigan, himself a cop. There is no hierarchy in which cops stand above criminals: they all inhabit a world in which reciprocal action and influence are permanent features and which cops and criminals live in symbiosis. The point is made in a brief encounter between the self-serving infiltrator Colin Sullivan and his ever-pragmatic boss in *The Departed*.

"Cui bono?" Sullivan is asked. He pauses momentarily. Who benefits? Can his questioner be serious? Does he mean the police? Or the public they are meant to defend? Or society generally? Or him personally? "Qui gives a shit?" he responds. His questioner, a senior police officer, approves. "I think you are a cop, my son." It might be a meaningless, light-hearted piece of banter; but it might also be a perspective on how criminal justice works in America – like a pageant, a public entertainment consisting of a procession that the public stands by and watches; it looks impressive and grand, but is actually nothing more than a spectacle demonstrating that something is going on. Exactly what doesn't seem to matter. "Honesty is not synonymous with truth," we are told in *The Departed*.

Perhaps everyone in America is greedy: they're all products of a vast environment that encourages acquisitiveness. The way people respond to this is, for Scorsese, less significant than what we popularly imagine. It actually doesn't matter that much because crime is a question of supply and demand and, where there is demand, there is supplier. What does seem to matter is the impression that the forces of law and order constantly struggle against the opposing forces of criminality. But it is only an impression. The reality is more ambiguous.

Criminal justice in America works like a pageant, a public entertainment. And the public spectacle of a high-profile bust reminds the American populace that the ongoing war on crime is being won.

For Scorsese, crime doesn't lurk in the unlit corners of American cities. The urban ecology provides a way of understanding how it starts, but crime is all-pervasive. It's also unstoppable, indestructible, and, if Scorsese is to be believed, quite healthy. After all, the motivations that drive criminals are perfectly consistent with mainstream American values, as we saw previously. Then there is the balance of supply/demand, which is kept in a stable equilibrium thanks to the efforts of purveyors of prostitutes, drugs, and any other imaginable commodity. And the public spectacle of a high-profile bust – like that of Gotti – reminds the American populace that the ongoing war on crime is being won. Perhaps it is; but there will never be a final victory.

This picture of crime misses a few details, of course, such as the extra few dollars American consumers have to pay on practically everything from food to cars. Bribes, sweeteners, protection money, and other kinds of payoffs to organized crime have to be paid for. Legitimate suppliers typically pass on the cost to consumers rather than pay it out of the goodness of their hearts. Substandard construction materials find their way into the building process if inspectors are sufficiently bribed. Victimless crimes, such as supplying illicit drugs, can, on closer inspection, claim victims if the users resort to violent robbery to feed their habits. It might also be argued that the very nature of democracy is stricken if political leaders, union bosses, or corporate heads succumb to corruption at the hands of organized crime.

Scorsese, as we know, finds the practices enthralling. So do we, his audience. He makes many of them visible in a way that is fresh and perhaps unique. But, in doing so, he has shielded his eyes from the victims. The people who suffer in Scorsese films are typically felons, dislikeable egotists, or greedy abusers of their positions of power. Perhaps this is exactly how Scorsese sees the effects of crime's liaison with the forces of order. If so, it is a simplistic and incomplete observation and one that complements the conservatism of his wider vision.

4

MINDS AND THE METROPOLIS

Cities are terrifying places, teeming with immoral and malevolent fiends who prey on unsuspecting innocents after dark. In the words of Travis Bickle, the protagonist of Scorsese's *Taxi Driver*: "All the animals come out at night: whores, skunk pussies, buggers, queens, fairies, dopers, junkies. Sick, venal. Someday a real rain will come and wash all this scum off the streets." Travis Bickle is sickened by the rancidity and neon squalor of New York in the early 1970s. Its degeneracy is manifest: he sees it every night through the windows of his taxicab.

Bickle is one of a number of Scorsese characters who are troubled, vexed, burdened, and sometimes haunted by *what they see* in the environments. All societies are in perpetual change, of course; though Bickle and the other characters who will soon heave into view have lived through periods of transition, when one state has become or is in the process of becoming another. It's the subjective impact the change has that matters. Bickle and co. are disturbed by what they see,

*Like other members of America's "lonely crowd," Travis Bickle is
tormented by the anonymous and, in his eyes, degenerate environment
he sees around him. The streets of New York inhabit as well as surround
him. (© Kobal)*

their perception and understanding of what's going on in
their cities, and what they would like to do about it. "Flush it
right down the fucking toilet," is Bickle's solution.

The terrors of city life have been the subject of intellectual
discussion practically since the modern metropolis arrived.
Many writers have been intrigued by its impact on the way
we think. Writing over a hundred years ago, Georg Simmel
contributed his classic monograph *The Metropolis and Mental
Life*, which charted some of the physical and social changes
wrought by modernity. Splintered friendships, disrupted families, monotony at work, and anonymity among neighbors:
these were all features of city life. Traditional, or pre-modern,
communities were characterized by a "lower, more habitual,

more smoothly flowing rhythm" and "deeply felt emotional relations" that matured steadily. The modern metropolis had a faster tempo and produced an "intensification of nervous stimulation."

Even a simple matter of crossing a street necessitated a different awareness. Residents of the cities became accustomed to the unexpected, like a horse-drawn carriage appearing suddenly. They were more intuitively suspicious of fellow residents, habituated to routine, and inured to the humorless tedium of modern life. They cultivated an exaggerated sense of individuality, even eccentricity, as a defense against the impersonality of the city. And, for Simmel, it *was* a defense: city dwellers were engaged in a constant defense of themselves in the face of a hostile, impersonal environment.

Travis Bickle's response is initially one of self-abnegation. It is but one of a number of reactions depicted by Scorsese to the experiences of the modern city. Each of the experiences I cover in this chapter is shaped by imperatives that seem to derive from external pressures more than internal drives. In their different ways, they express Scorsese's "antimodern tendency," as David M. Hammond and Beverly J. Smith call it, in their "Death, medicine, and religious solidarity in Martin Scorsese's *Bringing Out the Dead*."

Unrealistic hopes of being a savior or a conqueror of death are summarily dealt with by the unforgiving city in *Taxi Driver* and *Bringing Out the Dead*, the respective (anti)heroes of which bear witness to the casualties of the modern life. Compassion is often not sufficient; these men must make restitution. And when a computer operative tries to escape the "humorless tedium of modern life," he finds a labyrinth so full of hostility that he can't beat a path back to his life of conformity. His experience in *After Hours* is oddly similar to that of the haunted horror writer of the television film "Mirror, mirror," who imagines a zombie companion every time he sees himself in a reflective surface. All the experiences of the city are in some way haunting. All demand reparations.

Bickle is part Innocent, part Avenging Angel. He is someone's or something's agent. At least, that's how he sees himself: devoid of any control over his own actions, simply acting out instructions. "My whole life has pointed in one direction," he reveals midway through the film. "There never has been any choice for me." This has traces of Lionel Dobie's advice to his protégée in "Life lessons," as we will see in Chapter 8. Like true artists, Bickle has no choice. There's nothing to suggest he believes in the doctrine of predestination: Bickle's calling is of a more earthly nature – he must purify the "open sewer" of the city of its "filth and scum."

Bickle emerges as a mysterious character: he announces himself as an ex-marine, honorably discharged in 1973, presumably having served in the Vietnam War. His motivation for becoming a taxi driver is that he can't sleep and spends his nights riding subways and buses; so he "might as well get paid for it." Insomnia is one of the symptoms of what we now call post-traumatic stress disorder, some others being a dulled response to others and persistent emotional disturbance. While there is

> **"Betsy, in her incandescent loveliness and white dress, becomes Travis's icon of purity, plucked by his eyes from the engulfing evil of the city."** MICHAEL PHILLIPS ET AL. ON *TAXI DRIVER*

no recognized "Vietnam War syndrome" in the same way as there is now "Gulf War syndrome" that affects veterans of the 1991 conflict, it's conceivable that Bickle's sleeplessness is attributable to exposure to military hostility.

He has no educational qualifications but his chauffeur's license is, as he describes it, "clean, real clean." Twelve-hour shifts picking up fares in places such as Harlem and the South Bronx (described by another driver as "fucking Mau Mau land," in allusion to the violent anticolonial Kenyan nationalist movement of the 1950s) expose him to a landscape of conniving pimps, teenage prostitutes, their slimy clients, and homicidal husbands stalking unfaithful wives ("a nigga lives there and I'm gonna kill him . . . I'm gonna kill her with a .44 Magnum pistol"). Bickle observes all these through the windshield of his cab or in its rearview mirror.

He senses there is serendipity in his meeting Betsy, who works for a politician and appears "like an angel out of this filthy mess." She becomes, as Michael Phillips and his colleagues put it in *Film Quarterly*, "Travis's icon of purity, plucked by his eyes from the engulfing evil of the city" (p. 38).

Betsy's boss is a Senator Charles Palantine, who is seeking the presidential nomination. His aides approach their jobs pragmatically, as if they were selling mouthwash, as they put it. Palantine initially impresses Bickle, especially after he asks him, "What is the one thing that bugs you most?" Bickle's answer is "this city."

A date with Betsy goes grotesquely wrong when Bickle takes her to a soft porn movie house. She leaves angrily in the middle of the film and, despite his pleas over the next several days, won't forgive him. The misjudgment is due to Bickle's artlessness, disclosing a callow side to the world-weary character projected through the narration. Much of Bickle's thoughts are voiced aloud through his diary notes and letters: he despairs over Betsy, "I realize now how much she is like the others, so cold and distant."

The rejection proves to be the point at which a series of small, ineffective changes acquires enough pressure to cause a larger, more significant change in Bickle. He records the peripeteia in his diary: "My life has taken a turn again." He buys a small artillery of weapons (including a .44 Magnum) from a small-arms street dealer and resolves to get his body into shape by quitting smoking and starting an exercise regimen. Later, the exercises take on a more Spartan character: he holds his clenched fist over a flame to inure himself to pain, but perhaps also to purify his flesh (he has been a frequenter of the porn movie theater).

It's during this purification that Bickle rehearses his now-iconic "are you talking to me?" routine in front of a mirror. This is part of his preparation for purging and defending a city that he believes has been defiled and degraded. Bickle's vigilantism effectively begins during a visit to a convenience store where he witnesses a stick-up. Emotionlessly, he shoots the robber dead. Returning to his sparsely furnished apartment, he sits in front of his tv, which is perched on a fruit box and pushes gently against it with his foot. For a while, the tv balances precariously, like Bickle himself; then it crashes in a flurry of sparks.

Bickle resembles what David Riesman called an inner-directed man. An "inner-directed" person moves through life trying to obey his internal piloting. "Getting off course, whether in response to inner impulses or to the fluctuating voices of contemporaries, may lead to the feeling of *guilt*. . . . Overwhelmed with guilt, he will despise himself for his failure and inadequacies" (p. 125).

Bickle abhors his indulgence. "I do not believe one should devote his life to morbid self-attention," he writes before discovering his mission; and it really is a mission in the sense that Bickle believes he is carrying out an important assignment, if not for religious, then for social purposes. "Here is a man who wouldn't take it any more, a man who stood up against the scum, the cunts, the dogs, the filth."

He is riven by a combination of personal inadequacy and the sinfulness that comes of doing nothing; he begins, as an editorial comment in the Catholic *America* magazine put it, "desperately searching for a measure of grace" (March 5, 2007).

Riesman proposed a way of understanding someone like Bickle, a fictional figure of course, but one who seemed to embody the guilt-haunted post-Vietnam America, convulsed and humiliated by defeat in a war many believed unjust as well as unwise (if ever war can be anything but). While he was observing an earlier period (the Vietnam War did not begin until 1964, when two US destroyers were reportedly attacked), Riesman had already detected a profound change in what he called the American "character" (which equates to what we would now call social identity in the sense that it's shaped through actual experiences and reflected in our motivations and fulfillment).

Riesman called his book *The Lonely Crowd*, the title suggesting the solitariness that inhabits large gatherings of people in modern America. The incipient disappearance of inner direction, with a loosening of the sense of personal destiny, was due, at least in part, to the onset of large-scale institutions. Inner-directed people like Bickle had an internalized set of goals or ambitions. In Betsy, her colleagues and the politician she supports, Bickle encounters *outer-directed* people: they are sensitive to the expectations and preferences of others. The "others" in question referred not so much to people as anonymous organizations, including the media, political machines, and denominational religion.

Any faith the returning vet might have had in political parties, however, is quashed by his personal rejection. And, when he notices a sweet-looking child hustling on the streets, he finds a personal focus for his mission.

The epistolary parts of the film leave us in no doubt about Bickle's distorted purpose: he writes an anniversary card to his parents, claiming to be working for the government on a secret mission. In a perverse way, this is true: that *is* his perception of his task. He also claims to have been seeing a girl, who is probably an imaginary composite of Betsy and the child hooker he tracks down.

"Overwhelmed with guilt, he will despise himself for his failure and inadequacies." DAVID RIESMAN, *THE LONELY CROWD*

The child, whom her pimp claims to be 12, calls herself "Easy," though her name is Iris. Bickle proffers himself as her salvation, though the reason why anyone wouldn't want to work the streets escapes her. In her eyes, her salvation has already arrived in the form of Sport, as her pimp is known.

Somehow Bickle decides that, despite her adulteration, Iris is capable of saving herself if she returns to her family in the Midwest. "Life in the American heartland may be dull and repressive," is how Michael Phillips et al. summarize Bickle's pitch, "but at least it is not seamy or perilous" (p. 38). Bickle, it seems, hasn't lost faith in America: just its cities and perhaps only New York. Iris, however, prefers the street life and is soon back to Sport.

Scorsese's understanding of the peculiarly tight relationship between hookers and their pimps was recycled in *Casino*: in this and *Taxi Driver*, prostitutes are seen as brassy and independent on the surface, but unbreakably fettered to their pimps in a manner that suggests they – perhaps like most other women – are incapable of a genuine independence. Their gullibility combined with proneness to romance will always disable them. Iris melts in the arms of the sly and unscrupulous Sport ("I'd be lost without you," he tells her) and instantly forgets Bickle's warning about him: "He's the worst scum."

Taxi Driver was released in 1976, four years after Arthur Bremer's attempted assassination of presidential candidate Governor George Wallace. Wallace was left paralyzed. Earlier, in the 1960s, assassins had killed both John and Robert Kennedy. So, when Bickle prepares for what appears to be an attack on Palantine, there is an existing model. While not exactly commonplace, attempts on the lives on prominent politicians were fresh in the public mind.

In the film, Bickle is scared off by security guards and turns his attentions to more vulnerable targets. In actuality, John Hinckley became fascinated with the film and the character of Iris in particular, to the point where he mimicked Bickle's behavior. He tried unsuccessfully to assassinate President Ronald Reagan, believing he was acting as a proxy for Jodie Foster, who played Iris. (Scorsese later developed the idea of delusional love, or erotomania, in *The King of Comedy*, as we will see in Chapter 9.)

Having failed either to liberate the whore or kill the politician, Bickle pursues his purgative actions by shooting Sport ("How are things in the pimp business?" he asks before firing his .38 Special Smith & Wesson into his gut). Thus begins the slaughter: pursuing Iris, Bickle repeatedly shoots the proprietor of the squalid rent-by-the-hour motel she uses for her tricks, and her john too. In the process, he is wounded so that, when the police arrive, he is sitting, incapacitated but still defiant. He gestures suicide, holding his blood-soaked hand to his temple and making a "boom" noise.

Is Bickle a psycho, or a hero? After all, he does hardly anything a decent person wouldn't do if fervently bent on purifying New York City of those self-serving hypocrites who claim to be serving the people, and ridding its streets of vice-mongering parasites. The film's postscript leaves no doubt. Newspaper headlines read TAXI DRIVER HERO TO RECOVER and TAXI DRIVER BATTLES GANGSTERS, and the voiceover features a letter from Iris's parents in Pittsburgh, thanking Bickle for his redemptive act.

When, on December 22, 1984, Bernard Goetz wandered into a 14th Street subway station, he didn't realize that he was also wandering into popular folklore. Threatened by four African Americans, he fired his own .38 Special Smith & Wesson at them all, paralyzing one and brain-damaging another. They all survived. Goetz had previously been a victim of street attacks in Harlem in the 1970s, and again in 1981, when he sustained injuries.

During the 1970s and early 1980s, New York City's reported crime rate was more than 70 percent greater than the rest of the USA, homicide and other forms of violent crime featuring prominently. Goetz, the "Subway Vigilante" as he was known, pled self-defense, was found guilty of illegal possession of a weapon, and, after appeal, served eight months in prison. But he was popularly heroized for his action in facing up to violent robbers and, to this day, gives interviews on an incident that some still believe constituted a turning-point: perhaps coincidentally, New York's crime decreased over subsequent years.

When *Newsweek*'s Jack Kroll in his *Taxi Driver* review observed, "Travis Bickle, a man who fits nowhere in society, becomes an emblem of all those who are trying to become human beings while society lies in disarray," he failed to qualify his point (quoted in Kelly's 1980 collection, p. 188). Bickle sees himself as more of a misfit than he actually is. Let me explain.

Through his diary, Bickle describes himself using the American writer Thomas Wolfe's phrase, "God's lonely man." The import of Wolfe's essay is that, "loneliness, far from being a rare and curious phenomenon, peculiar to myself and to a few other solitary men, is the central and inevitable fact of human existence." This suggests Bickle's condition is more widespread than he suspects and that when he senses he "should become a person like other people," he already is.

Scorsese's grim story of self-help and urban vigilantism is hardly a manual on how to save cities, but it does convey a frame of mind that was prevalent in the immediate post-Vietnam period.

Before *Taxi Driver* ends, Bickle is seen back in his cab, picking up Betsy and appearing at one with the world as he gazes at her through his rearview mirror – at least until a momentary lapse when he seems suddenly distracted and changes the angle of the mirror, hastening a blaze of light from the surrounding night traffic. He might be imagining Betsy. Then again, the car's mirror, like its windshield, has provided a lens through which he sees reality. So, the ending, in which, like Rupert Pupkin of *The King of Comedy*, the eccentric emerges a luminary, might be a perception rather than a reality. Pupkin's fate is plausible: he served his time and became a celebrity. Bickle, like the real-life Goetz, could have been hailed as, in his own words, "a man who stood up" (though, of course, a plea of self-defense would probably not have flown for Bickle).

Reviewing *Taxi Driver* for *The New Yorker* in 1976, Pauline Kael wrote, "Travis wants to conform, but he can't find a group pattern to conform to. So he sits and drives in the stupefied languor of anomie. He hates New York with a Biblical fury; it gives off the stench of Hell, and its filth and smut obsesses him" (quoted in Kelly's 1980 collection, p. 183).

"He hates New York with a Biblical fury; it gives off the stench of Hell, and its filth and smut obsesses him." PAULINE KAEL ON *TAXI DRIVER*'S TRAVIS BICKLE

Kael's "stupefied languor of anomie" is a phrase worth unpicking. She means that Bickle is unable to think straight in his discomfort, a discomfort occasioned by a lack of rules or normal patterns of behavior. Riesman also used anomie to describe the condition of those who do not or cannot adjust to accepted standards and so find themselves "rule-less, ungoverned." Bickle's epiphany – and he seems to have a moment of revelation ("My life has taken another turn") after being rebuffed by Betsy – is a kind of response to the anomie. After it, he discovers direction and guidelines for his action. (The term "anomie" is from the Greek *anomos*, meaning lawless. I'll return to it in the Conclusion.)

For Bickle, evil reveals itself with clarity. And he sees it everywhere; it is endemic in the city. The city is, to use Andrew J. Swensen's term, a "quotidian horror." In his 2001 article "The anguish of God's lonely men," Swensen compares *Taxi Driver* with Dostoevsky's *Notes from Underground*. "The plots combine a lament on urban decrepitude [with] an indictment of urban predation and the would-be salvation of a prostitute victimized by society," he writes (p. 268).

Another Scorsese character has a more inclusive aim: *everyone* must somehow be saved, even those who are already lost. Swensen argues that the main characters of *Taxi Driver* and *Notes from Underground* grapple with "the metaphysical horror of a universe lacking a God" (p. 270). But Frank Pierce, a paramedic in *Bringing Out the Dead*, thinks he is God's agent caught between grace and damnation. "You wonder if you've become immortal," he reflects after saving a life. "For a moment there, God was you." And, presumably, vice versa.

Like Bickle, Frank Pierce spends his nights driving around New York City, in his case in an emergency medical service vehicle. Like Bickle, he is in his thirties and similarly burned-out. By the early 1990s, the Vietnam vets were well into middle age: Pierce meets them usually as they are suffering cardiac arrest or trying to commit suicide. Most of his working life is spent saving "lives" – and I use inverted commas because Pierce and his colleagues are trained to resuscitate, even in the complete absence of cognitive activity and even when they are effectively, as one of his colleagues puts it, "plant food."

Bringing Out the Dead was released almost a quarter-century after *Taxi Driver* and forms a natural companion. Paul Schrader wrote both from the perspective of young men etiolated by the experience of New York, a city to which they are drawn yet which repulses them. Pierce roams Hell's Kitchen, a neighborhood of Manhattan best known for its deprivation, waiting for his dispatcher to issue instructions, such as, "You'll be driving to the man who needs no introduction, chronic caller of the year three straight and shooting for number four. The duke of drunk, the king of stink, our most frequent flier." (Scorsese himself voices the dispatches.)

The mordancy is a way of maintaining a sense of humanity in a job in which life and death is a numbers game. Paramedics keep score. Pierce, as we learn in his voiceover, hasn't saved a life in months. Fate's arbitrariness disturbs Pierce much more than it does his colleagues, all of whom have become as anesthetized as their patients. They try to save lives, not out of any sense of spiritual calling, but because that's what they do. For Pierce, on the other hand, every day means a new apocalypse.

As Bickle was fixated on saving someone, Pierce is obsessively attached to someone he didn't save. She died a month before, just like one of the hundreds of other young women who overdose or are murdered in the city. Most of them, Pierce can erase from his mind as easily as he cleans the blood from his hands. But the face of Rose keeps re-appearing to him. She even talks to him. "Why did you kill me, Frank?" she asks. "*I didn't* kill you," he blurts, prompting his partner to wonder whom he's talking to.

When Pierce looks out of his windshield or side mirror, he sees much the same as Bickle had: tragic homeless figures stumbling and weaving between beaten-up cars, brazenly solicitous prostitutes, though now, as Pierce's colleague Marcus observes, they dress much like any other woman ("Whatever happened to go-go boots and hot pants?"), and junkies, now in the thrall of an especially pernicious narcotic known as "red death." But his scope is different: his life isn't "headed in one direction," as Bickle put it.

> **When Pierce looks out of his windshield, he sees much the same as Bickle had: tragic homeless figures weaving between beaten-up cars, brazenly solicitous prostitutes and junkies.**

At least, Pierce doesn't want it to; he habitually arrives late on shift, pleading with his captain to fire him. "I'll fire you tomorrow," his captain replies. "Your city needs you." He quits the job, only to return. Perhaps he only supposes it isn't headed in one direction; but from over the two plus days covered in the film, he seems as chosen for his Purpose as Bickle is for his. Screenwriter Schrader's Calvinist upbringing obviously familiarized him with grace of God and the doctrine of predestination.

The story that frames the film is that of a 60-year-old man who collapses while watching tv in his apartment. On arrival, Pierce and his partner discover that he has stopped breathing. They apply electrode patches, pry open his mouth, and turn to the electrocardiogram monitor, which shows a flatline. Pierce pushes a laryngoscope down the patient's throat, injects him with three sets of drugs, and activates the defibrillator. After several convulsions, the patient's daughter, Mary Burke, urges them to stop. But they proceed, asking the family to play some music until they unexpectedly find a pulse. The man lives, though without regaining consciousness.

Over the following couple of days, the man stirs briefly, at one point registering cognitive activity. Mary, a former drug user, who has been clean for a year, visits the hospital regularly and strikes up a rapport with Pierce. He escorts her to the apartment of Cy, a drug dealer who runs "Sunrise Enterprises, the stress-free factory," and is slightly resentful at the lack of recognition for "the work I've done in this community."

To the tranquil reggae of the Melodians' "Rivers of Babylon," Pierce takes a pill offered by Cy ("you can't believe how relaxing it is") and drifts off. Like Bickle, Pierce is a would-be savior who is in need of saving himself. The soporific has what Cy recognizes as a "paradoxical effect," and Pierce storms off, carrying Mary across his shoulder like a firefighter rescuing the casualty of a blaze.

Later, Pierce is called back to Cy's apartment after rival dealers have invaded it. Amid the wreckage he finds Cy impaled on the spike of a steel balcony railing and supports him while emergency service workers cut through the rail with oxyacetylene. At one point, Cy looks behind him at the cityscape, the sparks from the flame spurting into the night air, and sighs, "Isn't it beautiful? . . . I love this city."

Pierce hates it. When Mary says, "This city; it'll kill you if you're not strong enough," he agrees with the first part. "This city doesn't discriminate: it gets *everybody*." He means good and bad. Even people like him, who devote themselves to saving others, are damned.

In *Bringing Out the Dead*, Scorsese makes his protagonist's thoughts visible and audible. The audience sees Pierce's perceptions and hears the voices of the living, the dead, and those he commits to a crepuscular world – the brain-dead. "Let me go," he hears Mary's father imploring him toward the end of the film. He lies motionless in a vegetative state on a hospital bed. Pierce obeys the voice, disconnecting the patient from his life support, then waiting for him to die before reconnecting. "He's coded," a nurse eventually declares, meaning that he's finally dead.

You might suppose that having the capability to allow another human being to live or die is empowering. In fact, it renders Pierce almost as helpless as those he's trying to save. "Frank Pierce is as much in need of care as are his patients," conclude Hammond and Smith. "The suffering and dead haunt him and seem to be dragging him into insanity" (p. 116).

Madness and insanity are crude labels and are not helpful in understanding the way in which Bickle or Pierce engage with their worlds.

David Thomson disagrees. In his 1999 *New York Times* article "An offering to the ghosts of wildness past," he compares "Travis Bickle's descent (no, it's an elevation, really) into madness" with Pierce's frantic "clinging to ordinary decency."

Madness and insanity are crude labels and are not helpful in understanding the way in which Bickle or Pierce engage with their worlds. It could be argued that Bickle was clinging to ordinary decency too. After all, Goetz's sanity was never questioned.

Perhaps Bickle and Pierce represent two different types of social character. Pierce depends on the approval of others, including his colleagues, his patients, and their families. He even depends on the approval of people he only imagines he sees, particularly Rose, whose life he nearly but didn't quite save. He's sensitive, perhaps over-sensitive, to the expectations and preferences of others. In this sense, he resembles what David Riesman, in the study quoted earlier, called the outer-directed person.

Apart from a fathomless regard for human life, Pierce seems uncertain of other core values; he has friendly but shallow relations with fellow paramedics, and seems constantly to look to others for direction and endorsement. He can't even quit his job without his captain's say-so. As Philip Hopkins writes in his "Dead man walking," "Frank's compassion for the after-hours denizens of Hell's Kitchen is admirable, but his dedication to his job is less understandable in the movie."

Philip Horne provides a clue in his 2001 article "Martin Scorsese and the film between the living and the dead." As the film ends, "the frenzy of the streets at night is replaced by the calmness of companionship and a meditative dawn, and the tormenting spirit has been appeased" (p. 51).

There is, of course, no tormenting spirit, at least not in an objective sense. The source of torment for Pierce lies in the environment he patrols and which agitates his restlessness. His remark, "This city doesn't discriminate: it gets *everybody*," suggests a resignation. The voices he hears, the visions he sees, are all pushing him. It's as if he's lost capacity to control his own destiny.

Haunting in *Bringing Out the Dead* and, to a lesser extent, *Taxi Driver* is a trope, a figurative way of expressing how people absorb or internalize their surroundings. Scorsese characters are embedded in contexts: they make no sense as isolated individuals. They have to be understood but in terms of circumstances: time and place, events preceding and following, surrounding objects and people, beliefs and perceptions. Often, beliefs and perceptions are the most decisive influences. All these affect how we think; and thoughts themselves have a factual status. "They help shape our reality," wrote Riesman in the preface to the 1969 edition of *The*

Lonely Crowd. Hence my earlier use of italics in the phrase *what they see.*

Scorsese makes much the same point in "Mirror, mirror," a 1985 episode of *Amazing Stories*, a television series. Jordan Manmouth, a best-selling author of horror stories, not unlike Stephen King, appears on a talk show to publicize the latest screen adaptation of one of his books, *Scream Dreams*, the cover of which bears a reproduction of Edvard Munch's 1893 painting "The scream."

When asked whether he takes pleasure from disturbing his audiences, he confirms that he aims to excite people and adds, "What you see is what you get." It's a puzzling rider: most people don't see corpses breaking from their graves or zombies – apart from in movies. Most, but not all: Frank Pierce at one point in *Bringing Out the Dead* sees several patients he failed to save rising from the streets to clutch at him.

Things become clearer when Manmouth returns home to his Beverly Hills home and looks in the mirror, where he sees one of his own zombies standing behind him. Terrified, he seeks help, but he soon discovers that reflective surfaces are inescapable: in windows, camera lenses, shiny faucets, and other people's eyes. We see ourselves reflected everywhere. And everywhere the writer sees not just himself, but his zombie, which may or may not be a product of his imagination. In the episode's credits, the zombie is actually called a "phantom," indicating that he might have imagined this figure, who looks like an asylum seeker from Michael Jackson's 1983 "Thriller" video.

Figment of the imagination it may be, but it eventually drives the writer to throw himself out of a bedroom window in a desperate escape attempt. What Manmouth *sees* is what he ultimately gets: the reality he imagines for his novels affects him, though in a way he couldn't have anticipated. "This is not a book, Karen," he tells his lover and agent. "This is real."

Manmouth is undoubtedly one of the lonely crowd: he lives alone in his palatial art deco home, thrives off the patronage of his fans, but is contemptuous of them. Finding an autograph seeker who describes himself as his "biggest fan in the world," Manmouth snubs him. He does the talk show circuit but expresses his hatred of agents, journalists, and publicity in general. His life depends on the approval of people, most of whom are anonymous.

Like all the other characters of this chapter, Manmouth is haunted. When Hammond and Smith write of Frank Pierce, "The suffering and the dead haunt him and seem to be dragging him into insanity," they make a resonant point. Many of Scorsese's urban dwellers are persistently disturbed, not by ghosts, but by thoughts, specifically by thoughts of what is going on outside – not inside – them. This is the sense in which they are haunted.

Paul Schrader observed of his own text, "*Taxi Driver* involves a pathology of suicide" (quoted in Michael Bliss's 2000 interview, p. 8). He was alluding to his own forensic examination of the causes of self-destruction. Bickle's abnormal response to his perception of decay and stagnation in the city, rather than the material conditions, is what drives him toward what might in a different period be suicidal. In the climate of the 1970s, he is glorified. The causes of Manmouth's attempt are more opaque, though he too is driven by his thoughts rather than objective facts.

Unlike Bickle or Pierce, he lives well away from downtown – in the case of Los Angeles, an area generally known for its salubrity, this is Central City East, the lamentable trough of poverty better known as "The Nickel," where up to 8,000 homeless transients congregate. Manmouth might not like the streets, but, when he is arrested after reacting violently to an image of the apparition in the dark glasses of a police officer, he is forced to confront them head-on while locked in a holding cell with an assortment of "Nickel" lowlifes, one of whom demands money from him. It's a minor reminder of a world beyond Manmouth's usual scope and one with which he wants no truck.

While I'm cautious about endowing the films considered in this chapter with too much coherence or consistency, there is a compelling unity in the themes they convey. When Pierce jokes that Cy, transfixed on the balcony rail, is "our shish kebab of the night," he might as well have been referring to himself and the other anguished city dwellers whose torment Scorsese documents.

There is a continuity even in their use of mirrors, whether in a bathroom or a motor vehicle, or windows as metaphors for what Freud called the *superego* – the part of someone's mind that reflects social norms and, as such, functions as a self-critical conscience. At one point in *Bringing Out the Dead*, a slacker goes on a spree, smashing the windshields of a row of parked cars with a baseball bat. Invited to take a swipe, Pierce takes the bat and shatters a windshield. It functions as a symbolic gesture. Manmouth smashes a mirror in his own home with a vodka bottle in an attempt to rid himself of his unwelcome guest.

"The society *feels* to them like Kwakiutl or even Dobu." David Riesman's research prompted American participants to compare and contrast their own culture with that of the Kwakiutl, a native people of the northwest coast of America, and Pacific islanders from Dobu. The former was pictured as a culture of "conspicuous consumption," where canoes, copper sheets, and other items of value are ceremonially destroyed to display wealth, while the latter is "a society of paranoids," where economic life is sharp and sometimes fraudulent, property is sacrosanct, and theft is commonplace (p. 234).

Riesman's respondents didn't like what they considered the American character, but they felt powerless to do much about it: in fact, they felt coerced into conforming. The irony for Riesman was that no one was actually forcing them to behave. "It is they themselves," he concluded. Feelings of powerlessness were themselves powerful in inducing a state of conformity.

The 1960s and 1970s changed all that. The conflict in Vietnam started in the middle of the swinging sixties and provided a rallying point, bringing a generation together in protest. By the time the war ended in 1975, the American character had changed. Many other veterans shared the anomie experienced by Travis Bickle.

After the brief, shaky liberal period of Jimmy Carter's presidency (1977–81) came the reign of Ronald Reagan and a "return" to the values of muscular individualism, a preparedness to use force against weaker opponents, and boosterish self-reliance. "They summed up the code of the cowboy, the man in flight from his ancestors, from his immediate family, and from everything that tied him down and limited his freedom of movement," according to Christopher Lasch, in his *True and Only Heaven*. "Reagan played on the desire for order, continuity, responsibility, and discipline" (p. 39).

These were features of a new type of person who worked in an organized work environment with colleagues who were also trained to work to a consistent standard in a control-led manner and discharge their duties in a responsible way. Computer programmers, or word processors as they were sometimes known in the 1980s, keyed, formatted, and stored text in computers. They needed to be precise, accurate, and dependable. The computer programmer epitomizes Reagan's era much more dependably than the Wall Street dealer.

Scorsese's character Paul Hackett is one such

programmer: late twenties, educated, decently paid, he exhibits no strong political leanings, though he's probably satisfied with Reagan, now halfway through his presidential tenure. Hackett might not like the spiraling amounts spent on defense, or the cuts in social services budgets, but he feels better when he reads his salary slip and sees how little income tax he pays. He is as emblematic of the smug mid-1980s as Bickle is of the restless early 1970s.

Hackett is as emblematic of the smug mid-1980s as Bickle is of the restless early 1970s.

Hackett is the central figure of *After Hours*, a seriocomic story in which a wholesome and conventional young man grows bored and ventures out into the night. This is the same city that horrified Bickle and Pierce, though initially it holds no fears for the unworldly Hackett. Gullibility is apparently fortifying. But, as Hackett discovers, New York has an unfriendly core social order and he eventually comes face-to-face with the kind of vigilantism that had been legitimized to an extent by Goetz. In this case, Hackett becomes the quarry. (The film was released in 1985, the year after the Goetz shootings.)

"I don't intend to be stuck doing this for the rest of my life," a trainee tells Hackett, who is studiously instructing him in the use of format rulers, prefix codes, and suchlike. Hackett looks askance: chances are that *he's* going to be stuck long after his apprentice has moved on. It's a depressing thought to take home. When he gets back to his upper Manhattan apartment, television offers him no comfort: Hackett looks like another lonely man in the metropolis. He seeks relief in a nearby coffee shop, where he sits alone, until another loner catches his eye. After striking up a conversation, he discovers she shares an apartment in Manhattan's

SoHo, an area known for its artist-occupied industrial lofts and which was visualized in Scorsese's "Life lessons" (as we will learn in Chapter 8).

Later in the evening, Hackett contrives a way to get invited to the woman's loft and jumps in a taxi. There is a sense in which the drive to SoHo speaks for a decade, perhaps even a generation. Whereas Travis Bickle looked at his passengers and found demonic husbands with .44 Magnums or hookers going down on their johns, the driver of Hackett's cab sees a well-groomed middle-class professional whose most heinous act is losing the $20 bill with which he intended to pay the fare.

Hackett's pursuit of Marcy Franklin, as he discovers his fellow night owl is called, leads him to Kiki Bridges, the sculptor with whom she shares an apartment. The self-confident artist works in her underwear and looks every inch a maneater. Hackett admires and even assists in creating her current work, which is a three-dimensional papier-mâché representation of Edvard Munch's "The scream." The Norwegian artist's image featured, as we saw, in "Mirror, mirror," which was co-written (with Steven Spielberg) by Joseph Minion, who wrote the screenplay for *After Hours*. The Munch work is widely considered a potent expression of pain and frenzy, a visual equivalent perhaps of the literature of Franz Kafka, whose stories were characterized by a night-marish and elliptical reality, where the individual is lonely, confused, menaced, and often trapped.

Enamored of Franklin, Hackett heads unsuspectingly to his own entrapment. Little clues are ignored: why are $20 bills used in the sculptor's papier-mâché, and why is Franklin's account of a rape she says she experienced some time ago deliberately implausible ("he took his time . . . I slept through most of it")? And, perhaps, most enigmatically, why does Franklin volunteer intimate details about her ex-husband to someone she has only just met? "When he came, he'd scream out 'Surrender Dorothy!' . . . instead of moaning or saying, 'Oh, God,' or something normal like that." The exhortation is from *The Wizard of Oz*, where it's written in the sky by the broomstick-riding Wicked Witch of the West. Franklin's husband, it seems, was obsessed by the movie.

When he finally does exit the building and makes for the subway, Hackett is 53 cents short of the fare and refused a ticket by the vendor. "I could lose my job," he tells Hackett, who is incredulous. "Who would know, exactly?" he asks, pointing out that the rain is pouring and he will have to walk home. He despairs more at the vendor's indifference to his plight than his persnickety attention to pennies.

Lurking in the night are the kind of people Travis Bickle sought to exterminate. Sadomasochists, burglars, stoners, rentboys, and leather-clad bikers making out with each other are parts of a moving sprawl of nocturnal SoHo nightlife. At least they are alive. Hackett's biggest shock is a dead body: that of Franklin, who overdoses on Secanol, the barbiturate that contributed to the deaths of, among others, Jimi Hendrix, Marilyn Monroe, and Judy Garland, star of *The Wizard of Oz*, of course.

Death and mortality keep presenting themselves to Hackett. The death's head tattooed on Franklin's dead body also appears on her boyfriend's key ring and a nightclub patron's belt buckle. The bar he drops into is called Terminal. Eventually, he feels death encroaching himself.

The serpentine plot of *After Hours* involves Hackett's encounters with a series of women: after Franklin and Bridges, he runs into a waitress, an ice cream vendor, and a nightclubber, all of whom show ambiguous interest in him. Each woman, in her own way, assists Hackett's often comical attempts to get back to the safety of his own home. "The situation which is repeated over and over again in *After Hours* is this: a strange woman seems to offer something like love, and then turns on him [Hackett] threateningly," summarizes Lesley Stern in her *The Scorsese Connection*. "His perception of enmity, however, is articulated by the film as a possible reflection of his own hostile impulses" (p. 109).

This is one interpretation, though, when Hackett claims, "I have every reason to believe my life is in serious, serious danger," his perception seems accurate enough. After every attempt to escape has led him into an ever-less fortunate predicament, Hackett is falsely accused of burglaries he didn't commit and finds his face adoring amateurish posters: "THIS MAN IS A BURGLAR!! IF YOU SEE HIM, STOP HIM!"

Unlike Bickle's ruminative lone vigilante, those chasing Hackett are propelled by a kind of reflex action. As the mob bears down on him for crimes he didn't commit and a murder he suspects will be pinned on him, Hackett insists to a woman hiding him in a basement, "Those people up there want to kill me."

His cry of "What do you want from me? I'm just a word processor for chrissake!" is an appeal to no one in particular to deliver him from the "barbarians," as he calls the pursuant crowd, back to his "normal world" of computers, shirts, and paperclips. His escape is as surreal as the events that precede it: he is plastered in papier-mâché so that he resembles a sort of life-size Munch. When he falls off the back of a truck, the plaster cracks and he returns to his office, covered in powder, but seemingly unperturbed.

The familiar surroundings of desks, filing cabinets, and phones signal a successful resumption of normality after a night in the city's nocturne. As Cynthia Willett observes, in her 1996 analysis for *Cultural Critique*, "Hackett has fallen into a Kafkaesque-style maze of paranoid proportions, but with a difference. In yuppie America, there is one way out of terror, namely to return to work" (p. 150).

We might reverse Jack Kroll's point about Travis Bickle's being "a man who fits nowhere in society": Hackett fits practically everywhere. He just happens to find himself "in a nightmare where being a regular kind of guy is anomaly," as Esther Fein puts it in her 1985 review.

Riesman anticipated the coming of people like Hackett. He called them *indifferents*. "These new-style indifferents have some education and organizational competence and since they are neither morally committed to political principles nor emotionally related to political events, they are rather easily welded into cadres for political action – much as they are capable of being welded into a modern mechanized and specialized army. . . . Their loyalty is at large, ready to be captured" (p. 171).

In stark contrast, Bickle and Pierce are social hypochondriacs: they have an acute anxiety about apathy. Hackett is the kind of person who would have voted for Reagan, though without too much conviction. If this makes him conservative, then it doesn't prevent him from an occasional voyeuristic peek into the city's underworld. It scares him as much as it does Pierce and it did Bickle. But he has a safety zone into which he can retreat. Bickle, we suspect, would have used his Magnum on most of the people Hackett encounters.

Fein suggests that, in many Scorsese films, "the streets themselves became characters in the plot." Cities are not just places: they are living entities with mental and moral qualities that we infer through their inhabitants. Each of the three main characters featured in this chapter is a herald: they carry messages about life in the metropolis. Even the West Coast horror writer Manmouth makes a comment on city life, if only by his studious avoidance of it. Even then his stories evoke themes and motifs that Scorsese recycles.

For Scorsese, cities can and do strike dread as effectively as anything Manmouth can imagine in his books, which bear such titles as *Eyes of Terror* and *The Killer's Hand.* Jennifer L. McMahon develops this point in her 2007 essay "*After Hours*: Scorsese on absurdity," in

Conformity itself seems horrifying in a context of difference and diversity.

which she likens the film to the literature of Albert Camus and Jean-Paul Sartre, both of whom are closely aligned with existentialism. "Existentialists generally prefer to paint existence in alarming (rather than amusing) terms," she points out; "the truths that they are attempting to reveal are so unpalatable that an ordinary person simply will not acknowledge them unless forced to do so" (p. 121). Approached this way, *After Hours* and "Mirror, mirror" survey similar terrain. As McMahon suggests, "While not horror fictions in the manner of *Frankenstein* or *Psycho*, existentialist fiction often portrays existence in horrifying terms" (p. 122).

Hackett's existence seems hardly frightening, at first: living alone without wife or family and having a decent white-collar job affords him a certain desirable independence. But he's actually a total conformist; he's more likely to identify with the ghosts of an older generation than the one that experienced Vietnam. Not that he reacts to other people as if they were surrogate parents: he gets most of his guidance from contemporaries, or the media. He works in an institution and is, to a degree, shaped by institutions. It might be argued that the work organization is an elaborate kind of exoskeleton. Conformity itself seems horrifying in a context of difference and diversity.

Unlike Bickle, who despises himself for his inadequacies, and Pierce, who is consumed by guilt, Hackett has no cross to bear. He is at one with a city of anonymous people, none of whom will, as he puts it, "just sit and talk," but all of whom have some eccentricity. And all of them fit in with the heterogeneity of modern city life.

There is a moment in *After Hours* when Hackett is visibly repulsed by the sight of a rat caught in a rattrap but still wriggling. Perhaps it reminds him of his own entrapment in the less neighborly parts of the city, or perhaps in any part of town. Is this part of Scorsese's conception of the city? A humanly created device that entices but ensnares? In the three principal films considered in this chapter, the city is a paradox. It is an environment that encourages and releases individuality but captures and confines it in a way that frustrates sometimes to the point of implosion.

5

PAWNS IN THEIR GAME

In 1963, Medgar Wiley Evers, a civil rights leader working for the National Association for the Advancement of Colored People (NAACP) in Mississippi, was assassinated by a white supremacist. It was ten years after the landmark *Brown* vs. *Board of Education* case, which was meant to create the circumstances that would end racial segregation in America. But by the time of Evers' death, less than two percent of African American pupils in southern states attended integrated schools and the nation remained obdurately divided.

The Evers murder was one of a number of deaths attributed to a white backlash. With the civil rights movement and nonviolent protest gaining momentum, the nation faced the prospect of the most fundamental democratic change in its history. Martin Luther King's policy of nonviolent disobedience involved sit-ins, boycotts, and marches; it was often confronted with aggressive, sometimes deadly force.

Black protesters were frequently pummeled, kicked, and beaten by weapon-carrying whites, or bundled, carried, and dragged by police officers. In Scorsese's documentary *No Direction Home*, there is a silence in which hazy black and white images of incidents like these irrupt into the narrative, which tells the story of Bob Dylan. A black man curls up in a ball as a mob of white men and women take turns to hit him; baton-wielding cops heave bodies.

The voice of the artist and former inamorata of Dylan Suze Rotolo contextualizes. "I was working at CORE," she explains, CORE being the Congress of Racial Equality, an integrationist pressure group. "A call would come in and people would say, 'Oh my god, so-and-so was beaten to a pulp, so-and-so's in the hospital. These were traumatic times to live through . . . it was insane. Why should this be happening? And I'm sure Bob [Dylan] had that same feeling: you just can't live through this. You live in your own little world and have your own interests, but the outer world is definitely part of it."

Footage of Dylan performing at the historic rally of August 28, 1963 in Washington, DC, which became a defining moment in the civil rights movement, are followed by Mavis Staples, herself an African American, who asks "How could *he* write 'how many roads must a man walk down before you call him a man'? This is what my father went through: he was the one who wasn't called a man."

It functions as testimony to Dylan's empathy with the black people who were fighting for civil rights in the early 1960s. The first Civil Rights Act came in 1964. Dylan aligned himself with the cause fostered and pursued most eminently by King. "White people didn't have hard times," says Staples, perhaps oblivious to the fact that whites who joined the civil rights movement and participated in the sit-ins were treated much like black protesters.

No Direction Home is an epic film in the sense that it tells of what Dylan himself describes as his odyssey: in true Homeric style, it narrates the deeds and adventures of a legendary figure and locates his place in the history of the nation. It also makes sense of Dylan through the opinions and perspectives of guests who perform rather like a Greek chorus commenting and evaluating without ever intruding.

Dylan is described as a "sponge": he soaked up other musicians' mannerisms, their songs, and their motifs. But he also absorbed what musician Dave Van Ronk calls "the American collective unconscious." Dylan himself acknowledges his own eclectic approach; in the early 1960s, he strove to distil and convey what he calls the "essence of the spirit of the times." They were times that, as he famously sang, were a-changing.

Black and white flashbacks remind us of the hatred eating at America's soul as those changing times threatened to end an arrangement that had been in place for the best part of four centuries. America's postwar failure to deliver a semblance of equality for African Americans had been the subject of somber academic inquiry in the 1950s, though it took a prosaic incident to start what became a social movement. When, in 1955, Rosa Parks, a black seamstress, refused to give up her seat to a white man on a bus in Montgomery, Alabama, it was a small act of defiance with monumental consequences. The events that followed led to the formation of the Southern Christian Leadership Conference, led by King, and a sustained campaign that mobilized an entire generation.

Dylan was part of that generation; but the film portrays him as much, much more. Greil Marcus compares Scorsese's exposition to David Lean's presentation of the British soldier and writer T.E. Lawrence in the 1962 film *Lawrence of Arabia*. "He becomes the emblematic figure of his age," writes Marcus of Lawrence and, by implication, Dylan. "Not because he is a figurehead or spokesperson, but because in some essential and ultimately indefinable way, he *enacts* the age, acting out or performing the essence of its drama" (p. 50).

Dylan, for sure, was no leader or, as Marcus puts it, figurehead. In the film, Dylan makes this crystal clear: "The spokesman of the generation . . . *that* I couldn't relate to." *No Direction Home* discloses a remote man, often alone and detached from the struggle. His role seemed more that of a traveling troubadour, who dramatized events by setting them to music. For Scorsese, this doesn't appear to diminish Dylan's importance. If Dylan is "performing the essence" of America's drama, then civil rights and the fight against racism were part of that essence in the 1960s.

Scorsese's interpretation of Dylan accentuates this role, at the same time suggesting his opportunism in, for example, appropriating a collection of Woody Guthrie albums without the owner's permission, fabricating a personal history, and recording a track after consulting then ignoring its purveyor. The track in question is "The House of the Rising Sun," which Van Ronk was featuring in his act in the late 1950s and which was later recorded by the British band The Animals. In fact, Texas Alexander, a black blues player, first recorded the song as "Rising Sun blues" in 1928; given Scorsese's interest in blues music, it's surprising that Dylan's debt to this genre isn't acknowledged in the film.

Scorsese approaches Dylan as if he were at the center of whirling forces of social change. He is seen singing just yards away from Martin Luther King. Scorsese interposes a clip of Billie Holiday singing her elegy for the victims of racist lynching, "Strange fruit," even though Holiday died in 1959, before Dylan's emergence (and when Scorsese was making his high school project *Vesuvius VI*). And he introduces stills of the great Texas bluesman Huddie "Leadbelly" Ledbetter to strengthen the idea of a link between Dylan and the black American experience.

Certainly, Dylan surfaced in Greenwich Village at a time when civil rights was one of the two most powerful issues confronting Americans. The other was the atom bomb, the destructive power of which had been first realized in 1945 in Hiroshima, where a third of the Japanese city's 300,000 citizens were killed. A second American attack, on Nagasaki, led to Japan's surrender and to the end of World War II.

Scorsese's documentary features a contrary response from Dylan in an interview by the broadcast journalist and author Studs Terkel, who questions him about his allusion to nuclear fallout in his "A hard rain's gonna fall," only to be told, "It's not about atomic rain: it's a *hard* rain. Somebody else thought that too." This is a breathtaking understatement: *everybody* thought it was an anti-nuclear diatribe. In a later interview, Dylan says the song means "something's gonna happen."

The film includes reminiscences of friends of Dylan recalling the Cuban Missile Crisis of October 1962, which was the closest approach to nuclear war at any time between the USA and the former Soviet Republic. Friends of Dylan recall how bars and cafés were full of artists and musicians anxiously awaiting the response of Soviet leader Nikita Khrushchev, who eventually acceded. Whether Dylan consciously wrote lyrics that addressed such issues or not is less important than the undeniable reality that others believed he did. Dylan's music was either in or was brought into harmony with the times.

Dylan's keenness for writing on racism was equal to his apparent indifference to songs about nuclear war. Racial injustice was a seam that ran through the many layers of his work. Dylan's inspiration was what King, in his "I have a dream" speech, called "the fierce urgency of now."

The film also has footage of Oxford, Mississippi, about which Dylan sings in his 1963 track "Oxford town": "He went down to Oxford town. Guns and clubs followed him down. All because his face was brown." The reference is to an incident in 1962 when the University of Mississippi admitted James Meredith, its first black student at its Oxford campus. Protesting whites rioted in the streets, prompting President Kennedy to send in federal troops to quell the violence, which left two people dead. ARMY ENFORCES INTERGRATION reads a misspelled headline shown in the film.

Avoiding oblique or the kind of metaphorical attacks on racism favored by some blues musicians, Dylan pulled stories from newspapers and cast them into poetic compositions. His "The lonesome death of Hattie Carroll," in 1964, tells of an episode in Baltimore the previous year. William Devereux Zantzinger, an affluent white tobacco farmer, killed an African American barmaid named Hattie Carroll by beating her with his walking cane.

> **Dylan's "Only a pawn in their game" explains the murder of Medgar Evers in a way that deflects blame away from the individual killer.**

He served only six months in prison for manslaughter. Dylan spun the killing and the subsequent trial into a condemnation of American justice: "In the courtroom of honor, the judge pounded his gavel. To show that all's equal and that the courts are on the level . . . Stared at the person who killed for no reason . . . And handed out strongly, for penalty and repentance . . . a six-month sentence." (Zantzinger, who died in 2009, told Dylan biographer Howard Sounes that the song perpetrated "a total lie"; in 1991, Zantzinger was convicted of a scam in which he charged black workers rent for property he didn't own.)

Dylan might have been articulating a collective American unconsciousness, or perhaps, by 1963, a manifest consciousness, but it was not shared by everyone. While segregation might have ended legally with the 1954 Brown case, it endured *de facto* and was robustly defended by an assembly of whites who had vested interests in a divided nation, law enforcement agencies which reflected those interests, and politicians who depended on white votes. This was the import of Dylan's 1963 song "Only a pawn in their game," which is singled out in the film as one of his most influential pieces of work, offering an explanation of the murder of Medgar Evers but in a way that deflects blame away from the individual killer (who was, incidentally, not imprisoned until 1994, when new evidence came to light).

The exposition cites sheriffs, marshals, soldiers, and governors as the main beneficiaries of America's racist regime. "The poor white man's used in the hands of them all like a tool," sings Dylan to 15,000 people at the Newport folk festival in 1963. "To protect his white skin. To keep up his hate. So he never thinks straight."

This is a theory disguised as a song: racism, on Dylan's account, is perpetuated by a coalition of interest groups who profit from maintaining racial divisions: black people are cheap labor for white businesses and the criminal justice system reflects the powerful, not the powerless. White racists, like the killer of Evers, are "on the caboose of the train," the car at the rear that accommodates the crew, and not the plusher passenger carriages. When Dylan compares them to pawns, he means they are, in the wider game, pieces of the smallest size and value and so the most easily sacrificed. They are people used by more powerful groups for their own purposes.

In *No Direction Home*, black people are either blues musicians who provided the raw material on which later white artists capitalized, or the scorched remains of a fire fueled by economic interests. While it's never raised in the film, Dylan's own affinity with the blues almost inevitably meant that some of his music (like "The House of the Rising Sun") was sourced from black musicians, though not always with due acknowledgement. Muddy Waters features, along with Hank Williams, as an early influence. Another paradox that's absent from the film is the fact that Dylan himself, a white artist from Hibbing, Minnesota, should assume the mantle as a leading musical spokesman for racial justice, rather than, say, Richie Havens, an African American singer who also played in Greenwich Village in the early 1960s.

This changed as radically as the pattern of protest in 1965, when the Watts district of South Central Los Angeles was engulfed in a six-day conflagration. Frustrated by the gradual progress advocated by the civil rights movement, many black people took more direct, violent measures. The uprising spread to practically all major cities with black populations and, for two years, there were outbreaks all over North America, the last of these coming in July 1967 in Detroit, where forty-three people were killed after a week of violence. Detroit is, of course, the Motor City, home of the Motown record label, which had been started in 1959.

While Motown never endorsed the violent protest, several of its artists and their tracks were assigned political status. Singers such as Stevie Wonder, who in 1966 recorded a version of Dylan's "Blowin' in the wind," and tracks like Martha and the Vandellas' 1964 "Dancin' in the street" became the sounds of black protest. By 1969, Havens had grown in esteem and opened the famous Woodstock festival.

In 1976, with the release of "Hurricane," his crusading track about the seemingly unjust imprisonment for murder of the African American boxer Rubin Carter, Dylan seemed a slightly incongruous bard of racial issues. Carter was released after a long campaign that was assisted by Dylan.

While his alignment with the fight against racism was a feature of Dylan's early career, he later became associated more readily with protest against the Vietnam War, which started in 1957, US forces eventually withdrawing in 1973.

So much so that when a militant splinter of the Students for a Democratic Society (SDS) movement formed in 1969, it sought inspiration from Dylan's 1965 "Subterranean home-sick blues," which includes the supposedly prophetic lines: "Better stay away from those that carry around a fire hose. Keep a clean nose. Watch the plain clothes. You don't need a weatherman to know which way the wind blows." Thus the Weathermen were named and started their incendiary campaign against US involvement in Vietnam, as well as other issues, including racism.

No Direction Home is Scorsese's take on Dylan the phenomenon, rather than Dylan the man: he's as interested in other people's response to Dylan and the context in which he was afforded reverence as in the individual artist. This serves to give a definite form to his agreement with much of what Dylan was thought to represent. As Amy Taubin detects in her "From there to here," "Scorsese concretizes his identification with Dylan by re-recording in his own voice the confused, churlish speech Dylan made when he was given an award by the Emergency Civil Liberties Committee" (p. 33).

Scorsese himself has stated that, in order to situate Dylan in his time, he needed to recreate the cultural climate of the 1960s. "We're watching African-Americans having coffee at a luncheonette counter and white men pull one of them off the stool and start beating him up," Scorsese describes what he intends his audience to experience to Raffaele Donato in 2007. "That's absolutely awful, that's terrible. . . . That's the way it affected us then and that's how it should affect people now" (p. 206).

No Direction Home is a prism through which to view the Dylan phenomenon. Some writers, such as Paul Arthur in his "Please allow me to reproduce myself," argue that Scorsese's treatment invites comparisons with figures such as Jake La Motta and Travis Bickle. Dylan "exhibits some of the wariness and disaffection of an asocial outcast" (p. 50). Peter Doyle, in his "Citizen Dylan," concurs when he writes of Scorsese's Dylan, "he really was an artistic loner, a rolling stone" (p. 70).

Perhaps it's exactly this quality that tempted Scorsese into depicting Dylan as an emblematic character. After all, a rolling stone, in the proverb, doesn't accumulate status, responsibilities, or commitments. Dylan seemed happy for others to attribute these; though he never explicitly accepted any obligations for challenging nuclear armament, the war in Vietnam, or even the persistent racism that bedeviled America. He just wrote and sang about

> **It was an age in which those wishing to preserve what they saw as the American way of life killed many people, black and white, great and good.**

them. It's possible that Scorsese exaggerates Dylan's importance, particularly in civil rights. Was it possible for a white singer to "enact the age," to repeat Marcus' phrase? After all, it was an age in which those wishing to preserve what they saw as the American way of life killed many people, black and white, great and good.

Dylan bore no scars. If Joan Baez is to be believed, he rarely attended sit-ins (demonstrations in which occupants refused to leave a cafeteria or other public place), demonstrations, or other kinds of protests, although she actually sang with him at the "March on Washington" rally of 1963. It was enough, it seems, that he took a side at a point in history, when, as Baez points out, there was a stark, unavoidable choice to make. "You either: 'hated niggas,' or you supported King."

If there is, as Dylan suggested, a bogus kinship between the sacrificial pawns and America's powerholding kings, it is one that has afflicted the nation for decades, even centuries. Racism, prejudice, and other forms of discrimination based on purported physical differences aren't natural byproducts of ethnically mixed cultures. Scorsese is not renowned for addressing this issue full-on: he can't boast an equivalent of *Mississippi Burning* (1988), Alan Parker's fact-based account of the FBI's investigation into the disappearance of three civil rights activists in 1964, or Spike Lee's 1992 biopic *Malcolm X*, or anything resembling Norman Jewison's films, which includes the 1967 drama of racial tension in the South, *In the Heat of the Night*.

This doesn't mean Scorsese's vision of America is devoid of racism or that White Anglo Saxons are its sole perpetrators. On the contrary, Scorsese's films are reminders about the limitations of understanding racism as confined to one group or unvarying over time. This draws the approval of Jonathan Freedman, who, writing in *American Literary History*, singles out Scorsese's films as "rejecting ethnic nostalgia." "Such work seeks to think in complex ways about the place of ethnicity in larger social dramas including, but not limited to, those of race" (p. 526).

Racism and ethnicity are everywhere and in perpetual motion, changing continuously as circumstances change; though one form, more than any other, seems almost impervious to change. When, in *New York, New York*, Jimmy Doyle treads water while looking for a permanent job by guesting with a black jazz band at a Harlem nightclub, he raises a doubt. "Only one problem: do they let white cats in there?" he asks the band leader, who ironizes his answer: "You come round the back!" (Jazz enthusiasts often referred to each other as cats.)

Jazz provides a culture in which the music is superordinate: it represents an order over and above the petty differences between human beings, whatever their cultural origins. In *Boxcar Bertha* too there is a higher order that brings people together. Von Morton is a black union worker who is a member of the renegade gang in the 1930s, a period when Jim Crow was alive, meaning the segregation of blacks and whites was prescribed by law. This held sway until the 1960s, when, as we saw earlier, the civil rights movement attacked the moral as well as legal propriety of this arrangement.

The two instances of ethnic kinship stand in sharp contrast to the dominant tendency in American society. After the riots of the 1960s, a report authored by Otto Kerner described America as effectively "two societies, one black, one white, separate and unequal."

Scorsese sees more than two: America is more like a network of honeycombed cells, each with its own ethnic codes and protocols, which include prohibitions on transit. Passing from one cell to another, while not impossible, is contingent. One cell's racism is another's exclusivity, for Scorsese. If you defend codes, honor, respect history, observe ritual, and reciprocate favors, you are on the inside, entitled to call yourself a member and regard yourself as part of something. Those on the outside can legitimately be regarded with indifference or downright hatred: the insular code justifies taking any step to preserve the integrity of your own group, even at the expense of the others. Scorsese is less abstract in the way he brings these features of modern America to life.

In *No Direction Home* Dylan is reticent about his own background, though others reckon he fabricated much of his life story to fit circumstances. Perhaps it was circumstances that convinced him to change his family name from Zimmerman to Dylan. It's suggested in the film that he anticipated a Jewish-sounding name might be an impediment even in a milieu known for its liberal ideals. Scorsese's only Jewish character to encounter anti-Semitism is Ace Rothstein of *Casino*, who obviously saw no need to obscure his faith (the character on which Rothstein was based is, as noted earlier, Frank "Lefty" Rosenthal).

Throughout *Casino*, Nicky Santoro and his crew refer to Rothstein as a "kike" or "the Jew." At one point, Santoro mumbles, "Fucking Jews stick together, don't they?" with no dissent from his group. The county commissioner addresses Rothstein with the telltale, "You people . . ." a phrase loaded with bigotry. Rothstein never reacts, even when racially abused face-to-face. It's as if growing up in the Midwest has inured him to prejudice; his policy seems to be not to challenge it, just work around it. So when Santoro confronts him with, "You Jew motherfucker, you . . . every fucking wiseguy around will take a piece of your fucking Jew ass," he behaves as if he's been spoken to in this manner for his entire life. Perhaps he has.

> **Throughout *Casino*, Nicky Santoro and his crew refer to Rothstein as a "kike" or "the Jew." At one point, Santoro mumbles, "Fucking Jews stick together, don't they?"**

Jewish women are sneered at in *Mean Streets*: Charlie inquires, "Who's the girl?" and is bluntly answered, "Jewish." When he remarks that "she don't look Jewish," and seeks elaboration, his friend alludes to her promiscuity. "She's always in here with some different guy. You know the way they are." In *GoodFellas*, Henry Hill marries a Jewish woman, something that would have brought censure if not expulsion had he been Italian. But, he had an Irish father and, as such, was never accepted as ethnically Italian anyway. He enjoys the favor and grace of the *capos* and has enough money to lead an extravagant lifestyle. But he can never join the ranks of *Uomini D'onore*, or made men.

Ethnic borders are everywhere in Scorsese films. Italian ethnicity is examined mostly from the inside, especially in *Mean Streets* and *Raging Bull*, in which "outsiders" are regarded with mistrust and "insiders" are treated with respect unless they disrespect other insiders. When Johnny

Boy, in the former film, persistently violates the code, he effectively turns himself into an outsider. Even so, his close friend Charlie is shocked when he enquires how much money Johnny Boy owes his loanshark Michael. He regards them all as brethren. "You charged a guy from the neighborhood $1800 vig?" he asks incredulously ("vig" is short for *vigorish*, meaning a rate of interest on a loan from an illegal moneylender). The neighborhood is synonymous with the ethnic boundary, and Charlie does everything in his power to prevent a pesky dispute developing into a violent confrontation. He doesn't succeed, Scorsese's implied point being that money strains ethnic solidarity.

Scorsese's studies of Italian ethnicity in America are legion. In his 1974 documentary interview with his own parents, he records how, in the 1930s, America was regarded as "the land of opportunity" by Jews and Irish as well as Italians. This bred a sense of camaraderie according to Charles Scorsese. "Jewish and Italians used to work together," recalls the director's father in *Italianamerican*. Of all ethnic minorities in New York, only the Chinese were regarded with suspicion.

The Departed contains an episode that illustrates the longevity of this perception. Ever generous with his advice, Frank Costello reminds Chinese gangsters with whom he is dealing, "In this country, one guy brings the item. The other guy brings the money." He then adds a simplifying adage that draws on a centuries-old stereotype, "No tickee, no laundree." In one passage, Scorsese untwists an American prejudice that has its origins in the persecution of the 1880s when Chinese laborers working in mining and railroad industries became the focus of what was called the anti-coolie movement. (Scorsese is probably being mischievous: the film's plot is adapted from *Infernal Affairs*, a Hong Kong production featuring an all-Chinese cast.)

Costello functions as a scope through which Scorsese looks

at attitudes toward other ethnic groups, including Italians. Boston Irishman Costello reflects, "Years ago we had the church. That was just a way of saying we had each other. The Knights of Columbus were real true head-breakers. True guineas. They took over their piece of the city."

The Knights of Columbus is a fraternal benevolent organization started in late nineteenth-century America to help all Catholics, regardless of country of origin. Both Irish and Italians are predominantly Roman Catholics. "Guineas," in this context, is an epithet for Italian gangsters. It's not clear whether Costello is complaining or admiring the manner of the Italians' raid on what was once Irish territory, though the disparaging way he refers to them elsewhere in the film suggests his antipathy.

> **Far from being advocates of cultural diversity, Scorsese's characters usually pledge themselves to the cultures of their forefathers.**

An Indian convenience store owner objects to Costello's crew's language. "You keep calling me 'Babu'. It's Singh, motherfucker," he snaps, using a very American form of address. The reply is almost logical from the vantage point of an Irish American gangster, "Hey! You opened a store in an Irish neighborhood." So what does he, an Indian, expect? The scene is like an extension of a moment in *Bringing Out the Dead* when a south Asian taxi driver is referred to as if he were an unwanted pariah, "Hey, Swami . . . Raghead!"

Far from being the famed melting pot in which all ethnic groups blend and simmer in a rich and peppery casserole, America is more of a beat-up cauldron boiling over with acrid stew. Groups don't blend. They don't want to: far from being advocates of cultural diversity, Scorsese's characters usually pledge themselves to the cultures of their forefathers. The enmity expressed toward others is, in this sense, a defensive maneuver to maintain boundaries and ward off interlopers. Italians (the term preferred to Italian Americans), in particular, are prepared to work with and use outsiders when it suits their purposes. But they are disposable.

GoodFellas presents ethnic Italians' racism at its rawest. Stacks Edwards, an African American who is recruited for certain jobs, including the major Lufthansa robbery, serves his purpose adequately. But after the big heist, Tommy De Vito pays him an early morning visit and puts a bullet in his head. This is all very reasonable, even inevitable, to Hill and company. In contrast to the Italian wiseguys, who are sharp, sophisticated, organized, and practically untouchable, black gangstas are the ones who always take the fall. "Nigga stickup men" are like a different species, according to Hill, who assures his wife they are the only criminals who ever get caught. As we saw in Chapter 2, Hill dismisses blacks as indolent schmucks: "You know why they get caught? Because they fall asleep in the getaway car."

Italian wiseguys are united by their sometimes-lubricious contempt for African Americans. Scorsese allows a glimpse of this in *Mean Streets*, when Michael discovers that the girl he has been dating has been seen with a black guy. Mortified, he wipes his mouth, reminding himself with revulsion, "I kissed her."

But in *GoodFellas*, Scorsese permits a fuller display of offense at the Copacabana when Tommy De Vito's date reveals how impressed she is with the multitalented black performer Sammy Davis, Jr. De Vito and the rest of the group happily agree with her until she makes the mistake of remarking, "You could see how a white girl could fall for him."

De Vito is unwilling to let the remark pass. "So you condone that kind of stuff?" he asks. "I don't mean *me*," she explains. Like Michael in *Mean Streets*, De Vito is suddenly concerned that he's been intimate with a woman who is attracted to black men. In his mind, this would mean *he* has been involved with a black man. "I don't want to be kissing Nat King Cole." His date wriggles out of trouble by specifying that she admires Davis's talent, not him. "I understand what you're saying," says De Vito insincerely. "But watch what you say: people get the wrong impression."

De Vito is a very different animal to Jimmy Doyle in *New York, New York*, who is happy to make an accommodation with black musicians and fellow jazz aficionados. De Vito treats black people as articles that can be used then discarded. When assisting in a robbery, or singing for the delectation of whites, black people have use value. But that is all. So where is the grammar? Where is the structure or system that governs who befriends and who abhors?

The clue is in Scorsese's unchallenged presentation of Dylan's "Only a pawn in their game." Dylan, and we presume Scorsese, is interested in why lower-class whites seem to manifest more hostility toward blacks than more affluent whites. There's sharper economic competition at the lower levels of the economic ladder, of course. But, there is something else: status. In the traditional American hierarchy, especially in the South, black people as a whole were ranked below whites. This was enforced legally and, later, informally. Within the white sector, there was quite distinct class *ressentiment*, this being a psychological state arising from suppressed feelings of envy that can't be expressed openly.

John Dollard highlighted this in a classic 1937 study, *Caste and Class in a Southern Town*. Working-class whites were not much better off than blacks in material terms, but their skin served as some sort of compensation. Whatever the lowliness of their class position, the white is irrevocably ranked above the black in an American version of the caste system. The Dylan song conveys this: "Politician preaches to the poor white man, 'You got more than the blacks, don't complain. You're better than them, you been born with white skin.'"

In other words, racism, prejudice, and associated sorts of bigotry have origins in economic circumstances but are actually encouraged by politicians – and, we presume, the wealthy – who benefit from presiding over a weak and divided working population rather than a strongly united one.

In many Scorsese films, this remains obscured and there is a strong impression that ethnic divisions are part of the natural order. Italians hate Jews, Irish hate Italians, everybody hates Chinese, and so on. In *Gangs of New York*, however, Scorsese uses a conventional revenge tragedy to project a model of mutually destructive hostility in the nineteenth century. In this, he goes beyond the coordinates of human hatred and ethnic backbiting to present a wider perspective, which makes the racism and conflict of Scorsese's other work more comprehensible.

Between 1845 and 1849, famine in Ireland hastened a mass departure, a half-million Irish moving to Britain and over a million migrating to North America. They helped expand New York's population to a million by 1861, over 200,000 Irish and 118,000 Germans contributing to the developing new polyglot city. "With the growth, construction boomed and the Irish readily found jobs," writes Daniel J. Walkowitz in his article "'The Gangs of New York': The mean streets of history" (p. 206).

While many Irish found work, others perished during the Atlantic crossing, and the ones who stayed in New York, according to Eugene McLaughlin, "endured anti-Catholic hostility and were accused of taking jobs, undercutting wages, creating slums, and being political troublemakers" (p. 213). In *Gangs of New York*, Scorsese personifies this in the figure of Bill "The Butcher" Cutting, who gazes at the fresh arrival of immigrants at a New York port and declares, "I don't see no Americans. I see trespassers. Irish hawks who'll do a job for a nickel what a nigger does for a dime, what a white man used to get a quarter for."

Cutting and his followers were known as natives, or nativists, American-born people who believed in protecting the interests of established white inhabitants against those of migrants, slaves, or ex-slaves. Although slavery had ceased in New York State since 1826, the proclamation of Emancipation fueled poor whites' fear that freed black workers would migrate to the industrial north in search of jobs, adding pressure to the already competitive market for work. "Strains on these working people played into racism and ethnocentrism," Walkowitz observes (p. 206).

> **"I see trespassers. Irish hawks who'll do a job for a nickel what a nigger does for a dime, what a white man used to get a quarter for."** BILL CUTTING OF *GANGS OF NEW YORK*

By "played into," Walkowitz means that anti-Irish racism was already virulent among the English in the nineteenth century. The historian Edward A. Freeman, during his 1881–2 visits to America, observed, "This would be a great land if only every Irishman would kill a Negro, and be hanged for it" (quoted in Peter Gay's 1993 study, p. 81).

Freeman was probably reflecting deep historical sentiments of America's Anglo-Protestants. As Christopher Shannon points out, in his 2004 article for the religious journal *First Things*, "Anti-Catholicism has been called America's oldest prejudice" (p. 52). Cutting gives visible form to this prejudice and expands it to include others: he smiles disparagingly at a black man's dancing to the music of fife and drum. "Rhythms of the dark continent thrown into the kettle

Bill Cutting witnesses the collapse of a feudal estate based on ferocious ethnic rivalries. The modern bureaucratic state that replaced the feudal order introduced different kinds of bigotry, though their underlying causes remained. (© Kobal)

with an Irish shindig. Stir it around a few times and pour it out as a fine American mess."

Cutting is based on a figure from Herbert Asbury's book *The Gangs of New York*, first published in 1927 or 1928, and is accordingly a caricature. Asbury's tales of Old New York are, as James Parker puts it, "half-magical." But the sentiments Cutting expresses were widely shared. When he stares at Irish migrants and swears, "I'd shoot every one of them before they set foot on American soil," he summarizes the feelings of the Know-Nothings, a movement that was antagonistic toward Roman Catholics and recent immigrants, and which was active in the 1850s. Cutting's father, who, he states, died fighting in the American Revolution, was probably a Know-Nothing.

Cutting is the pivotal figure in *Gangs of New York* (as opposed to the book). Played by Daniel Day-Lewis, he is a fictional character with some resemblance to a real Bill Pool, who was killed in 1855. He features in a story of revenge: a boy named Amsterdam Vallon, played by Leonardo DiCaprio, is orphaned aged 8, in 1846, when his father is killed by Cutting while leading a coalition of Irish groups in an all-out battle against native Americans.

The orphan is sent away for fifteen years, after which he returns to New York's Five Points area bent on avenging his father's death. He meets and falls in love with a pickpocket called Jenny, who is also involved with Cutting, and insinuates himself into Cutting's inner circle. The plot is similar to many other tales of retribution, the vintage being Alexandre Dumas' *The Count of Monte Cristo* (1844/5). As in Dumas' classic, vengeance is exacted. Vallon confronts Cutting and kills him, listening to his adversary's final words, "I die a true American."

The story is what Scorsese himself has called a "motor" to drive a wider narrative about the historical divisions and conflicts that beset America in the nineteenth century and have vestiges that linger in the present. To this end, he concertinas history into brief periods, shifts the sequence of events, and voids some crucial events of proximate causes. Scorsese also tells a story that is entirely made up. But, he connects the events and the people together in a coherent manner and gives the sense of a continuous chronology of important events in a particular period. In other words, he provides an account of historical process: not a historically accurate study of past events, but a view of the past considered as a whole, or what Scorsese himself calls "an *impression* of a world."

It is a world rent with conflict, much of it directed by natives toward groups they regard as having no right in America. The conflict is exacerbated by the tendency of migrant groups to band together as a self-defense measure, establishing a segregated, sectarian environment with potential for confrontation. Social organization is "not just about gangs, but about *ethnic* gangs," stress Martin O'Brien et al.

in *Critical Criminology* (p. 21). "Notions of ethnic collectivity and gang membership are explicitly conjoined."

Religion also combines with ethnicity and gangs. The conflict between Irish Catholic migrants and Anglo-Protestant natives sometimes appears to be over religion, but Scorsese seems to suggest religious warring is a byproduct arising from a scramble over material resources, like shelter and money. It only looks like a conflict over religion because the churches provided sheltering canopies for migrant and indigenous groups alike in the nineteenth century. Remember Frank Costello's observation in *The Departed*, "Years ago we had the church. That was just a way of saying we had each other." Freedman comments on "the crucial role played by religion in the forging of ethnic self-understandings" (p. 527).

Religious solidarity made cultural difference – what Freedman calls "ethnic and racial self-understanding" – visible and provided a convenient basis for identifying groups designated unwanted. This complements Shannon's argument about anti-Catholicism; though American Indians, who have survived over 500 years of European, then white American, domination, hostility, and genocide, might contest Shannon's premise.

Native Protestants believed, as one of their political candidates puts it, that "invading hordes of Hibernians" were arriving. Hibernians themselves were worried about "hordes of ex-slaves looking to take Irish jobs," as Peter F. Stevens, of *The Boston Irish Reporter*, puts it. Hordes, it seems, were arriving from all corners.

While some critics assail Scorsese for airbrushing Irish racism out of his picture, Vincent DiGirolamo in *Radical History Review* disagrees: "No group is as badly misrepresented as the Irish. . . . They believed in free labor, if not Negro rights, and saw the planter class of the Confederacy as an aristocracy akin to the hated British" (p. 129).

The film also posits a Chinese presence in New York, though historians suggest that Scorsese exaggerates the numbers of Asians in the city during the period. Still, it gives the director the opportunity to expand nativists' range of targets and, in the process, disclose some of his own preconceptions. Chinese are depicted as whores and owners of establishments like "Sparrow's Pagoda," a brothel-cum-theater-cum-opium den.

But this is but one ring of conflict at the center of three concentric circles: a working poor, all sharing much the same material conditions, but set against each other by a perception of competition over scarce resources, the most basic of which was paid work. Housing was poor, with the Irish, in particular, living in insanitary slums known as rookeries. Cultural differences were reflected in faith, language, or physical appearance. In themselves, these were not sources of conflict; they functioned as badges of membership to different religious and ethnic groups. As such, some used them to identify "outsiders" and so provide substance to age-old as well as new prejudices.

A second ring of conflict involves the American Civil War, 1861–5, which is in the background of the film. It was fought over the issues of slavery and states' individual rights. The pro-slavery southern states seceded from the Union following the election of Abraham Lincoln on an anti-slavery platform, but were ultimately defeated by the North.

Irish migrants were sometimes conscripted into the Union army within hours of stepping off the boat. In the film, new migrants are handed two documents by military recruiters, "This one makes you a citizen. This one makes you a private in the Union army." The scene is played out to the sound of the traditional Irish song "Paddy's lamentation": "When we got to Yankee land, they shoved a gun into our hands, saying, 'Paddy, you must go and fight for Lincoln.'"

Lincoln's Conscription Act of 1863 was a draft to bolster the Federal Union forces during the Civil War, but included a clause that allowed those who could afford the then considerable sum of $300, about the annual wage of a manual worker, to avoid the draft ("for us, it might as well have been three million"). As Will Haygood points out in his "The battle of Old New York," "That exception was akin to creating class distinctions with an ax, especially for Irish immigrants, newly arrived and on fragile economic footing."

The draft was the catalyst for civil disturbance, natives and migrants alike causing mayhem in the streets of Old New York, an event popularly known as the Draft Riots. Scorsese's film climaxes with the riots, though the reconstruction has infuriated some historians.

"The Draft Riots were race riots as much as attacks against the government, and the factions were not white Irish versus white Protestants, but white Irish men, women, and children (and some white Protestants) against blacks . . . this was ethnic cleansing, on American soil." Benjamin Justice's verdict on the 1863 uprisings in New York is intended as a criticism of *Gangs of New York*, which, in his view, "is worse than apologetic; it's a denial" (p. 214).

Justice's article "Historical fiction to historical fact" presents one of a series of challenges to Scorsese's revision of history to suit dramatic requirements. Justice is piqued by the "denial" of racism as a motivation in the mass violence that closes the story. In his review of the movie for *The Journal of American History*, J. Matthew Gallman believes the portrayal "underplays the terrible attacks black citizens and institutions suffered, often at the hands of immigrant rioters" (p. 1125).

Gangs of New York shows a white mob in pursuit of blacks; it also shows the lynching and burning of a black man, though these appear to be random rather than systematic, as "ethnic cleansing" implies. The film doesn't reveal the well-documented attack on the Colored Orphan Asylum, which housed 300 African American children, and which was torched. Richard Oestreicher, one of a number of historians to criticize the film, uses the term "racial pogroms" to describe the event.

The violence subsided after three days, leaving a death toll of 119, including 11 blacks, according to Timothy J. Gilfoyle, another critic of the film, who describes the insurrection as "one of the two or three worst civil disorders in U.S. history" (p. 623). Bryan D. Palmer describes the displaced hostility in his review "The hands that built America,"

As with many subsequent urban uprisings in America, the anger was turned inwards against those with whom the rioters lived

where he writes of the rioters, "they resented the rich, but they killed their poor black brothers and sisters" (p. 330).

If the inner circle of conflict concerns religious, ethnic, or cultural hostilities, the outer circle involves a struggle against the government's attempts to conscript thousands into a war that had little relevance to the already beleaguered denizens of New York. As with many subsequent urban uprisings in America, the anger was turned inwards against those with whom the rioters lived rather than the inaccessible abstract government that was responsible for the conscription. Yet outside these two circles of conflict there is another encompassing circle that involves the gathering forces of history.

Modernization and the political structures it brings threaten a traditional order that has served Cutting and his kind well. Natives maintain a precarious authority through what Cutting calls "the spectacle of fearsome acts." Any attempt to usurp him is dealt with mercilessly. "That's what preserves the order of things – fear," confirms Cutting, as if delivering a memorandum to future gang leaders, such as those in *Casino* and *GoodFellas*. The natives, though, with their "backward-looking feudalistic understandings of American 'loyalty'," have a more formidable foe, as Palmer discloses. "A forward-marching bourgeoisie that would fashion its power and authority in production and exchange as well as out of the enticing carrot of 'democracy' and welfare provisioning backed by the violent stick of the state's repressive terror" (pp. 331–2).

Scorsese personifies this in William Marcy Tweed, who was one of the actual characters who ran the city. Neighborhood politicians were lifelines between the migrant and the new society. In New York, ward bosses were usually Irish, or Jewish. As a New York City official and state senator between 1867 and 1871, Tweed became the leader of Tammany Hall, the city's powerful Democratic Party organization, best known for its corruption. "Clerical errors" in the city finances cost the state treasury $200 million. Tweed was convicted in 1873, fled to Cuba, then Spain, but was extradited in 1876 and eventually died in 1878, imprisoned.

Tweed frowns on Cutting's primitive order: he represents the rise of the political machine in the modern bureaucratic state. "I'm talking about civic duty," he tells Cutting when the two men outline their visions. "Schools and hospitals, sewers and utilities, street construction, repairs and sweeping." He goes on to adumbrate the necessity that the city be responsible for its citizenry rather than allow them to remain self-reliant.

When Tweed tells Cutting that he's "turning his back on the future," Cutting snaps back, "not *our* future." Cutting's attempts to preserve his feudal estate against the strengthening state eventually bring the once-partners into conflict.

Politicians like Tweed were no idealists: their principles were based on practical rather than moral concerns, and, faced with the surge of unskilled migrants from Ireland and southern and central Europe, they responded in a way that suited their own requirements.

Industrialists, including the steel men and tin and railroad barons, encouraged the inexhaustible supply of migrant workers, who were prepared to work for less money than natives. And for migrants who were escaping from poverty, low wages were better than none. (Congress eventually tried to control migration with an ineffectual 1885 Contract Labor Law.)

Tweed has a mercenary approach to the Irish. When asked by Cutting to name "one thing they have contributed," he answers, "votes." He's prepared to pay Cutting a commission for securing him votes, though Cutting is true to his principles and refuses to help Tweed "befoul" his father's legacy. Tweed despairs at Cutting's failure to embrace what he sees as progress. "You can't fight forever," he tells him. And after Bill mutters, "I can go down doing it," he fires back, "You will."

Tweed sees politics as business: when Cutting rebuffs him, he turns to the Irish. "I'm offering, my boy, to form an alliance with you against Bill Cutting," he explains to Vallon, who responds by persuading Walter "Monk" McGinn to stand for Sheriff.

McGinn, a onetime hired fighter for Vallon's father, advises Amsterdam, *"An té nach bhfuil láidir ní folair dó a bheith glic,"* a Gaelic expression meaning if you're not strong, be smart. And, as if to demonstrate the value of this, he tries to outsmart Cutting, winning election (thanks to Tweed's rigging), then exposing him as someone who wants to fight instead of negotiating to settle political disputes. Cutting summarily kills him, signaling his resistance to the arrival of modern politics.

The murder does nothing to stop the inevitable tide of history, of course: little kingdoms like those of Cutting disappeared as the modern political machine envisaged by Tweed took over the running of major cities and eventually the country. When Cutting pronounces "civilization is crumbling," he is right: a *version* of civilization is falling to pieces. Its replacement is what Scorsese sees as the precursor of the modern American political system, a point he makes by featuring U2's track "The hands that built America" under the final image of the modern New York skyline (though, as Vincent DiGirolamo remarks, "all we see are the hands that try to tear it apart").

Modernity didn't usher in an idyll in which racism, religious persecution, and all forms of bigotry disappeared. As we've seen, Scorsese's America is marbled with inter-ethnic rivalries of near-barbaric intensity. So why do they persist? A return to the very start of *Gangs of New York* is instructive.

In portraying the 1846 confrontation which precipitates the recrimination, and in which Vallon's father is killed, Scorsese wraps up several less serious skirmishes involving native and migrant groups into a single climacteric. It establishes the lines that cleave the city and provides the film with its main theme. Workers and work-seekers do not oppose factory owners, political leaders, or landlords, but each other. The fighting is, as *The New Yorker*'s David Denby points out, "strictly along ethnic lines." Denby expresses reservation, "I can't believe that such a war would be fought without a material cause" (p. 166). He wonders whether the fighting was for control of the East Side docks, the whiskey trade, or gambling – the kind of resources that mobilized twentieth-century gangs.

From the perspective of natives, Irish migrants and their descendants are an unwanted presence. As Catholics, they're also the agents of Rome, representing papal interests instead of those of ordinary true-blood Americans. Ethnic conflict such as this is typically grounded in other struggles, so, when Denby solicits "a material cause" for the conflict, he is inquiring as to whether the cultural division is actually a byproduct of some deeper discontent. Were blacks and Irish blamed for the faults of others, such as capitalists who paid subsistence wages? Or for the schemes of others, like self-serving politicians, whose interests a disunited populace served?

Certainly, the only obvious groups to profit from conflict are politicians like Tweed, who bats for both teams, appeasing Irish with bowls of soup, while cozying up to Cutting. When the violence erupts, he stands back, calculating how he can gain. In a sense, blacks, Irish, and natives alike are all pawns in his game, to summon Dylan back to the argument.

Tweed was shrewd enough to realize that the growing Irish vote was crucial to his power. By strength of numbers the Irish eventually controlled the Tammany political machine engineered by Tweed. As Tom Deignan, of the *Irish Voice*, puts it, "The Irish climbed the American ladder, in part, because of the political clout they wielded thanks to their sheer, desperate numbers."

When Cutting states, "My father gave his life making this country what it is," he probably speaks for many more nineteenth-century natives: many had ancestors who had fought the British in the American Revolution of 1775–83. This helped shape their self-conceptions as Americans. Cutting's "patriotism and piety," as Sean Mattie calls them, are shared by a generation. But even age-old antagonisms fade with the generations and Mattie specifies three areas of the American landscape that were transfigured as "veneration for noble and heroic ancestors" receded.

In his "Blood, justice, and American citizenship," Mattie argues *Gangs of New York* discloses the end of a "tribal" era when neither natives nor migrants shared a view of the common good or acknowledged the same authority. As culture and politics became detribalized, there were agreements on what benefits the nation and what rules should govern the nation's behavior.

Several of Scorsese's other films suggest that the moral and political landscape of America didn't change quite as comprehensively as Mattie thinks. Tribal or ethnic rather than national loyalties continue to command the support and allegiance of individuals. The law is regarded as something that can be adapted, adulterated, or just avoided. And, if the enterprises exposed in films such as *The Departed* and *GoodFellas* are to be believed, Cutting's despotic regime, which was predicated on fear and maintained with the connivance of bribable politicians, was an exemplar for later generations.

"The old way of life – tribal, violent, and profoundly human – must pass away to make way for the cold, impersonal metropolis." This is a lesson author of "Melting pot" Richard A. Blake believes Scorsese conveys time and again. But the "old way" hadn't passed away by 1963 when Medgar Evers was killed; by 1993 when Rodney King was brutalized by four white Los Angeles police officers; by 1996 when Tupac Shakur was killed in a gangland drive-by shooting; or even by 1999 when unarmed Amadou Diallo was shot forty-nine times and killed by semiautomatic-weapon-carrying NYPD officers. The "cold impersonal metropolis" brought its own version of tribal violence.

Can tribalism ever die? Scorsese's main films are mostly jeremiads, their list of woes suggesting not. But, in his 2004 television documentary "Feel like going home," which was an episode of *Martin Scorsese Presents The Blues – A Musical Journey*, he portrays a slightly different image of an American culture. Here there are no antagonistic ethnic or religious tribes; just a mutual acceptance of different people with different tastes, all eager to enrich their own culture by absorbing those of others.

Blues music, Scorsese suggests, has deep roots in African folk rhythms. But it is an elementally American music, and the property of no one, no group in particular. Scorsese doesn't disguise the conflicts, particularly involving the church, which branded the blues "devil's music," or the racism that provided the music with much of its inspiration. Nor does he ignore the arguments over the propriety of blues. Black musicians are heard proclaiming it

Scorsese builds an America in which tribalism, racism, and ethnicity are not just discarded leftovers but integral parts of its construction.

as their own ("this is the one thing they could not take away from black people"), though Scorsese credits Alan Lomax, the folklorist and transcriber/recorder of blues songs, as the man who brought blues to a wider audience ("he came to realize music was as essential as human speech and just as precious"). He also acknowledges how white bands such as Led Zeppelin both cannibalized and popularized artists like Robert Johnson, whose music had calcified over the decades.

Without glossing over conflict, Scorsese proposes blues music approximates a paragon of ethnic fusion or, at least, incorporation in which peoples of diverse backgrounds, interests, beliefs, and outlooks contributed and cooperated even in a context of racial hatred and hostility. As R.A. Lawson puts it, in his 2007 "The first century of blues," "the coexistence of black acceptance and black rejection . . . allowed successive generations of scholars and enthusiasts to establish meaningful relationships with the sounds and personalities of the blues culture" (p. 60).

No metaphors are posed. Music, as Scorsese suggests in *New York, New York* and *No Direction Home*, is one of

those transcendent forces that has the capacity to amalga-
mate people. In his "Is 'The Blues' black enough?" Stephen
Asma concludes that Scorsese's "theme is that the blues
has become a universal language – that people of all races,
ethnicities, and classes find something meaningful in the
music."

People collaborate, working and melding together for a
specific purpose. Crime, Scorsese would have us believe, is
another transcendent force, though with direr consequences.
And, as I mentioned earlier, class – at least when filtered
through unions – is another. So ethnic unity is not a pipe
dream; it just needs, in the absence of a more precise term,
projects – undertakings or efforts that demand collaborative
not individual enterprise.

In Scorsese's films, the savage human consequences of
what Justice calls "ethnic cleansing on American soil" exist
in the past and present. The tragedy of racism might appear
to be part of America's history, yet Scorsese reveals the con-
tinuities. A remark passed unflinchingly by Frank Costello
in the presence of Chinese people calls to mind the same
sentiments expressed by Bill Cutting almost a century-and-
a-half before, and so recalls an entire history of bigoted
Orientalism. In *The Age of Innocence*, an observation by a
member of New York's *haut monde* in the 1870s that "the
whole tribe had rallied around his wife" anticipates the processes of unity and exclusion operated by American gangsters
in the 1950s. Images of black people being shot, lynched,
burned, intersect time and again throughout history. Around
these sounds and visions Scorsese builds an America in
which tribalism, racism, and ethnicity are not just discarded
leftovers but integral parts of its construction.

6

WHAT THE PEOPLE WANT

"Many of the expectations concerning the public behaviour of performers, sports people and politicians were predicated on splits between public and private life, front and back stage, which mostly no longer hold," writes Peter Doyle in his "Citizen Dylan," an assessment of *No Direction Home*. "Celebrity stalkers – of which the original obsessive Dylanologist A.J. Weberman offers a prototype – and paparazzi have helped put an end to that division" (p. 71).

In the 1960s, Weberman seemed less stalker, more haruspex – a soothsayer in ancient Rome who interpreted omens by inspecting the entrails of animals. Weberman foraged through Dylan's garbage for clues about the meaning of the man and his work. Doyle describes Dylan as being "as remote and enigmatic a figure to those who know him as he is to the rest of us," and this served to keep Weberman and lesser-known fans entranced.

The production of fame, the responsibilities it brings, and the consequences it has on both the famous and their audiences are themes that recur in several Scorsese films. Where else could an industry grow around the preposterous predicate that people will part with their hard-earned cash for anything as trivial as amusement? Only in America, seems to be Scorsese's aphoristic answer. And how come people who somehow contrive to amuse us have grown to the kind of prominence once reserved for Men of History?

Fame means something different today than it did a hundred years ago: then it was a kind of byproduct of a great accomplishment, such as leading a military campaign, or inventing something. President Woodrow Wilson was famous for taking the USA into World War I in 1917 and later playing a leading role in peace negotiations. Sir Alexander Fleming, the Scottish bacteriologist, was famous for discovering the effect of penicillin. Many politicians, literary figures, and religious leaders became famous, but, again, for doing something that made an impact on material lives.

Popular entertainers, like the Niagara-traversing tightrope walker Jean-François Gravelet, better known as Blondin, and Harry Houdini, the ingenious escape artist, were among the few showmen who became widely famous. Houdini, who died while still performing in 1926, was aided by an emergent radio industry. The first motion picture to include talking, Alan Crosland's *The Jazz Singer*, was released the year after Houdini's death. It heralded the start of

Scorsese has plotted the development of entertainment from a primitive method of distracting the masses to an all-conquering business

film, as we understand it today, and the rise of the modern film star, someone whose fame was predicated entirely on their ability to entertain us. (Silent films such as D.W. Griffith's *Hearts of the World*, 1918, and *Orphans of the Storm*,

1922, revealed Lillian Gish as a notable actor, as *The Kid*, 1921, and *The Gold Rush*, 1925, did Charlie Chaplin, who was actor/director of both films. Gish and Chaplin continued to make films into the 1940s, adapting to the changing demands of film to become modern stars.)

In the midst of a culture of Christian fundamentalism, Prohibition, and Model T Fords, amusement was turned from idle diversion into economic activity. Ian Christie believes Scorsese has a longstanding "fascination with the US entertainment industry." In his article "Fly guy," Christie suggests, "*The Aviator* . . . seems to have offered Scorsese a way to satisfy his own 'epic' impulses" (p. 20). Perhaps. Yet, that film is but one of a number in which Scorsese has plotted the development of entertainment from a primitive method of distracting the masses to an all-conquering business.

The industry responsible for the manufacture and distribution of organized amusement and its vital ancillary product, stardom, is seen in embryonic form in *Gangs of New York*. Blondin doesn't appear in the film, though he was only 300 miles or so to the northwest of Five Points in 1859. He was making the first of several crossings of Niagara Falls, each successive stunt getting hairier – he crossed blindfolded, in a sack, with a man on his back, and even cooked an omelet during one attempt.

Although Blondin wasn't part of the Greatest Show on Earth, you get the impression P.T. Barnum would have liked him to have been. Barnum appears in *Gangs of New York* as the proprietor of Barnum's American Museum on Broadway. He actually took over the museum in 1841 and converted it into a popular showplace, exhibiting live and stuffed animals from all over the world and human curios, like conjoined twins, dwarfs, and strongmen. Jugglers and conjurors were among Barnum's entertainers. It was effectively what we might today call a freak show, but, in the middle of the nineteenth century, the museum was the center of a primitive entertainment industry.

During the Draft Riots scenes in *Gangs of New York*, an elephant is seen stampeding along the streets, implying the museum was forced open during the unrest (Barnum paid $10,000 to London Zoo for a six-ton African elephant, which he shipped to New York to exhibit). In fact, the museum survived the uprising and lasted another two years, when it was burned. Barnum opened another museum, but that, too, went up in smoke (fires were commonplace in Victorian times).

Barnum then decided to take a version of his show on the road. "P.T. Barnum's Grand Traveling Museum, Menagerie, Caravan and Hippodrome" was the forerunner of the Greatest Show on Earth, with which Barnum is popularly associated. He is also associated with the phrase "There's a sucker born every minute," which sums up his approach to his audience: for him, people wanted to be entertained and, if it meant duping, hoaxing, or misguiding them in a way that didn't harm them, then it was acceptable. He drew the line at fake spiritualists, who were popular in his day.

Historian Bryan D. Palmer, in "The hands that built America," notes that Scorsese features a scene at "Sparrow's Pagoda" "in which Oriental acrobats bounce off the floor and caged prostitutes are suspended from the ceiling, auctioned off by none other than P.T. Barnum" (p. 327). The director seems to have taken some artistic liberty in this respect.

Neil Harris' 1973 book bears the title *Humbug: The art of P.T. Barnum*. Nowadays, we'd call it hype, and, in a sense, Barnum was a founder of hyperbolism (if by that we mean making exaggerated claims that shouldn't be taken literally). In his psychology of fame study *Images of Immortality*, David Giles cites Barnum as a showbusiness pioneer: the techniques he used for publicizing his shows were much the same as those used throughout the twentieth century. The Hollywood film industry's publicity machine refined and perfected what was for Barnum a rudimentary tool into a precision instrument. Art gave way to science. Barnum's legacy lasted long after his death in 1891, aged 80.

The *Los Angeles Times*'s Kenneth Turan believes Barnum is used merely as "window dressing" by Scorsese. This suggests he has no functional role in advancing the plot. Maybe not; but, in the overall context of Scorsese's films, he represents the presence of an incipient industry and, in this sense, he is a harbinger, signaling the approach of showbusiness – and the approach of a new type of mentality that we now take for granted, but which took shape only during the twentieth century.

Scorsese hints at this in *Gangs of New York* when Barnum stages a version of Harriet Beecher Stowe's antislavery classic, featuring Harry Watkins, an actual actor of the period. "In 1853 H.J. Conway's adaptation of *Uncle Tom's Cabin* played in the American Museum, directed by C.W. Clarke. Unlike the novel, this version had a happy ending," records Neil Harris (p. 106). Scorsese shuttles it into the 1860s. (Stowe's book was first published in 1852.)

> **"It was widely known in New York but never acknowledged that Americans want to get away from amusement even more quickly than they want to get to it."**
> NARRATOR IN *THE AGE OF INNOCENCE*

The event is uproarious, with the audience shouting, jeering, fighting, and pelting the actors with anything at hand. The auditorium resembles a moshpit, though with less decorum. The play seems insignificant: the crowd's amusement derives from their own activities, not the players'.

Similarly, in *The Age of Innocence*, set about a decade later but at the other end of the social scale (and, for intents and purposes, in a different world) – one described by its narrator as "balanced precariously" – there is staged entertainment, in which the audience seems little concerned with the performance and more concerned with who is escorting whom. Opera glasses serve as periscopes, offering gossipy patrons a view of interactions that might otherwise evade their gaze. "It was widely known in New York but never acknowledged that Americans want to get away from amusement even more quickly than they want to get to it," the narrator comments.

The "amusement" in this case is opera, and members of the audience leave during the "Jewel song," making their ways to the annual Beaufort Ball, which was a more important social occasion than the opera itself. In fact, even the entertainment is something of a ritual. The elite of Old New York watch the same opera every year whether or not they understand it. Charles H. Helmetag, in his review of the film, notes how "*Faust* was sung in Italian, of course, in fidelity to the novel, since in the 1870s New York society preferred to hear all operas sung in Italian, regardless of the language in which they had been composed. Even the programs listed the arias in Italian" (p. 164).

"The real thing was never said or done or even thought, but only represented by a set of arbitrary signs," observes the narrator. Appearing at the opera was an important social presentation; understanding, less still enjoying, it was immaterial. In this world, everyone follows everyone else.

In both events, the staged entertainment is only ostensibly the attraction. It provides an occasion for something more valuable, whether a cathartic blowout, or a careful observance of decorum. The actual productions on stage are of secondary importance and the players, singers, or actors are complete irrelevancies. Entertainment in this period is much closer to its earlier historical meaning: to receive others as guests and provide them with sustenance or enjoyment. Barnum was among those visionaries who saw that he could turn a penny by offering comparably agreeable experiences.

If, during his quests for exotica, Barnum had found a serum for everlasting life, he would have staged vaudeville in the early twentieth century, moved to Hollywood to start a film studio around 1910, a radio station in the 1920s, and expand into television in the early 1950s. Now, he would probably head a global multimedia corporation. His central insight was that popular entertainment offered opportunities to make money; he wasn't alone in realizing this.

"*This* is what the people want," says Howard Hughes as he stares at *The Jazz Singer*. Accompanying the flickering monochrome images of Al Jolson in blackface is the sound of his voice; it was, as I mentioned before, the first film to include synchronized dialogue. After its release in 1927, films progressively began to incorporate sound, ushering in the age of the "talkies." "Silent pictures are yesterday's news," Hughes declares.

Like many of his other prognostications, it is right; but it presents Hughes with a problem. He has just made one such silent picture at exorbitant cost to himself personally and against the advice of Louis B. Mayer, the head of Metro-Goldwyn-Mayer pictures. "Why don't you take your money and put it in the bank?" counsels Mayer, a Russian migrant who had moved from Boston to Hollywood in 1918 to become one of the film industry's early power brokers. But Hughes is undeterred. What's more he proposes to change his project. "We gotta reshoot *Hell's Angels* for sound . . . all of it."

The film eventually cost almost $4 million to make, most of the money coming from Hughes' engineering company,

Howard Hughes (left) was more of an irritant than a threat to the Hollywood establishment. He challenged conventions by featuring Jane Russell (background) in The Outlaw, *which was considered risqué in the early 1940s. (© Kobal)*

which he re-mortgaged to finance the project. The cost of *The Jazz Singer*, which was considered expensive at $422,000, pales by comparison. *The Aviator* is a study of megalomania, combined with a diatribe against US government and a sideways inspection of the Hollywood film industry in the late 1920s and 1930s. This was a "period of industrialization," as Joshua Gamson calls it. It yielded "a developed profession of public image-management, and an elaborate and tightly controlled production system mass-producing celebrities for a widely consuming audience" (p. 6). The title of Gamson's essay, "The assembly line of greatness," suggests how entertainment was being manufactured for mass audiences.

Hollywood grew with American culture: sown by enterprise, raised with capital, and capable of reproducing in every land in the western world. It was ruled by five major studios: 20th Century Fox, Paramount, RKO, MGM, and Warner Brothers. Up till 1948, these studios also owned cinemas, giving them effective control over the production

"*This* is what the people want. Silent pictures are yesterday's news."

HOWARD HUGHES, IN *THE AVIATOR*

and distribution of their product. As an independent operator, Hughes was challenging an effective establishment.

Paul A. Cantor, in his essay "Flying solo," suspects of Scorsese, "There has always been a rebellious and anti-authority streak in his movies that suggests an affinity with libertarianism" (p. 169). By this, he means that Scorsese seems to embrace an extreme laissez-faire political philosophy, which advocates as little intervention as possible from governments in the lives of citizens, a doctrine that has roots in the work of eighteenth-century Scottish economist Adam Smith.

"A rugged individualism . . . redolent of the frontier" is how Jerry Z. Muller describes the American adaptation of Smith's philosophy, in his book *Conservatism*. In *The Aviator*, Scorsese suggests that Hughes, a supreme individualist possessed of the entrepreneurial spirit and a schoolboy imagination, was stymied, at first by a Hollywood film industry that was effectively bossed by a cartel, then by a federal government peopled by odious politicians whose aim in life was to protect existing business interests. Scorsese documents palm-greasing greed, graft, and monopolistic corruption.

While Hughes is presented as a plucky rebel, he was actually a rich man at 19. His father died in 1925, leaving him control of the Hughes Tool Company, which made oil-drilling machinery. Hughes dropped out of university to run the business and soon began to entertain ambitions of becoming a filmmaker. Scorsese's film starts during production of *Hell's Angels*, with Hughes soliciting the loan of additional cameras from Mayer, who dispenses an entrepreneurial lesson when he tells him, "MGM isn't usually in the practice of helping out the competition."

Against all odds, *Hell's Angels* makes it to the screen and bolsters Hughes' sense of destiny. "Leave the big ideas to me," he tells his associates, to whom he entrusts only operational duties. His next big idea is to make a sexy western. A preposterous concept in the early 1930s, the project eventually became *The Outlaw*, a film completed by 1941, but which didn't gain theatrical release for another five years. Scorsese doesn't make this clear, but this film brought Hughes into further conflict with the Hollywood oligarchy.

The Outlaw featured Jane Russell replete with a specially engineered brassiere – what we would now call a push-up bra. "The picture appeals only to prurient interests" is the conclusion of the Motion Picture Association Censorship Board, though Hughes, in the film, marshals mathematical evidence to demonstrate that the amount of cleavage revealed in his film is not statistically abnormal compared to other releases. At this point Hughes appears as an heir presumptive to Barnum: he creates the hype to build interest well before the films reach the screens.

The Hollywood Production Code Administration ordered edits and, though Hughes initially resisted ("I'm not making a single cut"), *The Outlaw* was released with a poster bearing the legend THE PICTURE THAT COULDN'T BE STOPPED. In fact, it was: pulled from distribution, then re-edited, *The Outlaw* finally became a box office success. When Cliff Froehlich writes in the *St. Louis Post-Despatch*, "Scorsese's career is a conscious rebuke to Hollywood's safe, committee-approved formulas and narrow tastes," he suggests a parallel between the two directors.

Richard Alleva, in "It's cold up there," also discerns a comparison, though not a valid one, in his opinion. "Scorsese might have been drawn to Hughes because he identified the tycoon with visionary moviemakers like D.W. Griffith and Erich von Stroheim who defied studio bosses and often made unreleasable movies." But, he points out, "the parallel doesn't work since the moviemakers made films that, however overdone, contain treasures" (p. 20). Hughes, on this account left nothing of comparable value.

Scorsese sees Hughes differently: he spends less time on Hughes' hassle over *The Outlaw* and more on his struggle with the established airline operators and their government lackeys – at least, this is how Scorsese portrays them. He wins some, loses some; but all the time, he is striving against vested interests, institutional hierarchies, and time-honored practices. In the process, he becomes ever more bitter about how money and power lend elites a self-perpetuating dynamic.

Invited to the home of Katherine Hepburn's family, he hears amid the polite, though condescending dinner conversation, "We don't care about money here." His reply is like a whiplash: "That's because you have it . . . you don't care about money because you've always had it . . . some of us choose to work for a living."

Hughes might have started with the benefit of the business he inherited from his father, but he has no affinities with privileged classes that live off "old money" ("high hat, Ivy League pricks"). His values are proudly bourgeois in the sense that he upholds the principles of capitalism and feels that, good as money is, it should be honestly earned and used productively rather than fetishized. For Hughes there is no problem in inheriting wealth; the real problem lies in how to spend it: in his case, it was to finance his occasionally reckless projects. His 200-ton, eight-engine plane that was intended for World War II, but hampered repeatedly, was one such project, though, as the film indicates, the behemoth eventually did fly. The film closes shortly after this, showcasing Hughes as one of the last maverick businessmen in a corporatizing America.

In later life, Hughes succumbed to an obsessional-compulsive disorder compounded by a dependence on prescription drugs. The film shows some of his more bizarre practices, such as hiding himself away, storing his urine in milk bottles, or endlessly repeating phrases ("Show me all the blueprints. Show me all the blueprints"). Before his death in 1976, Hughes was a recluse with a severe anxiety over germs. His behavior in the 1930s and 1940s was anything but reclusive. He is seen at red carpet premieres escorted by Jean Harlow, whose career he launched in *Hell's Angels*, and dining with movie stars, such as Errol Flynn and Katherine Hepburn. When Hepburn complains that he is being photographed with other women in magazines ("Joan Crawford, Ginger Rogers, Linda Darnell, Joan Fontaine and now Bette Davis"), Hughes retaliates, "Since when do you care about scandal rags?"

It's an interesting counterpoint to an earlier scene in which Hepburn senses that Hughes is about to become a "name" in Hollywood, and, as such, should prepare himself for the media interest that was developing around film actors that came off "the assembly line of greatness." "I've been famous, for better or worse, for a long time now and I wonder if you know what it really means." He answers, "Yeah. I had my fair share of press on *Hell's Angels*. I'm used to it." (Hepburn actually made her film debut in 1932, two years after the release of *Hell's Angels*.)

Perhaps anticipating the onset of the invasive breed of

photojournalists, later to be known as paparazzi, Hepburn counsels, "We have to be very careful not to let people in or they'll make us into freaks." She complains that there were photographers at her brother's funeral. "They can always get in. . . . There's no decency."

Undeterred, Hughes continues his romance with Hollywood, acquiring the film production and distribution company RKO for a short period in the 1950s. By this time, the once-great studio responsible for classics such as *King Kong*, in 1933, and *Citizen Kane*, in 1941, was ailing badly and Hughes' tenure in command did nothing to reverse its fortunes. Hughes did, however, save the then promising career of Robert Mitchum, who, according to Lee Server, was arrested for marijuana possession in 1948. At the time, scandals such as this ruined many a showbusiness career. Mitchum was signed to RKO and Hughes assembled a powerful team to defend him.

In his *Robert Mitchum: Baby, I don't care*, Server records that Hughes agreed to loan Mitchum $500,000 at five percent interest. Mitchum was given a year's suspended sentence and placed on probation for two years, sixty days of that in the county jail. He emerged to make more movies for Hughes, including Josef von Sternberg and Nicholas Ray's *Macao* of 1952, in which he starred with Jane Russell. When he sold the company in 1954, Hughes effectively ended his relationship with the entertainment business, though not with entertainment itself.

Some have called it a golden age: a period when the Hollywood film industry rose to an artistic peak. Academy Award-winning films were released such as Victor Fleming's *Gone With the Wind* in 1939, Michael Curtiz's *Casablanca* in 1942, and William Wyler's *The Best Years of Our Lives* in 1946. Stars like Vivien Leigh, Humphrey Bogart, and James Stewart were untouchable, inaccessible, almost godlike beings who seemed to occupy a plane an unbridgeable distance away from fans. Hughes wasn't a star and spent most of the golden age breaking the rules Hollywood prescribed. Scorsese sees him as, at first, comfortable with the glamorous Hollywood lifestyle, then finding its excesses so unbearable that he hid himself not only from the media but from everybody.

Hughes might have enjoyed hobnobbing with the stars, but he never fully embraced their lifestyle. Not for him an afternoon's shopping in Rodeo Drive: he instructs his assistant to buy his clothes for him and insists they shop at J.C. Penney's, or Sears, according to Scorsese. Hughes saw himself as a star-maker rather than one of the countless stars who were, in the period, paid employees of the film studio. Not always well-paid employees either, as Hughes points out: "Actresses are cheap in this town."

The world outside Hollywood might be in awe of the celestial beings who grace the big screen. But Hughes regards them as inconsequential, like worker ants.

The world outside Hollywood might be in awe of the celestial beings who grace the big screen. But Hughes regards them as inconsequential, like worker ants, and he reminds Hepburn as much when she rises above her station, "Don't you ever talk down to me. You are a movie star. *Nothing more.*" (In 1950, Stewart, who, like other actors, was under studio contract, negotiated a different kind of deal for the Anthony Mann film *Winchester '73*: in taking a share of the profits as well as a flat rate, he paved the way for others to assert their independence from their employers.)

During the final two decades of his life (he died in 1976) – which are not shown in the film – Hughes was rarely seen. He also took to traveling, always in secrecy and always staying at hotels. While Scorsese's film doesn't cover this period, Jonathan Demme's 1980 *Melvin and Howard* suggests that Hughes took to wandering across Nevada in the guise of a penniless vagrant and became the benefactor of a milkman who loaned him a quarter. Such was the interest in Hughes that, when Clifford Irving claimed to have clinched his permission to write a biography, he was able to take his pick of the major publishing houses and negotiate his own advance royalties. Irving's fabrication is the subject of *The Hoax*, Lasse Hallström's 2007 film.

Once a highly visible Hollywood figure, Hughes ended life an indiscernible enigma. As often happens when interesting figures recede from public view, their myth outlasts and outgrows the person. In Hughes' case, the weirdness of the myth was not exaggerated: as Hepburn says, "There's too much 'Howard Hughes' in Howard Hughes." Although rarely seen, stories about Hughes continued to circulate and continued to captivate fans even after his kidneys failed, aged 70. By this time, showbusiness had changed dramatically from the industry he once sought to conquer. The stars had grown in stature, the media had grown more curious, and the fans had just grown. Not only were there more of them; they spent more money and, in return, made more demands.

Where fans would once have been content to see films and read about stars in magazines like *Photoplay* and *Modern Screen*, they turned into voracious consumers with a sense of entitlement. The stars were no longer "popularly elected gods and goddesses," as Gamson calls them in his *Claims to Fame*, and were seen more like ordinary mortals with whom fans could feel a sense of intimacy. Consumers became what Gamson calls "simultaneous voyeurs of and performers in commercial culture" (p. 137).

Fans became part of the whole showbusiness spectacle. After all, without them, film would be a very different medium, more like that of theater perhaps. Mitchum-like scandals captured the media's attention and, as such, were precious resources. Fans rather than studios or courts were the moral arbiters. Movie and, later, television stars became commodities: articles of merchandise that could be traded on the market. To have value, consumers had to *want* them: the films in which they appeared, the products they endorsed, and the values they seemed to personify. Fans devoted themselves to stars in a way that would once have been certifiable. By the 1970s, the outlandish behavior of fans was becoming more commonplace.

Johnny Carson, the doyen of late-night television for three decades from 1962, was the consummate showman: he reigned supreme dispensing slick one-liners or performing song-and-dance numbers with his guests on NBC's nightly "Tonight" show. Few of his audience knew how he lived in fear of his own fans – and with just cause. After his death, the FBI released nearly 400 pages of documents detailing dozens of threats against Carson in the 1970s and 1980s. A typical one came from a certain "Victor Lake" who wrote to Carson, explaining how he would blow him to smithereens, according to the *New York Post*'s Bill Hoffmann.

The threatened homicide didn't happen, but Carson must have been spooked by the thought that fans sometimes carry out their misdeeds. Robert Bardo, for example, was a worshipful fan of Rebecca Schaeffer, who played a sweet and virtuous young woman in the CBS tv show "My sister Sam." Bardo taped every episode and replayed them endlessly. He became upset, however, when he saw Schaeffer play a much juicier role in Paul Bartel's 1989 sex comedy *Scenes from the Class Struggle in Beverly Hills*.

Days later, he got a .357 Magnum and shot her dead. "I have an obsession with the unattainable. I have to eliminate what I cannot attain," he explained (quoted on p. 18 of Nancy Hooper's 1995 article "Celebrities at risk"). In custody, he insisted that Schaeffer had his name and number in her address book; she hadn't (a detail noted in Joseph C. Merschman's 2001 study "The dark side of the web").

Love–hate does not quite do justice to Bardo's tortured relationship with Schaeffer: adore–abominate comes closer. He was surely the incarnation of the extreme fan, a creature who isn't content to worship from afar, but who imagines he or she can have something like intimacy with whoever inhabits their thoughts. Television made this possible: seeing someone, even in only two dimensions, created the illusion that there was the possibility of a relationship. Someone like Johnny Carson, who was on tv screens five nights a week all year round, wasn't just a well-known image; he was someone with whom viewers identified, related to, or connected with, to use some of the terms we regularly use to describe a one-way association. And, of course, they are one-way, at least for the most part. Only a small proportion of fans ever get to see, less still interact with, the object of their devotion.

A 1956 article in the journal *Psychiatry* introduced a term to describe this imaginary relationship that viewers experienced with tv characters they regularly saw but never met. *Parasocial interaction*, according to Donald Horton and R. Richard Wohl, is experienced by only one party – the viewer. This doesn't diminish the impact of the interaction, at least not for the viewer, who is able subjectively to create a relationship, have conversations, exchange ideas, reciprocate favors, and so on. Rupert Pupkin has created one such interaction in *The King of Comedy*. In his case it's with Jerry Langford, a talk show host not unlike the previously mentioned Carson.

Pupkin's parasocial interaction is an elaborate affair, involving his own "studio" in the basement of a home he shares with his mother. He has positioned lifesize cardboard

cutouts of Langford and Liza Minnelli to create the impression of Langford's show. Pupkin acts out a ritual in which he
enters to applause (which only he hears, of course) and takes
his place after air kissing Minnelli ("Hi, Liza") and compli-
menting Langford ("Jerry . . . don't get up"), whose responses
only Pupkin hears. He goes through the kind of spiel heard on
any number of talk shows and with some aplomb. Working
the imaginary audience, he plays around with his guests as if
he were a pro. This might be a make-believe world, but it's
constructed in elaborate detail and played out with scrupu-
lous attention to authenticity. And Pupkin feels a familiarity,
even intimacy, with his "guests" ("He's a personal friend of
mine," he says of Woody Allen, with complete conviction).
Pupkin is integrated with his fantasy.

Yet, when Pupkin congregates with a miscellany of autograph hunters, star-crossed adulators, and rhapsodizing fans,
he is at pains to tell anybody who will listen that pursuing
stars is just a hobby. "It's not my whole life," he stresses.
Much of what he does suggests otherwise. So, when he manages to squeeze into Langford's chauffeur-driven car and tell
his idol "by nature, I'm a comedian," his meaning is clear:
autograph hunting isn't his whole life, but it is part of a more
consuming project, which is to emulate the stars.

"I've studied everything you did," he tells Langford,
without disclosing too much of his obsessional tendency.
Langford hands him a handkerchief to bandage a minor cut
he's incurred while negotiating his passage into the car. He
regards it as a priceless memento: Langford's handkerchief
stained with his own blood. Their meeting is brief. Langford
(as he later reveals) just tries to get rid of his unwanted passenger as painlessly as possible, so offers him a few faint
words of encouragement.

From Pupkin's perspective, the encounter proves momentous: the relationship is transubstantiated from parasocial to

social. Pupkin starts to act as if the words he imagines are Langford's directives. When he hears Langford marvel at his comic gift, describe him as a genius, and then invite him to dinner at his summer home, it's real – though only to him. "Jerry and I have a real relationship," he tells Masha, a fellow fan and, eventually, confederate in kidnapping. "No fantasy world." Seeing someone, even in only two dimensions, creates the illusion that there is the possibility of a relationship.

Pupkin's converted basement, his inner conversations, and delusions of friendship might seem extreme adaptations, but consider the case of Günther Parche, who gave his home a makeover so that it was a temple for worshipping the former tennis player Steffi Graf. Parche's obsession had a compulsive element: he charged onto a tennis court and stabbed Graf's rival, Monica Seles, in 1993. Seles was injured, incapacitated, and unable to play competitively for several months. Graf remained as the world's number one female player. If, as Parche later suggested, the aim of the attack was to prevent Graf from losing her status, then it was achieved. Parche was imprisoned but he achieved his ambition.

Pupkin, too, gets his own way at the cost of his personal freedom. Having interpreted Langford's modest encouragement as an invitation to appear on the tv show, Pupkin prepares for his big break; he believes he can regard Langford as a friend, someone he can call on unannounced at either his office or his private residence. He does both. A series of polite rebuffs at the former only serve to convince him that Langford's overprotective staff has failed to grasp the integrity of his new friendship. Even a forcible ejection from the office only reminds him that he should make a direct approach to Langford.

Arriving unannounced at Langford's home, Pupkin bluffs his way past a panicking butler, pours drinks for himself and his date – a bartender for whom he's held a torch for twenty years (he's now 34) – puts on some music, and starts dancing. When Langford returns from the golf course, he is, understandably, speechless. Eventually, he musters words, "You know I could have the both of you arrested." Pupkin dismisses it as a gag and proceeds to fool around. Even when Langford calls him a "moron" and insists he leaves, Pupkin is still trying to rationalize the shambles. The incident proves something of a turning point for Pupkin, however. After it, he resolves to rely less on Langford's patronage and more on his utility as a hostage.

The episode teaches Pupkin the difference between onstage personae and real-life people. Disillusioned though not deterred, he recruits Masha, a crucial Scorsese female whom I'll explore in Chapter 9, and together they execute to perfection a kidnapping that involves holding Langford bound and at gunpoint (an empty pistol, as it turns out) while Pupkin extorts a stand-up spot on Langford's show. Pupkin is arrested, but remains free long enough to see his tape-delay routine broadcast on national television. Langford escapes unscathed, his reputation presumably enhanced as a result of the experience. Hostage escapees and survivors frequently benefit from profligate media coverage.

In *The King of Comedy*, Scorsese provided a vision of the future. When it was released in 1982, it seemed like a portrayal of a wannabe stand-up comic who was so obsessed with a major tv star that he was prepared to go to spectacular lengths, not just to meet him, but to visit him at his private residence. Pupkin looked and sounded like a "wacko," which is actually the word he uses to describe Masha. In 1982, that is. Five years later, he didn't look so cranky; in fact, he looked representative of a generation of adoring fans, a great many of whom went to greater lengths than Pupkin to meet and, as we noted before, hurt the famous. Pupkin never seemed dangerous. Bardo probably didn't either – at first.

Pupkin is obsessive alright: he is fixed on becoming the host of his own show. Langford is not just his role model, but his idol, someone he reveres and strives to emulate. Pupkin might also be compulsive: he stops at nothing to get near Langford; he runs a gauntlet of security guards to get into his office, connives an elaborate bluff to penetrate his private residence, and outrageously but deftly pulls off a kidnapping to get a short spot on his show. All based on a putative invitation only he hears.

Pupkin gets his way, though at a cost. Immediately, after he's granted a "live" spot on national television, he's arrested and subsequently serves time in prison. During his period of incarceration, the Pupkin mystique grows, rather like Howard Hughes' did while he slid toward personal oblivion. As a result, on his release, he's able to capitalize on his fame. Far from denouncing his flamboyant stunt, consumers appreciate it. There is, as David Bromwich puts it in his "How publicity makes people real," "a curious shade of moral approval or fellow feeling that is elicited now by self-exposure of any but the most rancid and debasing kind."

> **In a perverse way, Pupkin is caught in a similar paradox to Hughes'.**

In a perverse way, Pupkin is caught in a similar paradox to Hughes': in making *Hell's Angels*, Hughes defied studio conventions, sunk in his own millions, and lost the lives of four people working on the film. Pupkin's sacrifice is less grandiose, though motivated by a similar kind of obsessional ambition. "The Pupkin gambit," as Richard Greene calls it, is unequivocally successful: his act is seen by 87 million viewers and Pupkin's image appears on the covers of *Newsweek*, *Life*, *People*, and *Time*, which carries the headline KING FOR A

NIGHT. In fact, it isn't just a night. Pupkin serves thirty-three months in a low-security prison in Allenwood, Pennsylvania, and, as a coda informs us, writes a best-selling book, secures a film deal, and becomes the kind of celebrity he wanted to be, leaving us to ponder how his bizarreries actually secreted a cunning rationality.

The King of Comedy, as Barbara Mortimer points out in the *Journal of Film and Video*, "emphasizes the extent to which Rupert's imaginary world has been shaped by television, and vice versa" (p. 36). Why vice versa? How has television been shaped by Pupkin? Before my answer, a clue: *The Jerry Springer Show*. This first aired in the US in 1991; since then it has gone global and spawned countless imitators. Its impact can scarcely be exaggerated: it changed tv.

By turning unexceptional people into remarkable television stars, the show took the unprecedented step of inviting audiences to *engage* with tv. They became involved in a way that just wasn't possible before. Of course, viewers were absorbed in drama and documentaries and the other fare offered. But seeing and listening to ordinary citizens with extraordinary stories involved them – whether they knew it or not – in a kind of quid pro quo. They watched intently as people poured out their secrets, many of them so shameful that the studio audiences gasped with embarrassment. In exchange, they made a deal with themselves, which went something like: if I were given the chance to go on the show, I'd divulge everything; no matter how much humiliation it brought on me.

Fame is a valued commodity, for all members of what Ed Siegel called in 1985 "the electronic family." "One can simply watch, and remain a distant cousin," announced Siegel in his article "Fame game becoming America's newest pastime." "Or one can be a doer, or victim, of pathological deeds and become an instant folk hero or folk villain."

In *The King of Comedy*, Scorsese glances at the former and concentrates on the latter: devotees and aspirants, those who worship the famous and those with ambitions to become famous themselves. Often, they are the same people. But during the kidnapping, Langford discloses his version of life in showbusiness. "I'm just a human being with all of the foibles, all of the traps, the show, the pressure,

The entertainment industry is not just an aspect of Scorsese's vision: it is an index to the social and cultural changes in America since the late nineteenth century.

the groupies, the autograph hounds, the crew, the incompetents; those behind the scenes you think are your friends, and you're not too sure if you're gonna be there tomorrow 'cause of their incompetence. They're wonderful pressures that make every day a glowing radiant day in your life. It's terrific."

It's hardly a soliloquy to induce sympathy, but it serves to round out the character of someone who is otherwise seen as either an oleaginous talk show host, or a gruff misanthrope, much like Jordan Manmouth, of "Mirror, mirror." When Pupkin promises to be fifty times as famous as he is, Langford's riposte reveals the depth of his animosity toward fans, "Then you'd have idiots like *you* plaguing your life."

If "plaguing" sounds like an overstatement, tell it to Björk, who, in 1996, was the addressee of a sulfuric acid-filled parcel bomb sent by a fan in Miami who videotaped himself making the package then shot himself in the head with a .38 revolver while the tape rolled. His reason: she had started a relationship with the African Caribbean dj and musician Goldie and he didn't like black people. Police intercepted the parcel.

Goldie's 1996 track "Letter of fate" is about this incident. Plagued, pestered, or persecuted: all seem appropriate.

When Langford explains, "I have a life, OK?" it is probably in a spirit of wishful thinking. In other words, he's expressing a hope rather than stating a fact. From the 1980s, showbusiness veterans and tv neophytes alike were forced into a Faustian contract: like the legendary necromancer, they had to surrender their souls, or at least their private lives. An increasingly invasive media commissioned by gossip-hungry consumers wanted every morsel of information.

Any showbusiness aspirant who wasn't prepared for total disclosure could kiss off their chances of becoming a celebrity. Part of the definition of celebrity is being constantly in the media. "Anyone can become a celebrity if only he can get into the news and stay there." Daniel Boorstin noticed this as early as 1961 when he wrote his *The Image: A guide to pseudo-events in America*. Even then, the media was flexing its muscles. By the time of Springer, it was able to make or break showbusiness careers. How might the Robert Mitchum contretemps, effectively smothered by Hughes, be covered today? "MY DRUGS HELL" BY HOLLYWOOD NEWCOMER or *OUT OF THE PAST* STAR CHECKS INTO REHAB maybe?

"The media's growth had outstripped Hollywood's ability to make stars in the 1980s, as the number of chat shows and magazine proliferated," writes Mark Borkowski in his *The Fame Formula* (p. 360). Television and the new media that followed it in the 1990s did not exactly compete with the film industry, though Hollywood needed them more than they needed Hollywood. The proliferation Borkowski writes of has introduced all manner of celebrities into the popular consciousness. Many of them are decried as talentless products of a lightweight celebrity culture that rewards anyone who can capture the public's attention. Someone like Pupkin, perhaps.

Earlier, I referred to Scorsese's "fascination with the US entertainment industry," as Ian Christie calls it. Christie writes of Scorsese's long-gestating plan for an "epic of American show business" based on Dean Martin, who was, for long, part of a comedy double act. His partner was Jerry Lewis, who plays Langford in *The King of Comedy*. John Gray's 2002 film *Martin & Lewis* examines the volatile relationship between the two entertainers.

It could be argued that Scorsese has fashioned his epic through various films; he has built a reference guide containing information about periods through entertainment. Sometimes just a film poster summons an entire era. In *Boxcar Bertha*, for example, there is a brief glimpse of three such posters, one being for Lothar Mendes' 1936 *The Man Who Could Work Miracles*, emblazoned with H.G.WELLS' SPECTACULAR MYSTERY. In *New York, New York*, every set evokes the atmosphere not so much of postwar New York, but of Hollywood's many visualizations of American cities in the 1940s and 1950s. Travis Bickle's apparently arbitrary destruction of his own television set in *Taxi Driver* conveys contempt toward a medium that had by the mid-1970s become, to some, frighteningly influential. The entertainment industry is not just an aspect of Scorsese's vision: it is an index to the social and cultural changes in America since the late nineteenth century.

7

FAMILY VALUES

It won't show up on any map, but *Cape Fear* is right next to Camelot. In the 1960s, the self-governing republic of America, it was thought, would be the source of moral and political inspiration to the rest of the world. Like the legendary court of King Arthur, it was a place associated with optimism, romance, and excitement.

At his inauguration in 1961, President John F. Kennedy delivered a speech redolent of the Gettysburg address. "Let every nation know, whether it wishes us well or ill, that we shall pay any price, bear any burden, meet any hardship, support any friend, oppose any foe, to assure the survival and the success of liberty."

It amounted to a global pledge to leaders of any nation, large or small, regardless of ideology, to help the American people in their pursuit of liberty. In many ways, the speech captured the country's conscience: there was no room for self-reflection, no questioning the rightness of its stance. America had assumed moral authority; it had self-confidence and a conviction in progress.

Residual bigotries would soon disappear, along with the violence that had pockmarked the nation for decades. Kennedy was elected with the strong support of African Americans. Despite the 1954 ruling that "the doctrine of 'separate but equal' has no place," America was still a divided nation and Kennedy had promised to hasten an end to seg-regation. Those who challenged racial laws were known as freedom riders. An abundant life lay ahead for all Americans, not just whites. They lived in a country where all the major institutions had proved their value.

Central among these institutions was the nuclear family. Marriages had been growing since the war and the family seemed in hale condition. Despite the upheaval of World War II, the family had emerged intact. Few seriously doubted its protective and nurturant values. The original film *Cape Fear* echoed these values: the family at the center of its plot was a hardy natural defense against a disease-like invader.

The other institutional rock was the American legal system. Enshrined in the US Constitution since 1789, it embodied the fundamental principles of justice that governed and regulated American life.

By the time Scorsese visited *Cape Fear* in 1991, institutional authority in American society had crumbled.

By the time Scorsese visited *Cape Fear* in 1991, everything had changed: institutional authority in American society had crumbled and those who ran major institutions had lost the public's confidence to the point where they had to rely on bribery, manipulation, intimidation, and secret surveillance. *Cape Fear* is one of a brace of Scorsese films directly inspired by films in the early 1960s.

While *Cape Fear* was a remake of British director J. Lee Thompson's 1961 original, *The Color of Money* was a sequel to Robert Rossen's *The Hustler*, from the same year. The early films were contemporaneous and Scorsese's films were both set on the cusp of the 1990s, leaving a record of social change over three decades. (Thompson's film is often mistakenly recorded as a 1962 release.) In assessing the conduct of American society in the early 1960s, the originals might have ended with "satisfactory progress," while Scorsese's conclusion is something like "could do better . . . but probably won't." I will move to *The Color of Money* in the Conclusion.

Scorsese's *Cape Fear* strains to be as different from its original in as many ways as it can without shattering the nucleus of the plot. That nucleus concerns two men: Sam Bowden (played by Gregory Peck in the original and Nick Nolte in Scorsese's version), an ostensibly respectable lawyer and devout family man, and Max Cady (played by Robert Mitchum and Robert De Niro, respectively), who is embittered by a long incarceration, and wants revenge on the man he holds responsible for his punishment. That man is Bowden, who is a crucial witness in Thompson's film and ineffectual defense attorney in Scorsese's. In both cases, his actions contribute to a guilty verdict.

While the crime isn't shown in either film, it involves, an "attack" on a woman, in the original, which is called more explicitly a rape in Scorsese's film. Thompson's Bowden has a clear conscience: he identified Cady as the perpetrator and stood up in court to tell the truth as he saw it. Scorsese's Bowden's conscience is much hazier: he deliberately withheld evidence that might have affected the outcome of Cady's trial. Worse: he was acting as Bowden's defense attorney. But he's rationalized his action by concluding Cady deserved his sentence.

On his release from prison, Cady heads toward the sleepy

North Carolina town where the Bowden family live. It's a white picket-fence world, black people hardly visible in either film. In the original, Cady solicits directions to a courtroom from an African American cleaner, whom he hails, "Hey, daddy! Where does Sam Bowden hang out?" It's an address that reflects the casual condescension of the South in the pre-civil rights period: Cady doesn't mean to patronize or insult him; otherwise he might have called him "boy." He neglects to add "please" or "thank you," as if reinforcing his right as a white man to demand service.

The Bowdens have a comfortable, though largely uneventful life until Cady unexpectedly appears and announces himself to Bowden, who assumes he has only to pull a few strings to have the annoying ex-con removed. Cady, however, keeps him off-balance: having studied law during his incarceration, he's educated enough not to put a foot wrong. So, in Scorsese's version, when Bowden argues to Cady that he actually did him a favor ("You could have been sitting on death row"), Cady is not buying it ("I'd have been up for parole either way in seven years").

In each version, Cady is both envious and resentful of the marital bliss Bowden seems to be enjoying. The marital bliss is genuine enough in Thompson's film, though it's anything *but* in Scorsese's rendition.

In Scorsese's film, Cady's envy compounds his anger at Bowden, though he's careful to remain polite and law-abiding in every personal encounter. His passivity actually goads Bowden into aggressive action. Cady, meanwhile, purrs contentedly as Bowden frantically tries to anticipate what he'll do. When the Bowden family dog is killed, Cady is an immediate suspect, though there is no evidence to link him to the crime.

What does he have planned for the Bowdens? The answer is uncertain, but second-guessing Sam Bowden is so spooked that he resorts to drastic action. He attempts to bribe Cady,

Behind the wholesome image of affluent suburban American family life, the Bowdens are riven with conflicts that are exposed by the arrival of an old nemesis. (© Kobal)

though without success. After his cozily close police officer friend fails to discover a pretext on which he can base action against Cady, Bowden hires a private investigator, whom Cady outsmarts, and then a bunch of hired bruisers, whom Cady outfights.

At this point, Bowden has violated his legal code of ethics, not to say the law, sufficiently to be beyond care: he even grabs his gun and takes off in pursuit of Cady, albeit briefly. Terrified, he contrives a plan that puts his family at risk, but also lures Cady into a trap at the Cape Fear River. When the final clash happens, it's less a case of good vs. evil: more honorable-but-imperfect vs. justifiably-resentful-but-depraved.

Bowden emerges as the victor in the final confrontation at the Cape Fear River. The climactic last act includes perhaps the only instance of disregard for physical reality in an American-based feature film directed by Scorsese (I'm excluding the tv episode "Mirror, mirror").

Cady has THE LORD IS MY AVENGER tattooed across his back and quotes the Bible, particularly the books of Esther, Psalms, and Job. "God tested his faith, took away everything he had," says Cady of Job and himself (Job was a prosperous man who remained committed to God in spite of undeserved misfortunes). Bizarrely, he also claims to be a devotee of Friedrich Nietzsche, the nineteenth-century philosopher who rejected Christianity's compassion for the weak and speculated on the rise of a race of people unfettered by the normal restrictions of human beings. Cady has spent his years in prison striving to be what Nietzsche called an *Übermensch*, "My mission in that time was to become more than human."

Cady's imperviousness to pain is just about believable: proficient yogis have achieved comparable states of insensitivity. But, when Cady is aboard the Bowdens' boat and holds an ignited flare while the molten phosphorus runs over his hand, credibility is thrown overboard. The phosphorus would in reality burn right through his hand. "Cartoonish terror" is how Remy Mackowski, of *Jewish Journal*, describes the scene, suggesting De Niro's portrayal of Cady wouldn't be out of place in one of the *Nightmare on Elm Street* films. "By the climax we're watching an Oscar winner play Freddy Krueger."

By contrast, Thompson's film ends with the far from invincible and mortally flawed Cady being shot and wounded by Bowden. The ending contrives to confirm Bowden's descent from an honorable defender of the law to a spiteful avenger, rather like Cady. "You're gonna have a long life in a cage. That's where you belong," he snarls at the bleeding Cady. "Count the years, the months, the hours until the day you rot."

Cady seems to die several times in Scorsese's version, though his Nietzschean indestructibility guarantees he keeps bouncing back. Ultimately, he drowns in the Cape Fear River.

According to Janet Maslin, Scorsese inherited the *Cape Fear* project from Steven Spielberg, who asked him, "What are you going to do with the family?" to which Scorsese replied, "They'll live. Otherwise there's no point to it." This was a *sine qua non:* the Bowden family had to survive.

Both films were based on John D. MacDonald's 1957 novel *The Executioners*. Thompson's original film reflects its time: the normal, ordered, safe, and mostly unremarkable American family exhibits none of the so-called "dysfunctions" we now associate with family life. Presenting a warm and comforting image of the conjugal unit, it honors values that have now disappeared. Of course, those family values themselves probably owe more to a cloying affection for the past than actuality; but the film never doubts the wholesome goodness of American family life in the postwar period.

As head of the Bowden family, Sam seems an incorruptible model of rectitude, who upholds and, in a way, personifies the law. Gregory Peck, as Bowden, also played the role of the righteous lawyer in several other films, including Robert Mulligan's 1962 *To Kill a Mockingbird*. In fact, Peck played a lawyer in Scorsese's *Cape Fear* too. Robert Mitchum also featured in both films: as the original Cady, he was the doomed malfeasant devoid of redeeming qualities; in the later version, he played a police officer. The casting suggests Scorsese wanted to strengthen links with the original.

The most obvious difference in the two versions is the plot's lever: Thompson's Cady is motivated by revenge. As a key witness for the prosecution, it was his testimony that clinched a guilty verdict and put Cady away for nearly eight-and-a-half years. Cady still holds him responsible. When

Bowden says, "You're not still blaming me for what you did," Cady laughs, "You still don't get the picture." He may mean his conviction was unsafe: the offense is cited as an "attack," censors in the 1960s regarding the word "rape" as unacceptable. Or he may be alluding to some sort of deception or artifice when he tells Bowden, "I wanted you to be just the same as the last time I saw you," then remarks about a nearby young woman, "Look at that wiggle! Maybe she thinks we don't know that's done on purpose, but we've seen a thing or two, haven't we counselor?"

Scorsese's Cady has an explicit reason for wanting revenge. Bowden buried evidence that might have cleared him. In the event, the evidence was never admitted and Cady was sent down for fourteen years. Bowden commissioned a report on the victim of the assault and discovered her "promiscuity." Whether such evidence would have been

Scorsese's Bowden is compromised from the outset, making his degeneracy more consistent with his character.

admissible is not certain. Rape shield laws that prevent evidence about a victim's sexual dispositions or past behavior were introduced in the 1970s. When Cady refers to his imprisonment at "a Georgia State correctional facility," he could be lying (he also claims he was imprisoned for hitting a sheriff during a nuclear plant protest rally).

It's possible that in the conservative southern state of Georgia around 1976 the evidence would be made available to the court. But it's also possible that the rape shield would have operated and the evidence would have been ruled inadmissible; in which case, Bowden's decision would have been irrelevant and had no bearing on the outcome. (In 2003, when Kobe Bryant, the basketball star, faced charges of sexual assault, personal details of the accuser were reported by the media and filtered their way into the courtroom, raising doubts about the effectiveness of rape shield laws in high-profile cases.)

Bowden, remember, was Cady's defense counsel: suppressing the evidence is a serious felony, especially when committed by a legal representative. "If you'd seen what this guy did to this girl . . . if it was your own daughter," he begins to unravel his mysterious motive to a legal colleague, who interrupts with a reminder of the sixth amendment of the American Constitution, "In every criminal prosecution, the accused shall have the assistance of counsel for his defense."

So, while Scorsese's innovation is in turning Bowden into a lawyer who is willing to bend the rules to suit his own purpose and thus provide Cady with an understandable grudge, in material terms it doesn't affect the plot. The original Bowden's corruption is a slow-burn process, his sanctimony gradually incinerated as he resorts to ever more drastic means of protecting his family. Scorsese's Bowden is compromised from the outset, making his degeneracy more consistent with his character and less of a surprise. So, when he bridles at his police officer friend for advising him to take unilateral action ("I can't operate outside the law; the law's my business"), it's hardly convincing. Even the officer is startled by the feigned outrage. "I'm a law officer; it would be unethical of me to advise a citizen to take the law into his own hands. I suppose you must have misunderstood me," he mocks Bowden.

The pressure Cady puts on Bowden is often more apparent than real. A hint here, an innuendo there is all Cady proffers. Bowden, on the other hand, is explicit. "I'll kill you off," he promises Cady in the Thompson version, a sentiment echoed in Scorsese's. Cady's only overt act of violence before either film's climax is when he picks up a woman in a bar, has sex with her, and then hurts her.

In Thompson's version, the woman's name is Diane and she is clearly attracted to what she sees as the "animal" in Cady. In the censorious early 1960s, Thompson's *Cape Fear* made no reference to a sexual encounter that we assume is consensual and which precedes Cady's violence. Diane ends up with a black eye. Scorsese turns the woman into Lori, who is a colleague of Bowden and who may have had an affair with him (it's never clear). Again they have what is this time clearly consensual sex before Cady gets rough. The violence in Scorsese's film is more gruesome: Cady bites a chunk out of Lori's cheek.

Cady later sets his sights on Bowden's teenage daughter, Nancy in the original, Danielle in Scorsese's version. Again the invisible hand of the censors seems to guide Thompson's depiction of Cady's prurience as he leers from a distance at the young girl. "Getting to be almost as juicy as your wife, ain't she?" Cady taunts Bowden. Scorsese's daughter is a nymphet with barely controllable pubescent sexual curiosity. She almost turns to liquid in Cady's physical presence. When he puts his thumb in her mouth, her response is promissory of fellatio.

For Scorsese, Cady's seduction of Bowden's daughter is part of his design to torment him. Thompson's emphasis is slightly different: Bowden's wife has a moment of realization when she tells her husband, "It's Nancy! He only wanted to get you away from her." In other words – and once more we should suspect censors at work – Cady's idea of revenge is to rape Bowden's daughter. This in itself might be sufficient. When Thompson's Cady heads for Cape Fear, he mistakenly believes Bowden is in Raleigh. So maybe he does have a different agenda to Scorsese's Cady, one that Thompson submerges slyly in his text.

In Scorsese's version, Cady resents the condescension of others. Bowden's private investigator calls him a "white trash piece of shit" and declares, "I don't give a rat's ass about your rights." Cady has been on the receiving end of this kind of comment before and appears to shrug it off. But it troubles him: educationally he regards himself as equal if not superior to Bowden or any of his colleagues. In one scene he sees symmetry between himself and Bowden's wife. "If your husband hadn't betrayed us both, who knows? We might have been different people."

He sees Bowden's breach of trust as having changed both their lives for the worse, consigning her to being a (probably neurotic) home-worker (she plans to start her own business) and him to being a powerless ex-con. This hints at the struggle that drives the plot of both films. Bowden exploits "Cady's poor, uneducated background," assuming his own class, position, status, and education "will protect him against Cady discovering the betrayal," writes Marc Raymond in his 2000 thesis *Martin Scorsese and American Film Genre* (p. 85).

There's no "betrayal," as Raymond puts it, in Thompson's original, though, as we noted earlier, there's an obscure allusion to deception. Ultimately, though, class, position, status and education do function as effective protection. Cady is damned and order is restored. Bowden's privileges protect him; he is reunited with his family and justice is seen to be served. Or is it?

Faith doesn't require proof. Confidence does. You can be confident that the American legal system is fair, just, and virtuous. But, without evidence, that confidence will wane. Americans have large resources of faith in their legal institution; they just don't have that much confidence in it. At least, that's the lesson the two versions of *Cape Fear* deliver.

The law is one of the two American institutions appearing in *Cape Fear*, the other being the family, which I will come to soon. In the early 1960s, at the time of Thompson's original, both faith and confidence were present. But over the next three decades came a series of destabilizing events.

Two years of rioting beginning in 1965 in the predominantly black Watts district in Los Angeles signaled the persistence of America's race problem even after civil rights legislation. Black Americans' complaints at the manner in which the police treated them reflected a wider discontent with what Stokely Carmichael and Charles V. Hamilton called "institutional racism," which, as they put it, "permeates society."

In 1966, at the height of the riots, the middleweight boxer Rubin "Hurricane" Carter was found guilty of the murder of two people in a bar in Paterson, New Jersey, and sentenced to life. The circumstances surrounding the case, particularly the eyewitness reports that were crucial evidence, turned it into a *cause célèbre*. Muhammad Ali aligned himself with Carter; Bob Dylan, as we saw in Chapter 5, recorded a campaigning song, "Hurricane"; and Carter's defense team continued to file for appeals. Eventually, after nineteen years, Carter was released. It seemed a wrongful conviction and one "based on racism rather than reason," in the words of the judge who ordered his release in 1985. *The Hurricane* was Norman Jewison's 1999 film of Carter's tribulations, based on Carter's own book *The 16th Round*.

Momentous fissures in the American institutional structure became visible in 1972, when five men were arrested for breaking into the Democratic National Committee headquarters at the Watergate building in Washington, DC. The name "Watergate" became synonymous with unethical behavior. The chain of investigation led all the way to the White House and ultimately to the resignation of Republican president Richard M. Nixon in 1974. Nixon, a qualified lawyer, had run against Kennedy in 1960, before winning election in 1969. He was reelected in 1972, much of his tenure being overshadowed by the Vietnam War.

Nixon's resignation – the first by a US president – was preceded by nationally televised hearings, making the disgrace public. The Watergate scandal was damaging, probably irrevocably damaging, to Americans' self-belief in the propriety of their political system. The purpose of the break-in, it was discovered, was to install wiretaps, so corrupting the fundamental principles and values underlying political conduct since 1787 when George Washington chaired the convention to frame the US Constitution. Only a naïf would believe Watergate was the first and only corruption; but the manner in which it was exposed before the world's media made it by far the most notorious.

The domestic political crisis was followed by international shocks. In 1983, President Ronald Reagan ordered the invasion by American troops of the Caribbean island Grenada, which had experienced an internal political struggle resulting in the deposition and execution of its prime minister. The propriety and legality of the American invasion and subsequent occupation seemed dubious. US troops defeated Grenadian resistance fighters, aided by Cubans, and overthrew the new military government, reinstating the old order. The United Nations General Assembly, along with several countries, denounced the action as a violation of international law. The US had intruded on the political affairs of a small independent nation because Reagan suspected a Soviet–Cuban presence would pose a threat to American security.

A far greater scandal followed in 1987, when the US, still under Reagan's presidency, was revealed to have covertly sold arms to Iran. The proceeds of the sales were then used by officials to give arms to the Contras, a Nicaraguan guerilla force opposed to the leftwing Sandinista government. The US government supported the Contras for practically the whole of the 1980s, despite congressional prohibition. The Iran–Contra affair occurred despite the suspension of official relations between the countries and was followed by the release of American hostages held in the Middle East.

Bookending these political events was an incident that served to remind America that the Rubin Carter case, far from being a remnant of a less enlightened age, was painfully representative of American justice. It was probably like hundreds, perhaps thousands, of other episodes: in March 1991, Rodney King, a black driver, was pulled over for speeding by Los Angeles police officers. The difference was that, on this occasion, an unseen video enthusiast was surreptitiously recording the incident. The tape showing an unarmed King curled up on the ground being beaten by four baton-wielding police officers was barely watchable. When the LAPD officers were cleared, rioting broke out across the nation. It was the most widespread violence since the 1960s.

There were other misadventures in the thirty years separating the two films, and I use the ones I've described as a father might savor photographs of his wife and children: to convey progression as his family matures. America matured, though not in the way expected during the Camelot years. Conspiracy theories aside, Kennedy's assassination in 1963 was blamed on reactionary undercurrents in American life – as was his brother Robert's murder in 1968 (during his campaign to become the Democratic presidential nominee). Far from developing into the inspirational liberal center of a new world, America became a symbol of bigotry, corruption, and overweening ambition.

The original *Cape Fear* disclosed the willingness of responsible people to act illicitly under conditions that disturb the order of their life. Thompson's subtlety was in showing how, despite the aberrant behavior of individuals, the legal system is essentially sound. It's even supple enough to accommodate the kind of maverick justice meted out by the vindictive Sam Bowden ("Count the years . . .").

In Scorsese's version there is no longer an unbreakable commitment to the rightness of the law. Bowden adapts it to suit his own sense of rightness and violates it feloniously when he senses the law doesn't work to his advantage. "I wanna gun," he blurts in desperation after arriving at the conclusion that "the law sees me as more of loose cannon than Max Cady."

As David Morgan writes, in his article "Nowhere to hide," "Bowden is stunned that Cady can exist and maneuver within the law, when his mere existence reinforces Bowden's belief that Cady belongs in jail" (p. 52).

There is evidence of a Watergate mentality in the way Bowden breaks laws to further his own aims.

Scorsese's Counselor Bowden is a product of the 1970s and 1980s: he's cynical and self-interested enough to use the law for his own purposes. There is evidence of a Watergate mentality in the way he breaks laws to further his own aims; a little of the Iran–Contra attitude in his deliberate concealment of evidence to suit his own interests; a hint of the imperious irresponsibility that guided the invasion of Grenada in his design to ensnare Cady by illegal means just because it suits him. He has no compunction about administering a kind of rough justice, however prejudicial it might be, just as long as *he* deems it equitable. He's even encouraged in this by an official guardian of the law.

Bowden, in Scorsese's version, has no confidence in the effectiveness of the law. "This lack of support paralyzes Bowden, and leaves him incapable of functioning," writes Morgan, who supplements his point by quoting Scorsese's scriptwriter Wesley Strick, who reveals his fascination with "the horror of discovering that this vast and intricate support system that we all kind of assume is there for you, is not there at all" (p. 51).

Perhaps it's not just Bowden's assumptions that have been shattered. Gerald J. Thain believes that the "travails of thirty years" between the release of the two films have "led to a public far more suspicious of authority of all kinds" (p. 44). In his scholarly article on the two versions, Thain concludes, "The 1991 version of *Cape Fear* seems consistent with the sceptical movie-going public of its day."

Events, home and abroad, since the early 1960s have hardened Americans: for Thain; they are no longer easily convinced by official authority, whether expressed in government or the law. Their doubts and reservations about the essential rightness of the justice system have multiplied. Urban uprisings and political treachery have combined with assassinations and government double-dealing to produce a populace in the image of 1991's Sam Bowden, described by Thain as "beset by moral ambiguity . . . whose moral compass is askew" (p. 46).

During her initial meeting with Cady, Lori, who is a very close – perhaps intimate – colleague of Bowden, drinks prodigiously and slurs a joke. "An unmarried woman. She meets a guy and he tells her he just got outta prison. 'What'd you do?' she asks. 'I cut my wife into fifty-two pieces,' he says. 'So, you're single?'"

It's not especially funny, though it does make a point about the hardiness of marriage: the killer's marital eligibility is more important than his homicidal background. Marriage and the family form a common theme in both versions of *Cape Fear*, and, while the joke occurs only in the Scorsese film, it would have worked in Thompson's too. Both versions situate the nuclear family at the center of the plot, and, while each offers a different portrayal of the institution, its value is never questioned. Bowden's family, in both versions, torments Cady. "One wife, one kid: that's what I had when you set me up," Thompson's Cady tells his adversary. "She dumped me. Never even visited." Scorsese's Cady expresses the same bitterness, "You're lucky, counselor. My own daughter, she don't even know me after I went inside; her mama told her I was dead."

For Thompson, the married life is an unqualified good; the family is a natural unit for the nurturance of love and the provision of security. This was 1961. Two years later, Betty Friedan's book *The Feminine Mystique* delivered a piercing attack on the traditional idea that being part of a nuclear family was essential for a woman's happiness. Could women really only find fulfillment through rearing children and making homes?

More attacks on marriage and the family came through Andrea Dworkin in her 1974 *Woman Hating* and subsequent broadsides ("like prostitution, marriage is an institution that is extremely oppressive and dangerous for women"). In her 1970 essay "Marriage," Sheila Cronan went so far as to declare, "marriage is a form of slavery." There followed the women's liberation movement, feminism, and, later, postfeminism, all of which contended in some way that marriage and the nuclear family were contrivances that kept patriarchy alive. The greater availability of birth control, especially the Pill, and legal abortion gave women much more power over their own reproductive functions. They also won more power over their professional lives, successfully winning legislation against sex discrimination and pay inequities.

> **"A portrait of a fractured, embittered family unit."**
> KIRSTEN MOANA THOMPSON ON *CAPE FEAR*

This created instability: as women entered the labor force in growing numbers, their dependence on husbands weakened. "A wife earning a salary herself is more easily disposed to get rid of a husband who has become a burden to the family or a hindrance to her own career," wrote Peter and Brigitte Berger in their 1981 book *Sociology: A biographical approach*. "The development of the modern family has not only been accompanied by a steady rise in separation and divorce rates but almost every individual family faces a peculiar crisis at the time its children leave home" (p. 102).

Women changed. So did their role in the family. And so did the family itself. Many of the features of the family visible in Thompson's *Cape Fear* were altered by legal and cultural changes in the status of women. "In the light of this drastically altered social landscape, Scorsese's remake instituted key character changes in the Bowden family," writes Kirsten Moana Thompson in her 2007 book *Apocalyptic Dread*, "creating a portrait of a fractured, embittered family unit" (p. 36).

Thompson pictured the Bowden family as if they had stepped straight out of a Norman Rockwell illustration. In Scorsese's hands, the family is a less ideal institution: infidelity, quarrels, unruly children, are in evidence and there is no sign of love anywhere. No wonder: Bowden's wife, Leigh, suspects he is having an affair with Lori ("You fucking her?" she asks him rhetorically) and almost reflexively brings up reminders of his past extramarital encounters ("I thought you promised to leave all that shit behind"). It's far from certain whether he has.

It transpires that after a previous affair, Bowden and his wife sought marriage counseling. Both found the experience uncomfortable, though Leigh, in particular, describes it as "humiliating." They uprooted themselves from Atlanta to try to start afresh in a new environment, but Bowden, it seems, has reverted to old ways. Convinced that he is lying to her when he denies infidelity, Leigh blames him for not leaving her years before. "You didn't have the balls to walk out," she screams at him as she throws punches. He claims her fragile psychological state ("crying every morning and evening") prevented his leaving.

It's inconceivable that the original Bowden would physically harm his wife, Peggy. Yet there is invisible harm. For example, Bowden believes both his wife and daughter are in peril and that Cady will be emboldened to attack (that is, rape) them. Why? Katie Reese provides an answer in her review "Scorsese's *Cape Fear*: The triumph of stereotypes." "When Cady explains to Peggy that coercion of her sexual consent through a bargain not to harm [her] would be considered legitimate consent, he is legally correct for that time period."

In other words, Cady would have claimed she gave him consent and, as long as he didn't beat her, the onus would have been on Peggy to prove he forced himself on her. Thompson's Bowden is aware of this and fears for both his wife and daughter. Even if he assaulted his daughter Nancy, he says – even hypothetically – he couldn't let her testify against Cady. So Cady is practically invulnerable, given the legal position in the 1960s. Hence Bowden is driven outside the law in his stricken attempts to defend his family. In both versions, he's advised by specialist professionals to adopt illegal means; though in the Thompson film, it's made explicitly clear that this is strictly out of concern for his family. "So, you're a lawyer, you believe in due process," his private investigator reminds him. "But it's *your* family, not mine."

Reese believes that, in its understated way, Thompson's film "actually engages in criticism of real laws prejudicing women." By contrast, Reese believes Scorsese's *Cape Fear* is a more traditional, conservative film. Sure, it offers a warts-and-all version of family life. But, it also "upholds the nuclear family by reinforcing the inviolability of women within the legitimate family." Reese means that the female members of the Bowden family appear to be in jeopardy, but never actually are; but Lori, as an outsider, gets brutalized. The family might be imperfect, but it provides a safe haven for its members. Bowden invokes his wife to unite in the face of an external threat. "The two of us together, working as a team," he explains, is the way to beat Cady. And so it is.

There is little immediacy in Scorsese's film; not in the sense of bringing us into direct involvement with the changes both in family structure and in attitudes toward the family. Given Scorsese's perception of women as capable of developing their character or abilities only through men, it's probably not so surprising. Certainly, "Scorsese's version exposes the chasms and ideological struggles over the constitution of the contemporary nuclear American family," as Kirsten Moana Thompson puts it (p. 34). But it eventually resolves them in a way that's reassuring, if not comforting.

At a time of Camelot-like hopefulness, with Watergate and Iran–Contra not yet parts of the popular vocabulary, Thompson's *Cape Fear* was based on sureties: the integrity of law and the family weren't in doubt. While Reese's point about Thompson's cunning critique of laws relating to rape seems a sound one, the original *Cape Fear*'s faith in the law's ability to repair itself overwhelms everything. In the event, the law did repair itself and afforded women protection in rape cases.

Scorsese might have anticipated the usual question asked of directors who remake serviceable films not quite old enough to be considered archaic. Why do it? To engage with heavy topics – rape, infidelity, child abuse, legal wrong-doing – perhaps? These decorate the plot as ornately as Max Cady's multiple tattoos. Scorsese even loads in a reference to homosexual rape when Cady tells how, in prison, he became a "fat, hairy hillbilly's wet dream."

But, in the end the anguish is dealt with as inadequately as in Thompson's version. Scorsese wrings a bruised optimism from an otherwise cynical tale. Our confidence in America's two great institutions has been shaken, but we remain faithful to both. Recall Scorsese's justification: "Otherwise there's no point to it."

The manner in which Scorsese closes his story brings applause from unlikely sources. Writing for *The Expository Times*, Reverend Dr. Robert Ellis applauds Cady's demise, which "demonstrates that he who takes vengeance to himself usurps God's place" (p. 307). Perhaps inadvertently, Scorsese restores faith in God, as well as two great American pillars.

But is Scorsese so conservative? Sometimes, critique and celebration become "intimately entwined and impossible to distinguish." The point has been made several times by several writers, including Roger Dawkins and his co-writers in their 2006 essay "Film theory." For Dawkins et al., irony can become a little bit too convenient for filmmakers: it functions as an "escape clause," allowing them to espouse the virtues of someone or something they would like to probe.

Scorsese despises *families*, but endorses the *family*.

Scorsese is, by turns, critical and orthodox about marriage and the family. "Marriage is a part of getting ahead," Lieutenant Ellery pontificates in *The Departed*. "People know you're not a homo; makes most guys more stable. Everybody sees the ring: they think somebody can stand the sonofabitch. Ladies see the ring: they know immediately you must have some cash and your cock must work."

In *GoodFellas*, the nuclear family is an integral part of the extended mafia family. When Henry Hill leaves his wife, his *capofamiglia* reminds him, "You got children. I'm not saying go back to her right now, but you *got to* go back."

Cape Fear is Scorsese's essay on nuclear family fission: the unit splits on impact, releasing its own kind of destructive energy. But this is how the nuclear family reconstitutes itself: smash it with a crisis and it reveals its power; ignore it and it atrophies. Scorsese portrays families as vile, hateful, and detestable; they are damaging units, driving their members to despondency. But, that's because the people in the family don't work together (as Bowden puts it). The actual institution is perfectly fine. Theoretically. Scorsese despises *families*, but endorses *the family*.

Maybe *Cape Fear* is an escape clause. But, if it affirms basic values, it also raises questions about the consequences of "living in a society that is depicted as exploitative, hypocritical and cynical," as Stephen Harper puts it. In his "Media, madness and misrepresentation," Harper is writing about *Taxi Driver*, though he might just as well be describing *Cape Fear*. Scorsese never despairs over the family: just the social milieu in which families operate and the human beings who operate them. For Scorsese, America is a land in which marriage and the family reveal their fragmentary, destructive potential, yet still retain their capacities to conscript men and women into what often becomes an infernal arrangement. Marriages are rarely made in heaven.

There are reasons for this to be found in Scorsese's work. Men are irrefutably men. Women, on the other hand, are many things; but they all want the same thing. This is why watching a Scorsese film can sometimes feel like being the invisible man at a wedding. You watch the bride fussing while she nervously rehearses her nuptial vows, then the groom as he ravishes a bridesmaid only minutes before the service is due to start. And you wonder: what does this tell us about how each understands love? Scorsese has an answer, as we'll discover over the next three chapters.

8

IDEA OF A MAN

Vickie La Motta is glamorous, even luminous, the kind of woman who turns heads. So when she walks in the Copacabana with a group of men, she gets the attention of several others, including her brother-in-law, Joey La Motta. It's 1947 and her husband is away at training camp in preparation for a big fight; he believes in total abstinence when he's training. Joey abruptly finishes his conversation with a boxing promoter, strides to the table where Vickie has settled, and yanks her out of her seat, reminding her that she shouldn't be out enjoying herself while her husband is out of town. "I feel like I'm a *prisoner*," she protests. "I look at somebody the wrong way, I get smacked . . . I'm tired of every time I turn around I got both of you up my ass."

Joey is unimpressed. "Get your stuff. You ain't making an asshole of my brother." Her escorts assure him that it's just an innocent social gathering and "nothing's going on," but Joey forcefully drags Vickie away. On his return to the table, ostensibly to relieve the tension, he begins, "We're good friends, we can straighten this out . . .," then suddenly smashes a glass in the face of his lifelong friend Salvy. The ensuing brawl continues outside, where Joey wedges Salvy in a cab door and slams it repeatedly.

Months later with the incident seemingly forgotten, Vickie's husband Jake asks Joey about the origins of his beef with Salvy. Joey talks vaguely and evasively about Salvy getting out of line, but Jake is still curious and asks whether Vickie has had sex with Salvy. The answer is no. "I'm your brother, don't you trust me?" asks Joey when Jake rejects his assurances. "No, I don't. When it comes to her, I don't trust *nobody*. Tell me what happened."

When the answers are not forthcoming, Jake changes direction. "You fucked my wife?" he says, making a question sound like an accusation. Astonished at the charge, Joey leaves, calling his brother a "wacko." Jake then climbs the stairs looking every inch a prizefighter entering the ring. After slapping Vickie several times across the face and pinning her at the throat, he persists with his interrogation. "Did you fuck my brother?" She's flabbergasted: his baseless allegations are commonplace, but about her and his own brother? Instead of her usual denial, she retaliates: "I fucked all of 'em . . . I sucked his [Joey's] cock . . . his cock's bigger than yours too."

It is, of course, a taunt, not a confession. But Jake believes his tyrannized wife's provocation, rushes to his brother's home, and beats Joey savagely. When Vickie arrives, he knocks her out with the kind of punch he's used to flatten many of his opponents in the ring.

Remember, this is the result of an incident initiated by Joey in a misbegotten attempt to spare his brother embarrassment. Somehow, it doesn't matter what happens, Jake La Motta is always going to react in a way that hurts people.

Raging Bull provides "one of the best records we have of white male masculinity," according to Judith Halberstam,

Jake LaMotta's aggression in the ring reflects a society in which
"violent masculine assertiveness is seemingly endemic." La Motta
authenticates his manly credentials, both in and out of the ring.
(© Kobal)

author of *Female Masculinity* (p. 275). It's not a view
shared by all scholars. Even if we set aside the question of
Italian Americans' ethnicity (were or are they "white"?),
which we'll return to in the Conclusion, there are other
objections. Fidelma Ashe, for example, finds the statement
far too reductive. The "white male experience," she argues, in
her "Deconstructing the experiential bar," is brought down
"to a single model of extreme violence toward others and
fails to explore the possibilities of resistance" (p. 193).

Vickie's resistance consists of answering back every so
often, for which she always receives a slap at very minimum,

or being seen in the company of other men, for which she gets worse, or, more effectively, just taking the two children and leaving, which is what she finally does, though not until several years later.

Vickie's husband Jake is one of those "boxers, made men, pool sharks, and other male subcultures forming the spine of Scorsese's dramas," as Paul Arthur puts in his 2008 article "Please allow me to reproduce myself."

"One of the best records we have of white male masculinity." JUDITH HALBERSTAM ON *RAGING BULL*

It's an interesting choice of words: spine means figuratively both a central feature and a source of strength. Of all Scorsese's questions, the one that extends through practically every film, from *Who's That Knocking at My Door?* to *Shine a Light*, providing support and protection for every storyline is this: what are the advantages of being a man?

Life is frequently wretched for those who, for some reason, aren't. Not that it's a Garden of Eden for those who are. But women seem to have few rights, enjoy no pleasures, and exist only to provide services for insiders, a point that leads Arthur to conclude that, if there is a project to be discerned in the films, it is – as we noted earlier – "Scorsese's wider mapping of masculine prerogative."

Actually, a map doesn't quite do justice to Scorsese's sprawling representation of men's subjugation and assumption of rights over places and people. His is more of a cinematic Bayeux Tapestry. Many of Scorsese's overly male-centered films, such as *Raging Bull*, *GoodFellas*, or *Gangs of New York*, resemble conquests: tales of powering American males who overcome the obstacles set by their social backgrounds and ascend through the ranks to positions of admiration and respect; or perhaps just awe.

Yet, curiously, it is in Scorsese's films where the focus falls on women that we find the most revealing expositions of men and masculinity. Here we're able to observe men adoring, detesting, schmoozing, and abusing women. The kind of fear-infused reverence they inspire is like that of someone holding a blade to your throat. "Has he got the *cojones* to use it?" you ask yourself; but you don't move in case he has. In Scorsese films, men don't inhabit people's lives so much as slice into them.

Unlike most rights and privileges, those exclusive to men aren't granted by anyone or anything, so much as seized and maintained. Men, in Scorsese's America, have an interest in preserving their prerogatives, and many of his films document their methods. In the process, they display and sustain a particular kind of manhood. By manhood, I mean the qualities associated with men. These, for Scorsese, include physical toughness, aggression, strength, virility, and striving. In short, he has a very traditional conception of manhood. For the sake of clarity, I should contrast this idea of manhood to masculinity, or *masculinities*, which refers to the whole spectrum of possible qualities that might be equated with being a man. Scorsese is attracted to only one segment of that spectrum.

There is no essence of manhood. It isn't transmitted through DNA. Some people have proposed that men are just chromosomally hardwired to be hunters, fighters, and defenders of their territories. But the caveman theory has pretty much been clubbed to death. More plausibly, scholars have argued manhood is something that's produced and reproduced, not just by men, or even by men with the help of compliant women. It's not as if they are busily working together to conserve or extend men's privileges. More realistically, it's that people only stop to reflect on them when for one reason or another the routine of their lives has been interrupted by something they consider to be a *problem*.

One person's problem is another's normal condition. Manhood precludes queries about the rightness or wrongness of dominating or molesting women. *Raging Bull* exposes many of the conventions and customs that governed women's lives in the postwar period. Vickie (or "Vicky" and, later, "Vikki" – her real name was Beverley), like most other women of the time, doesn't have a professional career of her own. Her duty is to behave as a devoted and helpful follower, supporter, and occasional attendant. She acknowledges her husband's authority and, at first, submits willingly to it. If Jake hits her, she usually takes it stoically. Her opinions are not so much disrespected as disregarded: her voice is ignored so that she's functionally mute. At one point, she actually conveys this: "I can't talk."

Maybe she can't; but she sees: we can examine and learn about La Motta's manhood through her tribulations. Drawn to her beauty when he first sees her, Jake conducts his background check with his brother. "D'you bang her?" he asks Joey, who answers no, but not for the want of trying. "I try to fuck anything," he qualifies his reply, adding, "You're a married man. It's all over. Leave the young girl [she is 15] alone." But, encouraged by her supposed virginity, Jake pursues her. In *Who's That Knocking?* J.R. is similarly encouraged, but is sickened when he finds out The Girl isn't a virgin.

La Motta's first wife, Irma, hazards herself in a moment of fiery disobedience toward the start of the film. When he cautions her against overcooking his steak, she hurls the meat across the table onto his plate. The gesture occasions a tumultuous incident in which he turns over the table and threatens her. It's a frightening response to a small act of insolence and a portent of what awaits Vickie.

Vickie is attracted to La Motta's ostentation and vulgar exhibitionism at first: he parades her around the Bronx as if she is a badge of his worldly success. La Motta stays embedded in his natural habitat enjoying the good life, part of which is patriarchal control of a beautiful woman who is the object of other men's desires. Vickie has two roles: as a ringside ornament for her husband and a domestic factotum. She sits graciously at ringside, shielding her eyes when La Motta takes a beating. She answers the call for "Coffee!" without ever considering responding with, "I'm busy, get it yourself."

The benefits abound: Vicky shops whenever and wherever she pleases; she enjoys a life of consumer choice and material comforts, having surrendered real control of her fate. Jake fulfills his duties: he pays the bills and sentinels her; and, when he can't, brother Joey keeps watch – as in the Copacabana episode.

Yet there is a paradox: Jake enjoys having a wife that other men find attractive, but that very fact fills him with doubt. "The right time, the right place, the right circumstances: anything's possible," he shares his suspicions of her infidelity with Joey, who agrees: "You're not wrong."

This emerges in his progressively severe interrogations of Vickie. An innocent visit to the restroom elicits an impatient, "What took you so long?" and a caution, "Shut up or I'm gonna smack you in the face. You embarrass me." An innocent goodbye kiss stirs him to wonder, "What was all that about? . . . You don't do that: you say hello, you say goodbye. That's all, you hear?" La Motta emphasizes his point with a hard slap across the face and a warning, "Don't ever have any disrespect for me."

For most of the time, Vickie must feel like one of La Motta's opponents, backed against the ropes and subject to a debilitating wave of attacks. Every time she goes down, she gets back up, only to take more punishment. There's no referee to stop the contest. Is she a masochist? Or does she imagine she can't do without the material benefits? What prevents her from throwing in the towel? Most probably, she just sees her husband's behavior as typically masculine, a natural state of affairs. All her female friends are equally as subjugated. By comparison, she is well off: she, at least, has money, albeit her husband's. But she is accountable to her husband.

When she carelessly describes one of La Motta's upcoming opponents as "good looking," Vickie finds herself in danger of a horrifying rebuke. His fury subsides, only to be roused again when Salvy calls the same fighter "a very attractive guy; all the girls like him."

> **"Should I fuck him, or fight him?"** JAKE LA MOTTA ON HIS OPPONENT, TONY JANIRO

With barely contained rage, La Motta jokes, "Should I fuck him, or fight him?" then widens his scope to include Salvy, "Maybe I should fuck you."

In this male subculture, symbolic emasculation is never far away: a humiliating put-down, a beating, even a rumor has the effect of depriving a man of his role or identity. The most withering assessment of a man is that he "takes it up the ass." Is this bellicose homophobia, or disguised homoeroticism? Robin Wood is one of a number of writers who have detected a "homosexual subtext" in *Raging Bull*.

Jake's good-looking opponent, Tony Janiro, is earmarked for brutal punishment. During the fight, La Motta deliberately props him up, just to administer a cruel battering. His intention seems less to win the contest, more to disfigure Janiro's face, which, as Salvy had earlier reminded him, had "no marks." In *Hollywood from Vietnam to Reagan*, Wood suggests that the "threat" Janiro posed for La Motta was not his attractiveness to his wife, but his "attractiveness to himself" (p. 113). Maria T. Miliora, in *The Scorsese Psyche on Screen*, agrees that La Motta "defends against his insecurities as a man by using his power to hurt others" (p. 88). Pam Cook's "Masculinity in crisis?" and David Friedkin's "'Blind rage' and 'brotherly love'" make a similarly subversive point.

La Motta's life is, in a sense, symmetrical: he realizes, or actualizes, himself as a man out of the ring just as he does inside. His remorseless brutal attacking style of fighting has a mirror image in the other main aspect of his life. He isn't a fighter first and a husband second: they mirror each other. And, in neither reflection does La Motta see anything but a true man. So, when he is comprehensively beaten by Sugar Ray Robinson, he takes his punishment *manfully*, his grotesquely swollen and blood-covered face a testimony to his courage. Immediately after the final bell, he follows Robinson to his corner to remind him that he stayed on his feet throughout the fifteen rounds, "Hey Ray, I never went down." He loses his title, but retains his manhood.

Were *Raging Bull* a prescription, its conclusions would be: the husband of the postwar era is expected to be the breadwinner and definitely not obliged to participate in the slightest way in the running of the household or the day-to-day rearing of the children. A woman's gratifications lie in being married, having and rearing children, and being a good wife and housekeeper. By contrast, the male realizes himself as a man outside the circle of his home and in the company of other men, the all-male subculture. He has his own circle of friends and associates, his own rights and aspirations, and his own life that is separate from that of his family. His wife does not: she is effectively his possession.

Why does Vickie accept it all? The short answer is: it meets her expectations. Young women of the time were under social pressure, from parents, especially mothers, as well as peers, to marry at an early age. Like her husband, Vickie is an Italian American. Roman Catholic values of the conjugal nuclear family greatly encourage the notion that marriage is to be pursued and preserved. So, while she feels she's held captive, she has the keys to unlock the jail door, but chooses not to use them. For most of the film, she appears to accept her position and supports and encourages her husband; any realization she achieves is always through La Motta's fame.

Jake and Vickie La Motta were actual people, stylized by the director to the point where they are indistinguishable from many of the fictional figures that populate the Scorsese landscape. Considering the former middleweight champion Jake La Motta himself cooperated with the making of the film, one presumes he found the wholly unsympathetic portrayal reasonably accurate. La Motta's 1971 biography *Raging Bull* (co-written with Joseph Carter and Peter Savage) provided the source material for the film. La Motta, in real life, has never publicly criticized Robert De Niro's portrayal of him. On the contrary.

As a record of white male masculinity, as Halberstam calls it, *Raging Bull* is a tour de force, a point developed by Leighton Grist, who, in his "Masculinity, violence, resistance," argues, "*Raging Bull* also situates Jake's resistance within a society in which reactive and violent masculine assertiveness is seemingly endemic" (p. 14).

> **Vickie performs as La Motta's foil: without her, his manhood disappears.**

While Ashe criticizes the film's occlusion of a female perspective, Vickie's role is vital. She performs as La Motta's foil: without her, his manhood disappears, at least until he can find another woman. Manhood is created and perpetuated with and against other people, male and female. La Motta is continually authenticating his masculine credentials, using Vickie as well as exhibiting her. The almost imperceptible awakening of Vickie manifests in answering back, refusing to remain imprisoned in her home, and eventually splitting completely. It may not look like resistance to a contemporary writer like Ashe, but Vickie's little shows of refusal were defiance in the 1950s.

There is plenty to be admired about the patience, resignation, even endurance of women like Vickie La Motta. She lived during a time when women were expected to grin and bear it: they suffered their entrapment and, in a housewifely expression of the Stockholm syndrome, felt affection toward their captors – perhaps with the resignation that comes of expecting no more.

A couple of decades later, women were less likely to accept this type of captivity.

Paulette's problem is that she aches to be taken seriously as an artist, but suspects she has no talent. Still only 22, she has been working as an assistant to the acclaimed Lionel Dobie, a Jackson Pollock-like figure who looks as if he's spent the night on a park bench with a bottle of hooch. Perpetually unshaven, his non-designer spectacles blotchy with paint, Dobie, played by a disheveled Nick Nolte, is fiftyish, but looks older. And, on his own admission, he is so in love with Paulette (she never gives a family name: "it's just Paulette," she explains) that he can't bear the prospect of her being with another man.

As well as assisting the great man, Paulette lives and sleeps with him at his studio apartment in New York, where he creates his masterworks as a lion tamer directs his beasts, slashing his brush like a whip across the canvas (though he actually calls himself a lion rather than a tamer). When he works, Paulette is mesmerized; she is awestruck – her feelings of respect blur and transmute to wonderment and passion.

His attraction to her is more transparent: she is over twenty years younger than him, has good looks, dresses skimpily, and prances coquettishly around the studio (she's played by the then 29-year-old Rosanna Arquette). Dobie persistently declares he loves her and would do anything, even kill, for her. This is the premise of "Life lessons," Scorsese's forty-minute segment of the triptych *New York Stories*. The "lessons" of the title are what Dobie delivers to his assistant, and they are, as he emphasizes, "priceless." But there might also be a pun about the diminishing satisfaction life offers men as they age – life lessens.

Paulette's ambivalence about her own abilities manifests in her leaving Dobie for a younger man, Gregory Stark, a performance artist of ambiguous talent. The story opens with her return to the studio after Stark has ended their affair. "I said I'm not coming back," she restates a message she has left on his machine. "We're still employer and employee, right?" answers Dobie, persuading her to continue her work, but with the proviso that they will no longer sleep together. He soon starts fantasizing about her, staring at her lying on the bed and confessing, "I just want to kiss your foot. I'm sorry. Nothing personal." John Morrone, in his review of *New York Stories*, interprets this as "symptomatic of this would-be lover's objectification of his love" (p. 21).

The relationship is unbalanced, but conveniently so: Paulette values Dobie's life lessons, his instruction, and the influence of his art; he values her as he might value a Vermeer – something to be collected, looked at, cared for, and protected, perhaps in an overindulgent way. He's prepared to let her see other men, bring them back to the studio, and even listens to them having sex. When she tells him flatly, "I don't love you," he shrugs, "So what?"

In fact, she *does* love him. Unbeknown to him, she stands enthralled as he paints, her eyes moistening in ecstasy with every masterly stroke of his brush. "Lionel," she beckons him, though he's too absorbed in his creation to hear anything. Perhaps she more than loves him: she wants to consume him, *be* him. "Will I ever be good?" she demands an honest answer from him. "Tell me right now." After a barely endurable pause, in which we assume a white lie would secure her fidelity, at least in the short term, Dobie prevaricates: "You're young yet."

Dobie tells her, "It's not about talent, it's about no-choice-but-to-do-it . . . if you give up you weren't a real artist to begin with." This is part of his "life lessons."

But, it is he who learns: the newly platonic relationship taxes Dobie. At a gallery, he sees her with a darkly handsome young man and rushes across to retrieve her. "I'm not your shepherd," he says, though his actions betray him. When he tells her the other patrons and exhibitors are laughing at her and then adds because of "that greasy-haired kid," she is relieved. "I thought they were laughing at me because of my work," she sighs. "This is kind of worse, don't you think?" asks Dobie. She doesn't. In fact, she spends the night with the greasy-haired kid, aka Reuben Toro, an aspiring artist.

Next morning, the piqued Dobie pours Toro coffee and sneers, "Are you a graffiti artist?" He cranks the volume of an audiotape of Giacomo Puccini's "Nessun dorma" by Mario Del Monaco, before taking up his brush and palette and standing triumphantly in front of his resplendent expressionist fresco (by the American artist Chuck Connelly, in fact). Dobie turns and gloats malevolently, mocking Toro with the majesty of his creation. Toro is wonderstruck, listening without knowing that the music he hears is that of another master artist who, in middle age – and composing *Madama Butterfly* – became entranced by a younger woman.

There is no visible violence, though, in a sense, this scene

is every bit as ferocious as the passage in *Raging Bull* where
Jake La Motta swaggers away from his prostrate rival, Tony
Janiro, having smashed him into an unrecognizable, bloody
mess. Recall that La Motta's wife had earlier incensed him
by calling Janiro a "good-looking kid." "He ain't pretty no
more," says a ringsider staring at the pulverized Janiro.

Dobie's barely managed possessiveness surfaces
whenever Paulette is near a younger man, especially Stark,
whom he grapples away
from her on one occasion.
If these demonstrations
are designed to validate
his manhood in the pres-
ence of younger and
better-looking men, they
might work for him, but
do nothing for Paulette.

**A good-looking young
woman wipes her palm
across the back of Dobie's
hand and expresses the
hope that some of his
talent will rub off on her.**

For her, it never needed validating.

If anything, Paulette doubts his sincerity. "You don't love
me: you just want me around. Sometimes, I feel like a human
sacrifice," she admits, as if, by staying with him, she is relin-
quishing her own chances of becoming a successful artist.
Eventually, she offers him a chance to prove his love and, in
an episode adapted from Fyodor Dostoevsky's *The Gambler*,
she tells him to kiss a police officer on the lips, or she'll know
he is "King Bullshit" and leave.

Despite his earlier declaration, he can't pull off the task
and skulks back to the studio. Paulette leaves him. (The
whole story has the tone of Dostoevsky, another great artist
who, when in his forties, had an affair with a much-younger
woman, also a writer, who dumped him unceremoniously.)

The trick in this tale of waning manhood and unrequited
passion is that the thing Paulette wants from Dobie is something he just can't give: his gift. But the thing he wants from

her is something that's readily available to a man of his renown. Scorsese saves this for the end, where two interactions remind Dobie that *ars longa vita brevis*. At least, his art is.

One: a sycophantic male grabs his hand and reveals, "I'm an artist myself, but, when I look at your stuff, I just want to divorce my wife." Two: a good-looking young woman wipes her palm across the back of Dobie's hand and expresses the hope that some of his talent will rub off on her; humbly, she introduces herself, "You're an artist, I'm a painter." During a brief conversation, Dobie's eyes wander lecherously to her lips, neck, ear, eyes, and hands (just one ring on her left index finger) and he makes an offer. "I need an assistant. I pay room and board, give life lessons that are priceless, plus a salary. You wouldn't know anybody that needs a job, would you?" She gasps, "Oh God!"

Unlike many other Scorsese females, Paulette's search for happiness does not involve romantic love, but a love for something she suspects she doesn't, nor will ever, have – talent. Her attachment to Dobie is conditional: she wants to be around him, to thrill at, be exhilarated by, become immersed in his creativity. What she realizes much more clearly than Dobie is that she is interchangeable: there is no shortage of doting young aspiring artists, female and male, who would gladly swap places with her.

"Heterosexuality is in *Life Lessons* an expedient of power," writes Ronald S. Librach in his 1996 analysis, "A nice little irony." He means that, for Paulette, it is a means of manipulating Dobie, though not always in the ways she designs. For Dobie, "its exercise is a response to the passage of time" (p. 130).

Dobie insists throughout the film that he loves Paulette, but, by the end, gets the message. For a male artist of his repute there are compensations for an aging body. The film closes with the insinuation that Dobie is about to repeat his maneuvers. The destination of Paulette is not known, though it would be no surprise to find her working as a curator, or as sales staff at a gallery. Probably not as an artist.

"It was my idea of a man: strong and dominating," says Alice Hyatt née Graham when asked to reflect on her attraction to her late husband, a man who categorically refused to let her pursue her childhood dream of becoming a singer. He was adamant: "No wife of mine is going to sing in a saloon."

After her husband's death in a road accident, the central figure of *Alice Doesn't Live Here Anymore* is forced into the role of breadwinner. She takes her 11-year-old son and sets off from Socorro, New Mexico, bound for a singing career in Monterey, California. On her way, she stops off in Arizona, where she circuits the bars in search of an audition. A promising introduction to a bar owner is brought to an abrupt halt when he asks, "Mind turning around for me?" a request Hyatt queries. "I want to look at you," he says matter-of-factly. "Well, look at my face. I don't sing with my ass," she snarls.

It's hardly an epiphany, but it's a little jolt, one of several unpleasant surprises that push Hyatt toward a different understanding of men. Determined not to allow men to ambush her ambitions, she rebuffs the 27-year old Ben Eberhardt with a curt put-down, "I don't date teenagers." She is 35. But his insistence wins her over. His surface amiability disguises a more minatory character, however. When a young woman approaches Hyatt and reveals she is Eberhardt's wife, the infuriated womanizer tracks them both down. "You bitch! I'm gonna cut you," he warns his wife, before cautioning Hyatt, "Don't ever tell me what to do. I'll bust your jaw."

Every time Hyatt, played by Ellen Burstyn, meets a new man, she feels like one of those dogs who are born and reared in controlled environments and, when eventually released, prefer the certainty of confinement rather than the world outside. Every venture into a world without men

> BAR OWNER: **Mind turning around for me? I want to look at you.** ALICE HYATT: **Well, look at my face. I don't sing with my ass.**

serves to remind her that she needs the sureness men seem to promise. Yet they never provide anything more than a reminder that they are all the same.

Surely men can't rule this world just like dinosaurs did 200 million years ago, i.e. with brute force. Can they? She soon discovers that, in fact, some women obligingly, even cheerfully, assist them. Take Flo, whom she meets when waiting tables at Mel and Ruby's. ("Ruby died fourteen years ago," we're told. "The place killed her.") Flo's outrageous flirting with the diner's customers is an embarrassment to Hyatt, especially when she tries to draw her into her teasing games. "Leave me out of your jokes . . . those routines you do for the fellas," she advises Flo.

Any hopes that this constitutes some sort of awakening are later dashed when Hyatt listens to Flo's earnest advice: "Undo the top button [of your shirt]. You get more tips that way."

Hyatt's education continues when she meets David, played by Kris Kristofferson, who confounds all her expectations of men: he is considerate, sympathetic, and willing to compromise on almost anything; yet not so soft as to ruin her assumptions about how real men should be. Perhaps not all men are like the hidebound misogynists who have stymied her. But only perhaps. One incident changes this. Hyatt's precocious son, Tommy, warms to David, but recoils at his often-demanding attempts to tutor him in guitar playing.

When Tommy brings a sudden end to a tuition session with "Screw you!" and cranks up T. Rex's "Jeepster" on the hi-fi, David strikes him. Hyatt reacts furiously and David justifies his action, "I expect him to do what I say in my house." She and Tommy leave.

Manhood takes many forms, but, for Scorsese, they share a common matrix. In Hyatt's eyes, the man she believed to be different is just the same as all the other men she has encountered. Her husband, in particular, used to bawl at Tommy for playing rock music. "Turn that shit down!" he bellowed at Tommy, who was listening to Mott the Hoople (like T. Rex, an English rock band of the early 1970s). So Hyatt has seen it all before.

Scorsese gilds his message by using the Rodgers and Hart song "Where and when" as Hyatt's signature number. The lyrics speak of déjà vu:

It seems we stood and talked like this before,
We looked at each other in the same way then.
But I can't remember where or when
Some things that happened for the first time,
Seem to be happening again.

The number was originally part of Busby Berkeley's 1939 *Babes in Arms*, which featured Judy Garland, who also appeared in Victor Fleming's 1939 *The Wizard of Oz*, of course. (Scorsese routinely cross-references his sources of inspiration.)

For Hyatt, it isn't just a case of history repeating itself. It's Manhood Recrudescing. Hyatt's lessons might instruct her as to the changing yet permanent forms manhood takes, but they don't release her from her bondage. "I don't know how to live without a man," she confesses to Flo before asserting proprietary rights, "It's *my* life. It's not some man's life I'm gonna help him out with."

While the film closes with Hyatt's apparent resignation to settle with David and scale down her singing ambitions, the conclusion is unclear. A CBS series based on the film, which ran between 1976 and 1980, centered on the diner and didn't include David in the storylines, though Scorsese was not involved in the show. In his vision, she *might* have stuck with David.

Marc Raymond, in his 2000 thesis *Martin Scorsese and American Film Genre*, notices a resemblance between *Alice Doesn't Live Here Anymore* and *The Age of Innocence* in the sense that both are "romantic melodramas" and feature women who either seek or find happiness through men rather than self-fulfillment. Actually, Scorsese's graceful adaptation of Edith Wharton's 1920 novel might qualify as revisionist melodrama in the sense that it tells a dramatic story that appeals to the emotions but with a modification of perspective, or point of view. Its subtitle might read: "The (mis)education of Newland Archer."

Archer is a lawyer in 1870s New York high society whose marriage to a pleasant but dull young woman is imperiled by his entrancement with an unconventional countess who has just returned from a failing marriage in Europe. Archer is a singular man. When he tells Sillerton Jackson, an older male friend, that he, at first, "supposes" that women should share the same freedoms as men, then later confirms, "Yes, I do," Jackson suspects an educative influence: "Well, apparently Count Olenski [the countess's husband] also takes a similarly modern view. I've never heard of him lifting a finger to get his wife back."

In the same conversation, Jackson alludes to the Count's sybaritism: "Handsome, they say, but eyes with a lot of lashes. When he wasn't with women he was collecting china. Paying any price for both, I understand."

I will explore how Scorsese handles the stricken romance at the heart of *The Age of Innocence* in Chapter 9, but for the moment, I want to explore how he essays an indistinct type of manhood. Intrigued at first, Archer becomes confused by his own sensibilities and, in an attempt to resolve his uncertainty, brings forward the date of his marriage to May Welland, who "anchors him" to the custom-governed elite culture of Old New York. Welland accepts that her true gratification can be realized only through a man. "Everything you do is so special," she fawns to Archer.

Most Scorsese men would understand and appreciate this. But Archer is frustrated at his wife's incapability for serious thought and realizes that he is constantly made to tolerate her ignorance and prejudice. After an absorbing dinner conversation with Riviera, a man he meets in Paris (and who is the Count's secretary), Archer calls him interesting and clever and suggests seeing him again. Welland isn't keen and calls him "common," but qualifies this, "I suppose I shouldn't have known if he was clever." Archer immediately resigns, "Then I won't ask him to dine."

Archer, unlike other Scorsese men, finds it less troublesome to conform to a woman and with tradition than to challenge either – which is effectively what he would be doing if he pursued the Countess. Scorsese portrays Archer as a weak-willed conformist unable to cope with an entirely different type of woman. The Countess is alluring yet prohibitive and, when he finally appears to summon the courage to tell Welland that he needs to make a break ("From the law?" she asks. "That too, yes"), she trumps him with the announcement of her pregnancy. In an instant, his future is affixed to hers and the consequences are terminal, as Gavin Smith et al. point out in their 1993 article "Artist of the beautiful." The tragic love story becomes "a bitterly ironic 'Paradise Regained,' featuring an American Adam who, neatly unmanned by a snake-in-the-grass Eve, stops short of sinning bravely and thereby loses his life" (p. 11).

Whether Welland's ploy actually unmans Archer – and, I assume Smith et al. mean deprives him of qualities traditionally associated with men – is not certain. She might have been girding him in anticipation that he was about to pardon himself from manly duties. In nineteenth-century America, faith in

As Newland Archer's world is rendered fluid and unstable, so is his understanding of what it is to be a man.

the power of manhood made it possible to believe that satisfaction would find its expression not by following passions, much less in the indulgence of the senses, but through the commitment of conscientious men to their wives and children.

Scorsese's men are always engaged in the pursuit of something; it's often an obsessional pursuit, as we've noticed earlier. Men obsess over things they want and contrive to get; women typically don't, which is why the ironically titled *The Age of Innocence* is something of an aberration. In Scorsese's vision, men typically value only other men, their values, beliefs, opinions, and perceptions. So, for example, in discussing *GoodFellas*, Matthew Kieran writes, in "Forbidden knowledge," of a "moral code which deems group outsiders to be morally insignificant."

Women seem to be just that – morally insignificant, by which Kieran means that they have no say in relation to standards of good and bad behavior or conduct – but they are insignificant for all practical purposes and significant only as ornaments. Wherever the codes operate, women are rendered unimportant at best, meaningless at worst. As

such, they are derisorily tolerated or degraded to the status
of mere objects.

Yet in *The Age of Innocence*, women are levers that operate
the mechanisms of change. As Archer's fixed and permanent
world is rendered fluid and unstable, so is his understanding
of what it is to be a man. A defender and protector, perhaps.
A provider, certainly. But not a warder. And if fearlessness is
an attribute of manhood, he is also left to contemplate what
kind of man he is.

How can this be part of Scorsese's enterprise to represent
the manifold features of men's rights and privileges – the map
of the masculine prerogative? Pat Gill provides an answer of
sorts in her 2003 article "Taking it personally." "Male suffering is nothing new to films," she opens her essay. "Male
characters have undergone torture and endured pain for
their beliefs, their country, their honor, their women, their
family, and their friends since films began to tell stories."

But, since the 1990s, Gill detects a shift in focus: films
gave up on trying to hide the failure of masculinity and
began to disclose men in despair. They despaired over their
own feelings and what they suspected about themselves.
They were prompted to "agonized acts of displacement and
amelioration," as Gill puts it, meaning, I suspect, that they
unconsciously transferred intense emotions from the original
object to other ones (i.e. the psychoanalytic version of "displacement") in their efforts to improve dire situations.

"The kind of movies I've made over the years have been
about people who expressed themselves in a certain way,"
Scorsese told Lewis Beale in 1998 – "through violence."
This is, as we've seen already in this chapter, not accurate; though many of his characters, like La Motta and
Alice Hyatt's admirers, both express and, in the process,
validate their manhood through aggressive action. If Gill's
argument makes sense, these "agonized acts" would be

desperate but ineffectual efforts to make a bad situation better. But, even in the absence of physical violence, there seems to be a violation, or failure to respect in the case of Newland Archer, or an irreverent disregard in the case of Lionel Dobie.

Sometimes, Scorsese's documentaries are revealing in this context. Joni Mitchell is only one of two women soloists in *The Last Waltz* (Emmylou Harris is the other; Mavis Staples sings one verse and backing vocals). Immediately preceding the appearance of Mitchell, there is a backstage conversation in which Scorsese asks The Band (whose farewell concert is at the center of the film), "What about women on the road?" It's a question that probably sounded less sexist in 1976 when the film was made. "I love 'em. That's probably why we've been on the road," answers The Band's Richard Manuel.

Bass player Rick Danko endorses his point, "Since we've started playing, just like we've all grown a little bit, so have the women." And laughter erupts. Cue Mitchell, who sings "Coyote," her own composition about a carnivore hunter's encounter with a female ("He's got a woman at home. He's got another woman down the hall. He seems to want me anyway"). When, in the same film, Muddy Waters sings, "I'm a man. I'm a natural born lover's man," from "Mannish boy," he sounds as if he actually could be that coyote.

Manhood isn't so much won as inherited, but the challenge lies in trying to substantiate, corroborate, or justify it. The forms this takes are varied. The only invariable feature about them is the presence of women. But mapping men's rights and privileges is only part of the story. How those rights are made to seem natural, those privileges maintained, entitlements dispensed, and advantages defended: these provide relief and contour to Scorsese's cartography.

9

WOMEN LOSE

"When it gets tough, you cry." If the argument is turning against you, take charge by issuing a reminder. That's what must be going through Jimmy Doyle's mind when his determined wife suggests plans that cross his own. Francine Evans wants it all and she has it within her grasp. Her singing is awesome: agents and record companies clamor after her. So, when she wants to take time off to have a baby, you remind yourself that the likes of Madonna, Britney, and company all did the same and that it's a perfectly reasonable segue for a diva.

Evans, however, lives in the 1940s, when it's temerarious to resist the whims of a husband. So, in moments of conflict – and there are many in this relationship – Doyle calls on nature to back him up: despite his wife's artistry, her brilliance, and the adulation she commands, she is still a woman and has a woman's weaknesses.

New York, New York, for Cliff Froehlich, of the *St. Louis Post-Dispatch*, "weaves in several threads that stitch together many of Scorsese's works." It is one of the two Scorsese films that "provide a virtual catalog of his directorial obsessions and approaches," the other being *Raging Bull*. Writing in 2005, Froehlich argues that one of those obsessions is in offering "disturbing insights into male–female relationships."

The film centers on Francine Evans, who soars to stardom, and her husband Jimmy Doyle, who zigzags in and out of work in middling jazz bands. As Scorsese films go, this is easily his most synthetic: there's no invitation to enter a world of skuzzy streets or well-upholstered dining rooms; the streets are all curiously clean, the lighting is patently artificial, and the romantic anguish of its characters is curiously unmoving. Conflicts and resolutions seem inconsequential in the greater scheme of things. In a sense, this is probably the whole point, as the lyrics of one of Evans' songs explain, "Somebody loses, somebody wins. One day it's kicks, then it's kicks in the shins. But the planet spins. And the world goes round" (from John Kander and Fred Ebb's "The world goes round").

The film is set amid the jubilation of the immediate postwar. Having been forced to serve in the war effort, whether in munitions factories or in the military, women became more independent. Men returned from the war to find women had taken their jobs. One of the ideological exercises of the late 1940s was to persuade women that their natural place was in the home. Conveniently, the proliferation of household appliances, like refrigerators and washing machines, abetted by a fast-growing industry to advertise them and a new apparatus to goggle at, pulled women back home.

But some women were ambivalent. Evans is a WAC: she's first seen in her Women's Army Corps uniform, drinking and watching the festivities of VJ-Day, 1945, at the close of the war. She's approached by Doyle, who cornily uses the line, "I know you from some place." She firmly and repeatedly snubs him, but he refuses to go. He's an itinerant saxophonist looking for

Francine Evans reflects American women in the postwar period: she stands steadfastly behind her man; later, she discovers the empowering effects of independence. (© Kobal)

a gig in New York City. When his loud playing and then-new bebop style impresses no one, Evans jumps in without invitation and sings to his accompaniment. She outshines him, but the surprise move clinches him a job as part of a double-act. Like Alice Hyatt, in *Alice Doesn't Live Here Anymore*, she learns that musical talent is not quite enough for a female performer. "Let's see your legs," says the club owner.

This was the Big Band era: bands led by the likes of Benny Goodman, Tommy Dorsey, and Count Basie were dominant purveyors of popular music. Rock 'n' roll didn't emerge until about 1955. Evans, being a proficient singer in her own right, soon takes off on a national tour with a dance band. Desperate to re-establish contact, Doyle tracks her down

in Asheville, North Carolina, gets a job with the band, and
starts an affair that leads to an impromptu marriage by a
Justice of the Peace.

The band is billed as THE FRANKIE HARTE ORCHESTRA WITH
FRANCINE EVANS, Doyle being a nondescript tenor player with
a penchant for overin-

American women glimpsed the possibilities of an alternative to the prewar sex role of dutiful wife and housekeeper.

dulgent solos. Evans'
professional status counts
for nothing in her rela-
tionship. There's never a
doubt over who has the
authority. Doyle talks to
Evans in imperatives:
"Come here!" "Get your shoes on!" The marriage is his idea;
she just goes along with it. The decline of the Big Band age
is reflected in the dwindling audiences. Dismayed, Frankie
Harte himself contemplates retirement. He sees "parking
lots, skating rink, theaters" springing up in places where
ballrooms used to stand.

When Doyle takes over, Evans gets an even bigger billing:
FRANCINE EVANS AND JIMMY DOYLE AND HIS ORCHESTRA.
Still, there is no diminishing Doyle's prerogative, even if
Evans is the one drawing ample plaudits. Doyle becomes
a troubled guest in his own band, watching impotently as
Evans becomes a star. (The film was inspired by the 1949
Anthony Curtiz film *My Dream is Yours*, which effectively
launched Doris Day as a major Hollywood star.)

Evans, played by Liza Minnelli, unintentionally starts a
zero-sum game, her every success seeming to be gained at
the expense of Doyle's fortunes. His love for her is spliced
with the kind of envy Jake La Motta felt for Vickie, who drew
desirous looks from all quarters. Like La Motta, Doyle (also
played by De Niro) becomes restively possessive. Evans, like
Vickie, avoids the kind of confrontation we might expect of

a contemporary woman. She endures what becomes humiliation with exasperated commitment to the band. Yet beneath that stoic exterior, there is a woman of some authority waiting to break through. She occasionally does.

In perhaps the film's most piercing scene, Evans heedlessly completes the bandleader's count to start a number: "One . . . two," intones Doyle, only for Evans to jump in with, "One, two, three, four." Doyle stands transfixed, scarcely believing her unwelcome contribution. He halts the band and publicly scolds her, "Come here! Do not kick-off the band. I kick-off the band, understand? Don't ever do it again. *Ever* again." And then he turns her and smacks her on the backside, not hard but as a father might discomfort a daughter who has misplaced his car keys. It's not as brutal as many other moments in Scorsese films, but, if any scene reveals the macho incubus in his full diabolic malignancy, this is it.

Much of the film revolves around the efforts of Evans to pursue her career, burdened by an ungracious lover who struggles to accommodate his partner's talent, recognition, and success. The struggle intensifies when she gets pregnant and decides to quit the tour in order to return to New York. "Doctors say I could lose this kid if I travel," she tells him. Even this doesn't convince him that she should stop touring. Later, he reveals he never wanted a child.

Without her, the band founders and Doyle signs it over to his pianist, resuming his sax playing in Harlem as the only white member of an African American sextet. Meanwhile Evans attracts the interest of a record label boss. Doyle's resentment at his wife's success becomes vilely manifest when he turns up for a dinner meeting off his head on smack and sporting for a fight. Mortified, Evans sits with the head of Decca Records as bouncers wrestle her husband to the exit.

Evans later confronts Doyle: "You care about your drugs, your friends and your music . . . all you care about is *you*."

This is confirmed when he visits her in the hospital. "Did you see him?" she asks. "Who?" replies Doyle. "The baby!" He looks dumfounded. "It's a him?"

Evans resumes her career with her hitherto long hair bobbed. A bid for freedom, perhaps? The hairstyle has been something of a symbol of emancipation since the 1920s when F. Scott Fitzgerald's hero of "Bernice bobs her hair" cut her long hair into a short boyish style hanging above the shoulders. Evans' portrait appears on dozens of magazines and her records sell, enabling her to get a lead role in a big Broadway show called "Happy Endings." The ending of her relationship is far from happy. In Evans' eyes, showbusiness success barely compensates for a failed marriage and, when Doyle, after a break, tentatively tries for a resumption ("wanna have Chinese?"), she agrees, then pauses as she approaches the stage door, where he waits. The hesitation becomes a demurral. Doyle leaves alone.

More dramatic shifts in the values and ambitions of women came later in the twentieth century, specifically in the 1970s with the advent of what was then called Women's Liberation. But in the late 1940s, American women glimpsed the possibilities of an alternative to the prewar sex role of dutiful wife and housekeeper. Evans is abundantly talented and clearly intent on a career in the entertainment industry. Not for a second does she suspect that becoming a mother will involve sacrificing her showbusiness interests. She sees no necessary contradiction in being a working singer and a mother. By examining womanhood through an unusually successful and widely fêted figure, Scorsese shows the difference between independence and independent-spiritedness.

Only at the very end of the film does Evans summon the inner strength to defy Doyle. In practically every aspect of her life, he has commandeered, governed, and directed her. Even when she announces her pregnancy and asks for confirmation that he is happy about becoming a father, his answer is feeble and unconvincing. So that later, when he discloses his true feelings ("Did I tell you to have that goddam baby? No, I didn't tell you. You had it, now keep it"), she is barely surprised.

As we'll see in the next chapter, the anti-romantic ethos that runs like a river through Scorsese films often yields curiously two-dimensional women. Either they are docile and ready to accept the control of the men they love, or they're forceful, strident, and occasionally aggressive – and still willing to accept the control of men. There is no inconsistency: even the most determinedly independent women are, for Scorsese, flawed by their preoccupation with men. Evans is probably unique in the Scorsese collection: a woman who finally realizes some measure of control over her life and, in the end, waits on the precipice long enough to calculate that throwing herself off is not her best option.

Evans waits on the precipice long enough to calculate that throwing herself off is not her best option.

The moments while she considers whether to meet Doyle at the stage door for a late supper are probably spent rerunning their past at high speed. She waits silently and does nothing, but there is little doubt she is remembering what was and what will probably be again should she succumb to another one of Doyle's corny lines.

It's difficult to imagine Scorsese presiding over a project such as, say, Stephen Daldry's *The Hours* (2002), which brought immediacy to the lives of three women linked by the fate of Virginia Woolf, or the harrowing *Monster* (2003), in which director Patty Jenkins unflinchingly portrayed the man-killer Aileen Wuornos, let alone *Thelma and Louise*

(1991), Ridley Scott's fable of ill-starred defectors from domesticity. There are dimensions in these films that are either unknown to or perhaps beyond Scorsese's range. In his world, women are either passive and yielding, or assertive, but willing to accede to a man's demands. On the odd occasion when they are genuinely weaponed, they're disarmed by their own mania.

Lusty and obtrusive but possibly deranged, Masha, who appears in *The King of Comedy*, makes her partner in crime – kidnapping, in this instance – seem rational by comparison. Celebrity-worshipping fan Masha (her other name is never revealed) aligns herself with fellow celeb-worshipper Rupert Pupkin as they conspire to take tv talk show host Jerry Langford hostage.

Masha is fixated on a man you might confuse with Jay Leno or Britain's Jonathan Ross. In other words, not conventionally handsome, but with a slick line in repartee, a few million dollars in his bank account, and a late night show to showcase his talent – a talent that, he reminds us, is not God-given, but has been diligently honed, working for years at small clubs.

We've seen in Chapter 6 how Pupkin's outrageous surmise that he can use Langford as a negotiating tool to get what he craves yields an appearance on national television and subsequent showbusiness success. Masha, by contrast, is borne on more fanciful but limited aspirations: she wants sex with Langford. But, while there is some symmetry in the fans' idolatry, the manner in which they express their consuming passions differs. As Ed Sikov put it in his *Film Quarterly* review of the film in 1983, "While Masha's obsession takes the form of hysteria, Rupert channels his energy creatively into becoming an image himself" (p. 19).

There is a method, however hare-brained, in Pupkin's madness, but there is none in Masha's folly. She goes along with Pupkin's scheme enthusiastically, covetously stalking Langford before eventually forcing him into captivity. Pupkin eventually gets his spot on the show, does his routine, then makes everyone wait before the prerecorded shtick is shown on national tv. The police comply with his every stipulation, even allow him to stop off at a bar and buy everyone a drink to toast his success while under arrest.

Scorsese intercuts scenes from Pupkin's unfolding stratagem with Masha's amorous débâcle. Mummified in white tape, Langford is seated at a dining table in a romantically candle-lit apartment where Masha lays bare her expectation that they will consummate their relationship. "I really love you," she tells the captive Langford, who is rendered helpless and speechless. This makes Masha's declaration no less sincere. Somehow, she seems to have ascended to a new level of self-delusion, conducting an intimate personal conversation with another living human being, but one who is effectively inert.

The scene is tender, but also frightening. Masha's announcement that she wants to be "impulsive" and go "nuts" sounds ominous, especially when she smashes a crystal wine glass just to demonstrate that, if there is even a tiny detail to mar the perfection of the occasion, she'll destroy it. "Wouldn't you like to see me outta my head?" she asks Langford, then strips down to her underwear and prepares for sex, singing a solicitous version of Ray Charles' "Come rain or come shine" ("I'm gonna love you. Like no one's ever loved you").

Meanwhile, Pupkin cool-headedly prosecutes his plan, anticipating every move as he connives his way onto television. Every new scene involving Pupkin shows him nearing his endgame. Masha, meanwhile, appears to be advancing sinisterly toward her erotomaniacal climax. While Pupkin skillfully evades all attempts to trick him, the painfully gullible Masha falls for Langford's first transparently insincere gambit. When she removes the sticking plaster across his mouth in order to kiss him, her internee asks her to release him. She tamely complies, only for Langford to strike her and flee. Even then, she chases him like a spurned lover, racing down the street in skimpy underwear and stiletto heels crying, "Jerry! *Jerry!*"

Masha, for all her purposefulness, becomes a disposable accomplice; her fate doesn't rate a mention. "Unfortunately, Scorsese does not take this sexual and ideological aspect into account at all," writes Sikov (p. 19).

Perhaps he does. By absenting her from the final passage of the film, Scorsese again invites the impression that he sees a woman as largely irrelevant. While Sikov doesn't spell out what he means by the "sexual and ideological aspect," we can presume he means the ideas, or ideals, behind the conception of women that lurks in this dramatization and the manner of characterizing women in a certain kind of way. One feature in particular of that characterization involves *agency*, by which I mean their actions or interventions in producing a result of one kind or another.

Imagining women as engaging, organizing, interrupting, or in some way making things happen, rather than just responding to others or a set of circumstances, vests them with the potential to initiate action. Masha, like the other women featured in this chapter, is far from passive: well, only in the way a quiescent volcano is passive. Physically energetic and ready to engage wholeheartedly in Pupkin's grand plan, she becomes integral to its success. But, it is his plan and its success is *his*, not hers. As with the other Scorsese schemes featuring women, this one brings no triumph for Masha. Remember: all Scorsese films are about collapse and change. The catalyst for change, in Masha's case, is Pupkin, or, more specifically, his project. One result of the project is that Masha is simply removed.

Masha doesn't want fame, or her own television show. It's never clear that she wants anything beyond an amorous union with Langford. But she pursues her prey determinedly and, when she traps him, communicates her deepest feelings: "I love you, baby. I love you *so* much."

Critics might spot a pattern here: yet another ballsy Scorsese female whose gratification can only derive from some sort of relationship with a man and who is, ultimately, prepared to subordinate herself to the priorities of men. Maria Miliora, herself a psychoanalyst, gives Masha short shrift in her book *The Scorsese Psyche on Screen*. "A rather silly woman [who] loses her hold on reality and slips into insanity," is her disparaging description (p. 173).

True, Masha is poised about one synapse from frenzy and appears to leap across the neurological gap when she realizes one of her heartfelt ambitions – to get close to Langford (even if he is tethered to a chair at the time). But Miliora is too dismissive. Masha's sly percipience is clear enough in her early stalking when she wheedles in and out of crowds, contriving to get her love letters to Langford. She starts the film as a fearless, if frenzied, autograph hunter and ends it as a madwoman, a dangerous madwoman. Another way of conceiving Masha would be as what some psychologists call an "extreme" celebrity worshipper who "over-identifies" with celebrities and who behaves compulsively and obsessively toward them in a "borderline pathological" manner.

I take this from the research of John Maltby et al. in the *British Journal of Psychology*, which concludes that this group share many similarities with most other fans: they just follow their favored celebs in a more enthusiastic way. They might be borderline pathological when it comes to celebrities, but they are able to function effectively and integrate anonymously into society. Initially, Masha seems to fit this description, though Scorsese's handling of her development consigns her to psychotic oblivion.

We never learn of her fate; we're never invited to care. A prison sentence, possibly; more likely detention at some sort of psychiatric facility. Pupkin might have been deluded, but he has enough good sense to figure out how he can realize his ambition. Masha is just deluded in a way that offers no hope.

Unlike men, who break rules with impunity, deviant women usually have to pay for their transgressions. Excitement, freedom, and even a limited autonomy are valuable resources, and getting them typically involves violating some sort of standard or protocol. There is always atonement. Ginger McKenna, for instance, pays a dear price: she dies after overdosing in a cheap motel, having spent her last few years in the company of "pimps, low-lifes, druggies and bikers in LA."

McKenna, like Masha, is a hysterical woman, prone to erratic behavior, often violent. In *Casino*, she starts as a hustler in the Las Vegas hotels, living on her wits and the gullibility of her clients. Her fortunes rise when she meets Sam

McKenna is like Masha: obsessively in love with a man who is indifferent.

Rothstein, the notional boss of a hotel controlled by the mob. And here is the twist: when the helplessly besotted Rothstein asks her to marry him, settle down, raise a family, and promises to set her up for life, she's dismissive, "You know a lot of happily married people, Sam? 'Cause I don't . . . I'm sorry. I'm not in love with you."

Rothstein persists. "What is love anyway?" he asks. "It's a . . . it's a mutual respect." McKenna uses her hustler's logic and agrees to marry Rothstein and bear his child in exchange for a life of garish abundance amid the western fantasyland. Knee deep in Bvlgari jewelry and Anna Nateece furs, she does her stuff, functioning like a designer label on one of Rothstein's pastel-colored suits.

But Scorsese introduces a further twist. Just when McKenna appears to have adjusted to the role of the obediently disempowered wife with $2 million in her own safety deposit box and a husband who works seventeen-hour days at the hotel, she is drawn back to her former pimp, an LA cokehead named Lester Diamond. She is like Masha: obsessively in love with a man who is indifferent. In Diamond's case, he is indifferent to McKenna, but extremely interested in her access to Rothstein's money.

For all his influence, Rothstein is powerless to dampen McKenna's passion for Diamond. When he has him beaten up, it serves only to strengthen her misguided commitment. She, too, is powerless: time and again, she is drawn back to Diamond, who barely disguises his mercenariness. In one scene, he woos McKenna on a long-distance call while snorting coke with a half-undressed woman. Rothstein dotes on McKenna. McKenna dotes on Diamond. Diamond dotes on no one – though he is partial to money and drugs.

McKenna, who once turned tricks for a living, is streetsmart, tough-minded, and painfully honest about the limits of her affection for her husband. She enters a bargain and seems to have what she wants: a life of abundant wealth and all the stimulants money can buy. But her Achilles' heel is a man. Worse: a calculating, manipulative, underhanded man who treats women as articles of trade – he is a pimp, remember – and sees McKenna as little more than a signatory to a joint bank account.

Over a ten-year period, she meets, marries, leaves, returns, then again leaves Rothstein, without ever giving the impression she has approached happiness. Her first appearance in the movie features her at her most joyous, giggling while she throws dice at a craps table and sneaks chips from her john's

rack into her purse. But this is not a woman for whom con-
tentment comes easily. If she isn't chasing Diamond, she is
seeking solace in booze or blow. And her trailing of Diamond
is at once pathetic and ruinous.

Deviant females are not a Scorsese specialty, of course;
which is why the dramas I'm highlighting in this chapter
are integral to Scorsese's vision. The point is: they *are* deviant; they think and behave in ways that depart from usual
or accepted social standards. Even Francine Evans, while
no maverick in the mold of Virginia Woolf or Simone de
Beauvoir, manages to break a few rules. After all, she successfully pursues a professional career in entertainment, has
a child, and disburdens herself of the man she loves, and,
we presume, continues to love long after they have split.

So how does Scorsese handle women who are out-and-
out deviants? As we've noted before, men who prosecute
an outlaw lifestyle have often been glorified retroactively.
We never learn of Billy the Kid's fixation with a woman, or
Butch Cassidy's fatal infatuation, and Al Capone never sim-
pered over a woman (or, if he did, it was never recorded on
film). Women, though, as we are learning, are different.

There is a cabal of American folk heroines known for the
prowess in endeavors typically associated with men. Martha
Jane Cannary, or Calamity Jane, was noted for her proficiency at shooting and riding as well as her heavy drinking
and wild excesses in the second half of the nineteenth century.
Annie Oakley regularly outscored skilled marksmen in shooting contests and campaigned for the admittance of women in
the US military's combat operations. Violent outlaw Bonnie
Parker, with Clyde Barrow, terrorized the American south
in the 1930s, as Arthur Penn's 1967 film *Bonnie and Clyde*
recorded.

Bertha Thompson left an account of her life, *Sister of the Road: The autobiography of Box-car Bertha*. The book's integrity is open to doubt: first published in 1937 as a biography "as told to Dr. Ben L. Reitman," it was later re-published as an account based not on one person, but on "sisters of the road" with whom Reitman conversed when doing his research. But it gave Scorsese source material for his *Boxcar Bertha*, a film that envisions Thompson as an uncommon, even rebellious, woman who was condemned in her own times, but later idealized, particularly by feminist writers. Thompson was, in her own words, "a hobo, a radical, a prostitute, a thief, a reformer, a social worker and a revolutionary."

In early 1929, Americans might have been forgiven for thinking they lived in an earthly paradise. The economy flourished, with real estate, banking, and manufacturing all doing good business. Even the church thrived, its pulpits heaving with members, presumably thankful to a most providential God. It really must have seemed that God blessed America. By October, the protection had disappeared: the collapse of the Wall Street stock market started a concatenation. The factories, big and small, closed their doors; car firms alone laid off half their workforces. Farmers who had grown rich feeding European armies no longer had any markets for their crops and fell bankrupt. Truckers were left with nothing to transport, shops nothing to sell. The skyscrapers that had sprung up during the buoyant years and which were, in many respect, testaments of American prosperity were left uninhabited. This was, of course, the Great Depression.

The number of transient, homeless women spiraled during this period, the causes lying in economic circumstances rather than wanderlust. In her 2006 article "Transiency and transgression in the autobiographies of Barbara Starke and 'Boxcar' Bertha Thompson," Christine Photinos informs us that, for men, transience is associated with a certain dignity. She cites writers such as Jack London and Jack Kerouac, both of whom embody a sense of pioneering adventurism that is truly American. This is not so for women.

Photinos points out that women who left home for a life on the road were often dispatched to the marginal categories of deviants or tramps, both of which bore stigmas of a "degraded kind of sexuality." Actually, during the Great Depression, "tens of thousands" of women were forced to travel in order to survive. Their motive might have been to search for work, or to escape a violent marriage – a condition often precipitated by the loss of work and the hardship that follows.

Scorsese portrays Thompson as neither a job-seeker nor a domestic fugitive: when her father is killed in an accident that could have been avoided were it not for the avarice of his boss, she has something of an epiphany and becomes a sort of labor union groupie. No mention is made of Thompson's mother, who, according to her own memoir, inspired her maverick approach. Instead, it is her father, or rather his death, that incites her urge to hit the road with a crew of labor unionists.

There follows a kind of *Pilgrim's Progress*, though John Bunyan's allegory of a spiritual journey is replaced with a directionless wandering through the West, evading the law and picking up money, legally or illegally, as the opportunities arise. Every so often, the unionists get into scrapes with the police or entrepreneurs.

Photinos is dismissive of Scorsese's treatment of Thompson, relegating her critique to a footnote, in which she indicates that Thompson is depicted "in search of a replacement father figure." She argues that Bill Shelly, the union organizer with whom Thompson becomes intimate, "becomes the focal point of the film."

Shelly certainly features in the most remembered scene in the film, where he is literally crucified, his hands nailed to the side of a railroad freight car. He is also endowed with a kind of Robin Hood benevolence, robbing from the rich to give to, in his case, the union.

So, there is little doubt about his essential goodness. But, it seems unfair to say he replaces Thompson at the center of the film. If anything, Scorsese gives Thompson an active presence comparable with that of her contemporary Bonnie Parker: she is unromantic, unafraid, and uninhibited about using violence. She also defies segregationist custom by befriending Von Morton, an African American union member. At one point, she hugs him in a "coloreds-only" bar in Texas, a punishable act in the 1930s.

Scorsese doesn't use Thompson as a way of evoking what Barbara Jane Brickman, in her 2007 essay "Coming of age in the 1970s," calls "an active, even aggressive feminism that most popular films of the era, even films by the new auteurs of American cinema, worked to silence" (p. 43). This aggressive approach came to fruition in Terrence Malick's *Badlands*, released in 1973,

"BOXCAR BERTHA" THOMPSON: **Look at the baby doll. Daddy gave me one like that once. She lost her head.** TILLIE PARR (A FELLOW PROSTITUTE): **Probably over some no-good man.**

a year after *Boxcar Bertha*, featuring "a female viewpoint and a female consciousness" that is missing from Scorsese's film.

Thompson's perspective is perhaps less that of a feminist, more that of a unionist, and, while the two are by no means incompatible, there is no indication that Scorsese invests Thompson with the desire to challenge traditional sex role arrangements. Photinos might be overstating the case when she argues, "Bertha's role is largely reduced to staring at [her

lover] adoringly while he makes his fiery [pro-union] speeches"
(p. 668). But it raises a valid point: Thompson's friends, associates, comrades, and lovers are, in all but one case, men.

The exception is Tillie Parr, a prostitute with whom
Thompson works at a brothel in Baton Rouge. During an
afternoon stroll around the shops, Thompson points at a
shop window and remarks, "Look at the baby doll. Daddy
gave me one like that once. She lost her head." Parr sneers
back, "Probably over some no-good man."

Thompson is less cynical about men as a species: some men
command her respect, even her love; others are there only to
be used. The latter are easily manipulated. Thompson, played
by Barbara Hershey, responds coyly when a gambler compli-
ments her. "You have a remarkable body. Quite full." Her
admirer is ignorant of Thompson's intention to con him, but
when he eventually realizes, he pulls a gun on her fellow con
artist. Thompson has no hesitation in shooting her fan.

When Thompson is working as a prostitute, one of her
clients is an Alfred Kinsey-type researcher, "an anthropolo-
gist," as he describes himself. His questions include: "Have
you ever been in love?" and "Was your mother a whore?"
Thompson quickly tires of his questioning and decides to
seduce him. "You can put away your pencil now," Thompson
advises as the surveyor succumbs.

On another occasion, she plays up the helpless woman stereotype when she enlists the help of a deputy sheriff to repair
a flat tire. "I'm just no good at them mechanical things,"
she confesses while her confederates escape the deputy's
surveillance.

Shelly complains that Thompson has been too comely
in offering her "ass on a platter." Thompson seems
uplifted by Shelly's idealism. He gives away his money to
the Brotherhood of Workers and despairs at the banditry.
"I ain't done an honest day's work in months," he moans.

Thompson argues their robberies are not crimes. "I think it's honest work," she tells him before offering to give it all up. "I'd do anything you want. You want to quit? Quit."

It's a revealing moment: for all apparent self-fulfillment she's found on the road, unfettered by convention, she's prepared to accept Shelly's decisions unquestioningly. He seems indifferent and answers, "If *you* wanna leave, there's no claims on you, honey."

Thompson stays and continues to involve herself with robberies. Before one especially dangerous job, Shelly advises, "Bertha, you just stay here: we'll go on ahead without you." "Like hell, I will," she responds.

Thompson is devoted to Shelly; Shelly's devotion, though, is to the union. Imprisoned and condemned to work on a chain gang, he manages to flee and lives reclusively. He never tries to find her. She finds him after meeting Von Morton, who leads her to his hideout. Shelly is recaptured and Thompson is beaten up in the struggle.

Amid the bleakness of the 1930s, Thompson emerges as a willful minx, able to use men to her own advantage, but ultimately reliant on them for support and, when needed, consolation. This is actually not too far removed from the way Scorsese imagines many, if not most, women in America, whether nineteenth-century countesses or dipso-maniacal whores in the 1960s. Their destinies are usually twinned with those of the men in their lives, rarely shaped by their own imperatives. Sometimes, they are shaped by men and other times by social orders. As we've noted before, Scorsese's orders have a tendency to crumble like dilapidated manor houses.

Thompson, like Alice Hyatt, of *Alice Doesn't Live Here Anymore*, is an exceptional character on Scorsese's map: they are both women who struggled for something they wanted and whose struggle forms the shape of the respective films.

There is evidence in Scorsese's other work to suggest that he continued to remain interested in exploring women who were either inadvertently or self-consciously attempting to defy social conventions and popular expectations. But he never again situated such women at the center of his dramas or documentaries. Francine Evans' struggle is certainly the focus of *New York, New York*, as we have seen; but it's a study less of her, more of her interactions with Jimmy Doyle.

There are, however, prodigious women elsewhere. The trouble is: the women in question are either undermined by a combination of their own mania and men who outwit and outmaneuver them to serve their own egotistical ends, or they allow men to take control of their lives in a way that retards rather than advances them.

Scorsese's America is a place in which there are plenty of submissive women; but there are women who are or become agents of their own destinies, headstrong mavericks and generously gifted artists, all equipped with the resources to defend themselves or gain an advantage over men. Yet they invariably choose not to. Their choices tell us more about Scorsese's understanding of women than it does about women themselves.

So what do women really want? Probably not independence: freedom from the control or influence of men might be superficially attractive, but it never manages to bring women happiness. In the next chapter, we'll discover why.

SUBMISSION TO ROMANCE

"I'd be just as happy if I never saw a man again," Alice Hyatt née Graham confides to a friend, adding that she might make an exception for Robert Redford. But, like most other women in Scorsese's America, she's drawn to another man, then another. And, like most of Scorsese's men, none of them seem capable of love, at least not in a genuinely reciprocal way, not in a way that brings happiness on women. Only in a way that involves treating them "as objects of comfort and fear, creatures that [Scorsese's] heroes desire and despise themselves for desiring," as Roger Ebert puts it in his *Scorsese by Ebert* (p. 90).

In fact, men, for Scorsese, are a bit like the fabled scorpion, which secures a ride on the back of a frog in order to traverse a river, but fatally stings his carrier halfway across, prompting the frog to ask, "Why d'you go and do that? Now we're both going down." The scorpion has no logical explanation: "I can't help it. It's my nature."

Women are like the frogs: willing to accept men's word

and prepared to see the rationality and desirability of a joint commitment. Men, like the scorpion, also see the sense. But they just can't help themselves. This, for Scorsese, sets up a deeply disillusioning concept of man–woman relationships. But the relationships are integral to Scorsese's vision: America is obsessed with romance.

Romantic love is an ideal: desirable but unlikely to serve any common benefit; perhaps something that exists only in the imagination – or other people's films. Of course, it's an extraordinarily potent ideal, particularly in Western cultures, where it has held sway since at least the eighteenth century and inspired artists, musicians, and writers as diverse as Goya, Liszt, and Byron. The union of two people spontaneously attracted to each other by an irresistible concoction of intuition, emotion, and sexual passion and strengthened by commitment, care, and mutual respect has been a singular feature and one that has provided filmmakers with a stock theme.

Scorsese is no exception, though his treatment of romance is that of an embittered cynic, who sees evidence of its presence all around him, but finds no proof of its virtues to women and suspects it's become something of a male connivance. This leads Marc Raymond, in his 2000 thesis, to discern what he calls "the anti-romance trend prevalent in all of his [Scorsese's] work, rigorously opposing the mainstream of Hollywood production" (p. 62).

The glorious romantic liaison has, of course, been a fertile soil in Hollywood's landscape. In Scorsese's, it's like the parched Arizona desert Alice Hyatt née Graham endures in her quest, not for love, but for a career as a professional singer. Hence her solemn pledge at the start of this chapter. It comes to nothing, of course. Like most other Scorsese women, she has neither the fortitude nor, eventually, the inclination to veer away from the female force field, that invisible barrier of impetus that deflects women away from their careers and toward an ill-starred search for love. Hyatt's experience is exemplary.

When David, a divorced man, offers her the chance to settle with him on his ranch, rather than continue her pursuit of a singing career in California, she says, "I want both. Can't I have everything?"

Scorsese thinks not. In fact no female in a Scorsese film has actually managed to change her life in a way that we might describe as successful. Even Francine Evans, of *New York, New York*, loses the man she loves. *Alice Doesn't Live Here Anymore* follows an escapee from a loveless, hostile domestic environment, and though the attempt is ultimately completed, it's not unqualified. Hyatt's maneuver is less liberation, more a case of jumping from the fat into the fire.

After a series of uncomfortable, sometimes violent escapades with men, she appears prepared to ditch her plans to be a singer/pianist, even though she's harbored this dream since a child. In fact, the film opens with the young Hyatt crooning the last lines from "You'll never know," from the 1943 film *Hello, Frisco, Hello* ("If there is some other way to prove that I love you, I swear I don't know how. You'll never know if you don't know now"). She then reminds herself that she's as good a singer as Alice Faye, who starred in the film. She looks and sounds more like Judy Garland in *The Wizard of Oz* as she fantasizes against a red sunset about becoming a singer.

But her yellow brick road leads only as far as Socorro, New Mexico, where the film finds her nearly thirty years later. Now married with an 11-year-old son, she isn't singing for a living. She's mending her husband's clothes, preparing family meals, and acting as a makeshift referee in the frequent feuds between her husband and son. At mealtimes, she almost begs her husband's approval. "Is it good?" she asks. "It's OK," he mumbles. Hyatt seems to have stopped a long way short of realizing her ambition. So when she takes flight to chase her professional dream, there is an inevitability about the way her story will end. She never does become a professional singer. "If I'm going to be a singer, I can be a singer anywhere, right?"

As Marc Raymond concludes, "Alice finds happiness not in self-fulfillment but through a man" (p.87).

Hyatt's predicament is germane. All women in Scorsese's America have a similar if not exactly the same problem: they *believe* in romantic love. So do some men, of course; though, like Scorsese, they are aware of its limitations and try to lead lives that exploit those limitations. Like the scorpion, they seem naturally disposed to destroy relationships with serial infidelities, periodic intimidation, outright violence, or a combination of all of these. They often do so in the knowledge that women are so smitten by the prospect of romance that their own injudicious behavior will do no lasting harm to their relationship. They are usually right.

Why is anti-romance so central to Scorsese's vision? Clearly, Scorsese identifies the pursuit of romance as one of the principle motivating forces in American culture. Everyone, regardless of class, ethnicity, or gender, wants to fall in love. This message creeps through every movie, whether it concerns nineteenth-century avengers who try to ingratiate themselves with charming pickpockets; flaky women who overdose on prescription drugs, still pining for their lovers; homicidal cab drivers who chase wholesome political workers; or reformed hookers who leave their husbands and run back to their pimps.

Alice Hyatt is one of several Scorsese women who thinks she is looking for a career, but is really looking for love. When she senses her professional career ambitions are about to evaporate, she turns to romance and settles for a more restricted and conventional lifestyle. She's a textbook Scorsese case of a woman who thinks one way and acts another. After all, she is probably not going to crack the big-time as a singer and will most likely be waiting tables for the rest of her life.

At least she doesn't meet the same fate as Marcy Franklin, in *After Hours*, who reports that her former boyfriend had a sort of *idée fixe* about the *The Wizard of Oz* when it came to sex, which eventually forced her to leave him. "I still love him very much," she confesses. When she later over-doses on barbiturates and dies, we wonder whether it was an accident, or whether the split distressed her more than she revealed.

Even professional women with established high-powered careers can succumb. In *The Departed*, a female attorney practically surrenders her career by getting pregnant and compromising her integrity with a corrupt cop. Scorsese's depiction of Katherine Hepburn, by reputation a strong-willed woman, highlights her vulnerability in the presence of her onetime beau Howard Hughes, in *The Aviator*. Status doesn't affect a woman's fixation with romance.

There is a perfectly sound theory behind Scorsese's anti-romance ethic, if we can call it that – after all, an ethic relates to moral principles, though it does influence conduct. His critics have often accused him of featuring women as "companions, sometimes mere appendages, to the men around whom the stories revolve."

Maria T. Miliora makes the charge, though there are several other writers who have, as we will see later in this chapter, claimed Scorsese treats women as men's accessories. In her

2004 book *The Scorsese Psyche on Screen*, Miliora develops this argument. "In their relationships with the more dominant male characters, the women are subordinate or submissive, often having no life of their own except in relationship to their husbands or boyfriends" (p. 159).

Scorsese's theory seems to be that, far from being forced by patriarchal imperatives or tyrannical men into subservience, women become their own worst enemies. If men are the scorpions whose nature dictates their destructive actions, women are the frogs who can't seem to avoid believing them. The far side of the river looms perennially as a Garden of Eden.

Scorsese first advanced this idea in 1969 in his commercial debut film *Who's That Knocking at My Door?*

As if to objectify the woman he idolizes, she is called only The Girl. I use "idolizes" with care: J.R. adores and exalts her initially, then becomes uncomfortable with her preparedness to have sex, perhaps for fear of dishonoring her.

The Girl was to reappear in several subsequent films; she acquired names, identities, and partners, but there was something enduring about her. She isn't exactly an archetype, but the manner in which she puts up with J.R.'s changes of attitude, mood, and character, the adjustments she makes to please him and the rebuffs she withstands all return in characters of later films.

Premarital sex with The Girl of his dreams is not something the Catholic J.R. wants to countenance, though he is enthusiastic about having sex with another, less revered woman and the film features him in sex scenes (which were, incidentally, shot some years after initial production was completed and were interpolated to add commercial value to a film that had only a lukewarm reception when shown as *I Call First*).

The pivotal moment in the developing relationship between J.R. and The Girl comes when she reveals that she was the victim of a sexual attack years before. J.R. instantly turns against her. But, The Girl sees J.R. as marriage material and is prepared to make flexible accommodations. What violence she suffers is emotional rather than physical, though Scorsese provides enough inferential evidence to suggest she is never far away from a physical beating.

Who's That Knocking at My Door? is not one of Scorsese's major films. It does, however, carry one of his major themes and, perhaps, one of his major types – not so much the woman, but the unattainable ideal that incites self-destructive behavior in her. She doesn't know it's self-destructive, of course; she thinks she is just following convention and that romantic love is something to which all young American women should aspire. In a sense, she is right.

> **"Scorsese shows how male violence is a precursor, almost, in fact, a prerequisite, to marriage in American culture."** MARC RAYMOND IN *MARTIN SCORSESE AND AMERICAN FILM GENRE*

Scorsese reincarnated The Girl in *Raging Bull*, in which, as we saw in Chapter 8, Vickie La Motta occupies a penumbral role, overshadowed by her brutish, misogynist husband. The "bull" of the title refers as much to Jake La Motta's animalistic manner outside the boxing ring as his style inside. Having met her future husband when she was 15, Vickie stoically accepts years of infidelity and physical abuse. Her unflinching acceptance has a disintegrating effect on her, at least until the point where she sues for a divorce and wins custody of their three children.

Habitual insults, offenses, and physical beatings recur in many Scorsese films, giving rise to the troubling suspicion that the director understands them as essential requirements. "Male violence is a precursor, almost, in fact, a prerequisite, to marriage in American culture," concludes Marc Raymond. An exaggeration? Perhaps Raymond's conception of male violence is somewhat wider than conventional comprehension.

Failure to respect someone's rights, privacy, their peace; treating them with irreverence; trespassing on their individuality; trampling on their dignity; defiling, degrading, damaging their sense of selfhood; disregarding the formal vows to love, honor, let alone obey. If this wider conception of male violence is what Raymond has in mind, it is a stark interpretation of how Scorsese sees violence, particularly male violence, and its place in American marriage, an institution indissolubly linked to romantic love, of course.

Time and again in Scorsese films, men readily betray and harm women, usually without intending to jeopardize their marriage or wreck their romance. There is no paradox here: in *Raging Bull*, in particular, the male protagonist sees no necessary contradiction in his role as husband and abuser; nor perhaps in his behavior as a husband and a boxer. There's no evidence that La Motta doesn't feel a powerful desire for idealized romantic love. He probably has a meat-and-potatoes type of conception: romance is having a wife whom other men ogle at, and who has his food on the table when he returns home from the gym.

Women like Vickie La Motta or The Girl survive in Scorsese's America; they rarely prosper. Much more often they either accept their subservience, or accept the consequences of challenging it. Their ambitions, or lack of them, define or constrain them. To describe the relationships they have with men as restricted is too charitable. Scorsese has defied conventions in so many ways, yet, when it comes to gender relationships, he shows no inclination to stray from what Jeffrey A. Brown, in a 2002 article for *Men and Masculinities*, calls "the comfortable monolithic dichotomy that aligns masculinity with dominance and femininity with submission" (p. 127).

Robert Kolker detects an exception: "Karen and Henry's relationship in *GoodFellas* is on a more equal footing, though 'equal' in Scorsese's gangster realm means that, while Karen has her own voice, can answer back, can confront Henry's mistresses, and help hide the cocaine, she remains relegated to the position of gangster's wife and subject to scorn and abuse."

Perhaps this should be equality*, the asterisk, in this instance, denoting: "of a limited kind, relating to the dispensation of gifts, including domestic appliances and the provision of material benefits." Admiration and respect do not figure in the definition. Being intimidated but in love does.

In *Cape Fear*, as we saw in Chapter 7, lawyer Sam Bowden's wife Leigh is tormented ostensibly by an ex-con bent on wreaking revenge on her husband. But she also suffers from a debilitating commitment to Bowden, who had an affair several years earlier and appears to be reverting to old habits (we never know for sure whether or not he is unfaithful to her). Still troubled by his initial infidelity, Leigh has been unable to pursue her career, but is preparing to do so when the suspicion of her husband's latest extramarital affair intrudes.

Why doesn't she just leave him? In fact, why hasn't she left him long ago? Her doubts have played havoc with her emotions ("Do you remember crying every morning and evening?" Bowden asks her hard-heartedly), and now they are threatening her plans to start up a new business. Yet her commitment to romantic love and the marriage and family it promises endures.

In the obsessive culture of America, romantic love has become a fixation: an arresting ambition that stirs us to

irrational and harmful action. Men believe in it, but can live
without it. Women can't. For Scorsese, women are hell-
bent on chasing romantic love and men callously exploit this
fruitless pursuit in a way that maintains their masculine prerogative. It's an unequal and damaging type of arrangement,
yet one that perpetuates itself through courtship, marriage,
and the nuclear family, all of which feature in some way in
Scorsese's work.

Let's return to Miliora's critique. While she doesn't
suggest why Scorsese habitually portrays women as sacrificial lambs, we might surmise it's because they are so
dazzled by the prospect of romantic love that they forget
themselves as individuals. Men might believe in it, but
women chase love more than men; in the process they
seem to give up most of their rights, do without their
pleasures, and allow themselves to become service provid-
ers for men. This sounds a harsh appraisal, but this is how
Scorsese seems to see it and it goes some way to answering
Miliora.

Scorsese's men, on the other hand, don't seem equipped
to get close enough to form anything beyond a expedient
attachment; one that suits their own interests. Maybe romantic love is a manmade subterfuge, a deception used by men
to contain women and preserve their own patriarchal grip
on society. You could be forgiven for thinking that Scorsese
designs his films to create this impression. After all, women
are scarce and, when they appear, they are usually depicted
as victims, if not of men, then of constraints of some kind.
Sometimes, they are little more than possessions in the
custody of men.

The problem with this argument is that not all Scorsese
women are as ancillary as Miliora contends. Women are not

just pulled in to make up the numbers: they have roles and manifest different responses to the predicaments men or fate forces on them. Some women show almost inhuman forbearance, others cave in, and some others just take off. Those who make accommodations to romantic love do so at a cost, becoming lifeless, apathetic foils.

Sometimes, as we saw in the previous chapter, we witness women asserting themselves, taking flight from oppressive or restrictive relationships, and striding out on their own. But, even when they strive for fulfillment outside a conventional relationship, they find themselves restrained by men, or sometimes bashed, either emotionally or physically, into resignation. It is a pernicious conception of romance and, indeed, the hopelessness of women seduced by the ideal.

But, while Scorsese certainly has a knack of portraying women as inhibited, long-suffering, and undemonstrative "appendages," as Miliora calls them, they're far from inert. And, in at least a couple of cases, Scorsese peoples his plots with women who are not involved in a search for the warmth, satisfaction, and stability that they think only romantic love can bring. Quite the opposite: they might look for suitable men, but, failing that, they'll settle for passable men who will satisfy their needs while they pursue their other business.

> **"Women are subordinate or submissive, often having no life of their own except in relationship to their husbands or boyfriends."** MARIA T. MILIORA, *THE SCORSESE PSYCHE ON SCREEN*

Sometimes they obsess over men who embody something completely different to romantic love. Paulette, of "Life lessons," may not be romantically attracted to Lionel Dobie, but she is stricken with a mixture of awed admiration and a schoolgirl crush. She both dotes on him and wants to leave him. Perhaps more than anything, she wants to be him, have his talent, enjoy the respect he commands from practically everyone. If she had all these, she could fully realize her own ambitions rather than live vicariously through him.

Would Paulette settle for romantic love? After all, when she says, "You don't love me: you just want me around," she implicitly suggests that, if Dobie *did* love her, she may relegate her own artistic ambitions and contrive an accommodation. Perhaps she would continue with her art, but as Dobie's partner or even wife. The great man would no doubt eclipse her, but there would be satisfaction in being loved by him.

For Scorsese, it doesn't matter whether the woman is a creative individual like Paulette, who craves the freedom of expression that an intimate relationship restricts, or a submissive adjunct like Vickie: women are smothered, imprisoned, or assaulted because they want to be in love. So, we know Scorsese's answer when Alice Hyatt asks, "Can't I have everything?"

Francine Evans, in *New York, New York*, like Hyatt, wants everything. In the event, she keeps her singing career, has a baby, but loses her husband whom she loves. She also finds a kind of self-fulfillment, but it's incomplete and, even at the end of the film, she remains indecisive about whether to go back to Jimmy Doyle.

Is this Scorsese the sociologist finding in each film a reason to make subtle *aperçus* on the cultural politics of gender? Or is it the secular Catholic, crafting dramas that reflect social reality as he thinks it should be? In 1993, when David Bromwich remarked of Scorsese, "He has always cared too much about the approval of both the neighborhood gang and the priests," he must have been thinking about the portrayal of women. In other words, he suspects Scorsese the social commentator is always constrained by the traditions of his own background.

Bromwich was *en route* to praising *The Age of Innocence* as "a genuine attempt to win the esteem of the rather different priests," that is, not the church authorities, but a constituency sympathetic to feminism. Though he didn't necessarily have in mind the likes of Germaine Greer, Betty Friedan, Judith Butler, or any of the other ordained ministers of the movement.

> *The Age of Innocence* **might properly be called a romantic story, though, in Scorsese's hands, it becomes a clinical examination of the *limits* of romance.**

There is, however, an understandable delicacy in the way Scorsese handles relationships in the film. Understandable because it is an adaptation of Edith Wharton's acclaimed novel about what we might call today a love triangle involving an estranged independently minded woman returning to New York after living in Europe, a gentleman-lawyer who is bewitched by her but too respectful of social norms to make it known, and the shallow and dutiful 22-year-old to whom he has pledged himself.

It might properly be called a romantic story, though, in Scorsese's hands, it becomes a clinical examination of the *limits* of romance. In some senses it is a highly unusual element of the Scorsese *oeuvre*, yet, in others, it is consistent with the anti-romance motif that informs much of the director's work and, for this reason, I'll explore it in some detail.

As we saw in Chapter 8, *The Age of Innocence* concerns a lawyer in the New York high society of the 1870s, whose marriage to a pleasant and well-connected girl is threatened by his love for her cousin, an unconventional countess with European ways. The members of the triangle are all, in their own ways, obsessed by romantic love. Countess Ellen Olenska, who is played by Michelle Pfeiffer, is worldly, cosmopolitan, cultured, supersensitive, and elegantly beautiful. This is how Wharton, herself American, but a blazing critic of America, saw Europe, where she spent the last twenty-five years of her life. The Countess reflects on her life in Europe, where she enjoyed the company of singers, actors, and musicians. Now, however, she plans to settle back in New York: "I want to cast off my old life to be American and be like everybody else because I want to put all the old things behind me."

The Countess's worldliness captivates Newland Archer, played by Daniel Day-Lewis, who is delegated the task of managing her divorce. "Our legislation favors divorce, but our customs don't," he counsels. "What could you possibly gain that would make up for the scandal?" he asks. "My freedom," answers the Countess. When Archer responds, "But aren't you free already?" he knows she is constrained by the invisible pressures of convention. It is her penchant for challenging custom and convention that both attracts and educates him and serves to remind him of the limitations of his unremarkable fiancée, May Welland. The virtuous Welland is, according to Sarah Kozloff, in her 2001 essay "Complicity in *The Age of Innocence*," "the epitome of that [New York] society's virginal wholesomeness."

Marriageable she might be, but Welland is bland, characterless, and uninteresting compared to the illustrious Countess. This allows Scorsese to address romantic love from what is for him a highly unusual perspective: that of a man, albeit a man in the late nineteenth century and one encrusted in upper-class traditions.

Described as a "proto-liberated woman in revolt," Ellen Olenska gives up her nascent romance with Newland Archer, and obeys the social imperatives of nineteenth-century America. She believes "morality is superior to romantic self-fulfillment." (© Kobal)

The smitten Archer is a product of the very things he can't control: his social class, the expectations others place on him, history; the decisive customary procedures, known as good form. Having entered into a formal agreement to marry, he's subject to compelling forces that surround him. Inner forces are inclining him in other directions. The conflict becomes intolerable when he realizes that the Countess has reciprocal feelings. She actually makes the first move when, in a mild subversion of etiquette, she tells him, "Tomorrow then, after five. I shall expect you."

The tryst is an occasion for Archer to ask, "Do you really

like to be alone?" The Countess, by way of reply, concedes, "Perhaps I've been too independent. All I want is to be cared for and safe." Later she jokes, "Does that mean I'm so helpless and defenseless?" after he offers her his protection.

Like most period films, the recreations of time and place look authentic, but the characters are very much of our time. (The story is set in the 1870s, though Wharton's book was published in 1920. Scorsese's film was released in 1993.) Geoff Andrew, of the *Time Out Film Guide*, describes Scorsese's adaptation as "expressionist," meaning that the attempt is to disclose emotional experience rather than offer an objective account of the world as it was.

> NEWLAND ARCHER: **Do you really like to be alone?** COUNTESS OLENSKA: **Perhaps I've been too independent. All I want is to be cared for and safe.**

Archer might look as if he has been plucked from history, but his responses are comprehensible in terms of the customs and conventions of today. The content and imperatives of the mores have changed, but the manner in which they prescribe behavior and penalize violations has not. Pamela R. Matthews, in her review of Susan Goodman's book *Edith Wharton's Inner Circle*, believes, "Scorsese understood some important connection . . . between contemporary audiences and the fiction of Edith Wharton" (p. 462).

So when Archer asks Welland "to advance our engagement," hastening the date of the wedding, we understand why, but not in our terms. In other words, today we suspect someone who is engaged but who falls in love with another would be likely to strive for personal fulfillment rather than obey the requirements of prior commitments. Today's practices and habits prioritize personal happiness over social convention. Yet, Archer's doomed bid to place himself above temptation is

meaningful, as is his torment, which motivates him to uncon-
scionable deeds. He follows Olenska and declares his love.

There is more guile to May Welland than she shows: when
she declares to Archer that she is pregnant, the announcement cuts asunder the provisions Archer had made for a long
trip to Europe and Asia. He becomes curious when his wife
tells him that she told the Countess the news two weeks
before. "I wasn't sure then, but I am now. And, you see, I
was right."

Countess Olenska, having gracefully come to terms with
her passions and prepared herself to succumb to them, is jolted
by the news of Welland's pregnancy and leaves hurriedly for
Europe. Only when she's preparing to go does Archer realize that he is at the center of connivance. He senses that his
wife and her Family (Wharton uses the capital F to empha-
size its preeminence and perhaps the unconquerable status
quo it represents) have outwitted and outmaneuvered him.
They knew all along that he was involved in a clandestine
affair, though perhaps presumed it had gone further than it
actually had.

To rescue the situation and smother its effects, the
Family has coordinated what Richard Grenier in his 1993
Commentary article calls "a conspiracy of rehabilitation and
obliteration." Nuptial stability is resumed and Archer's
errancy wiped out. "The silent organization which holds this
fashionable world together is also determined to put itself on
record as never for a minute having questioned the propriety of Countess Olenska's conduct, or the completeness of
Archer's own domestic felicity" (p. 50).

The order of things, or at least the appearance of order, is
restored, not so much by any individual, but by the stealthy
operations of a silent organization, by which Grenier (and
Wharton) means the elite culture of New York, a culture Wharton considered restrictive and deficient, unlike

Europe's *haut monde*. Any vestiges of hope for a romantic relationship are vanquished when Archer, groping for a sign, bids farewell to the Countess with a promise that he'll see her in Paris, which she qualifies with, "If you and May could come."

The film's epilogue depicts Archer twenty-six years on, now a 57-year-old widower and father of three. The Countess is also widowed, living in France. Archer travels to meet her. Tantalizingly close to reuniting with the love of his life, Archer decides against it, preferring to sit outside her Paris apartment while his son, Ted, visits her. *En route* to her home, Ted divulges a secret: his late mother had told him on her deathbed that Archer "gave up the thing [he] most wanted," in clear allusion to the Countess. He denies it, but finally realizes that his wife had guessed of his yearning.

There are no concessions to romance in either the book or the film; instead, there is a victory of social codes over human passions. Norms, conventions, standards, and principles that govern conduct usually prove irresistible. Wharton, like Scorsese, understood what Grenier calls the "equivocal demands of order, tradition, respect, loyalty and the fulfilling of commitments."

In bringing Wharton's tale of sacrifice to a different age and audience, Scorsese maintains the Old New York landscape but populates it with characters who seem familiar: pious denizens to whom a star-crossed romance is no more than an irritation, lovers grappling with irresolvable dilemmas. So faithful was Scorsese to the original text that even pedantic Wharton scholars were impressed. In a memoir of the film written with co-scriptwriter Jay Cocks, Scorsese revealed how scrupulously they had pored over the minutiae of set design. Buttressing this fidelity, there is an authorial voice, that of Wharton herself.

The story is not told by an omniscient narrator, but by an onlooker, who happens to be a woman and, as such, allows Scorsese to infuse his work with Wharton's own ideas of romantic love. For example, Archer is indecisive: he equivocates, falters, and perhaps even dithers as he seeks a solu-

> **"A woman who grimly insists that morality is superior to romantic self-fulfillment."** SARAH KOZLOFF ON COUNTESS ELLEN OLENSKA

tion to his quandary. His commitment to Welland is a watery type of fidelity, an obligation imposed on him. Too weak to resist, he conforms ritualistically. When he finally decides he needs a break from his wife and, indeed, the environment of which they are both part, his intentions to travel are stymied by the news of his wife's pregnancy. "I'm afraid you can't, dear. Not unless you take me with you," she tells him. Even then, he doesn't suspect his shallow but reliable wife has a design.

There is much more shrewdness and resolve in the women. The Countess is what Kozloff describes as "a woman who grimly insists that morality is superior to romantic self-fulfillment." In this sense, she is startlingly different from any other Scorsese woman. Welland is closer to the Scorsese norm. "I couldn't be happier," she declares to Archer as she prepares for marriage. "I do love you, Newland."

She becomes a damsel sensing distress, in love with Archer, suspecting she is about to lose him, and trying – successfully – to keep him by foul rather than fair means. She knows where Archer's true affections lie, but she is prepared to settle for being his second choice.

Emily J. Orlando, in her article "Rereading Wharton's 'Poor Archer,'" sees her as working with the Countess as opposed to against her, to dismantle Archer's world. For Orlando, Archer is Wharton's exemplar of "male blindness to women." He is so absorbed in himself that he fails to grasp the sensibilities of either the Countess or Welland. Both, in their ways, are responsive to Victorian demands for respectability; so much so that Welland is prepared to confine Archer to an arid marriage in order to satisfy those demands.

Richard Alleva sees the Countess as "the proto-liberated women in revolt." Reviewing the film for *Commonweal*, he concludes Olenska is "the most ambiguous character. She expresses a need to be alone and yet is eagerly social; seems to lead Archer on, yet sternly reminds him of his obligations to others; desires to be protected by her lover yet can find a way out of a desperate situation without his help" (p. 16).

Her strengths are apparent to Deborah Knight: "Intelligent, independent minded, sexually experienced, interested in the arts and culture. . . . She is a woman with ideas and opinions." In her 2007 essay "*The Age of Innocence*: Social semiotics, desire, and constraint," Knight calls Olenska "a woman willing to initiate action" (p. 95).

The view isn't shared by Belén Vidal, who, in her 2006 article "Labyrinths of loss," argues that Olenska as a "desiring subject is effectively barred from the relationship [with Archer]" (p. 427) and, as such, is denied subjectivity. In other words, her personal thoughts, feelings, tastes, and perceptions exist, but give rise to no action. Her movements, like those of Archer, are initiated by "the context of social pressure." Family, probity, chastity, manners, are the most potent sources of motion. "Woman's agency and self-expression are locked up in an image from the past," concludes Vidal (p. 422).

Deborah Thomas concurs when she highlights "the film's tendency to see woman as the main victims of social constraint and control." In her 2003 analysis, Thomas reveals, "The bad treatment meted out to Ellen ignores her blamelessness in such an intolerable marriage in which Jackson [Archer's friend] tells Newland, she was practically a prisoner" (pp. 28–9).

Earlier, I referred to Pamela R. Matthews' suggestion that there is a "connection" between Wharton's readership and today's cinemagoers. She speculates that this is maintained by a "yearning, perhaps, for a mythic, imagined past of elegant, stable gender relations guided by fixed rules" (p. 462).

There seems little evidence of feeling of loss or longing for a bygone age in Scorsese's film. Quite the contrary: beneath the elegance and stability of late nineteenth-century gender relations (a term that would have made no sense to Wharton, as it acquired its contemporary meaning in the late twentieth century), Scorsese shows confinement and desolation.

This seems consistent with his cynical take on romantic love and his contemptuous way of treating marriage. While *The Age of Innocence* is an unusual feature of the Scorsese portfolio, "it is a romantic melodrama [and] the one film it does recall from this perspective would be *Alice Doesn't Live Here Anymore*," according to Raymond (p. 87). Alice Hyatt's "happy ending" was, as I've pointed out, an accommodation rather than a fulfillment. All three main characters of *The Age of Innocence* are obliged to make significant compromises.

For every Ellen Olenska in Scorsese's America, there are women who scamper about men tending to their needs, or accessorizing men like ambulant suitcases, or even functioning as human punch-bags. Even the exceptional women who reach if not grasp success are frequently floored by their own shortcomings, or stymied by their own quirks as they scramble toward the elusive romantic relationship.

This reason alone makes *The Age of Innocence* illuminating. Wharton's sourcebook releases Scorsese to imagine a man unlike any of his other men. True, Archer responds to his circumstances, their codes, customs, and rituals, like many other Scorsese men. But no other man is prepared to break them in the pursuit of love. Perhaps Scorsese is signaling that such men no longer exist. Archer is strictly a nineteenth-century character with nineteenth-century values and nineteenth-century ideas.

Throughout the film, Scorsese drops hints that Archer's culture is in its last days. Bougeureau's "Return of spring," a painting featuring nudes and considered risqué in New York, if not in Paris, is given pride of place in the enfilade (itself a modern design) at a post-opera ball (in the book, it is, anachronistically, the same artist's "Love victorious," which wasn't exhibited until 1887; the opera is Gounod's *Faust*, which warns of the torment that awaits those who succumb to earthly temptation). Archer's use of a "new stylographic pen," a forerunner of the ballpoint, faintly suggests his tentative embrace of modernity, a point restated with more emphasis when he prepares to defy propriety in pursuit of love.

When asked, "Do you suppose a woman should share the same freedoms as a man?" Archer affirms, "I suppose I do. Yes, I do." Yet he never encourages his wife to disenthrall herself. "There was no use in trying to emancipate a wife who hadn't the dimmest idea she was not free."

The Countess is another type of woman altogether. "She was different," says Archer from the vantage point of the early 1900s. In reality, she was by then probably indistinguishable in her attitudes from many other women. The National Woman Suffrage Association had started in America in 1869 and was prying open new areas in politics and education for women. World War I would soon (1914) force women to play vigorous roles in the war effort and, in the process, strike at the Victorian image of women as delicate creatures in need of men's protection. A woman who valued independence and remained sensitive, even sacrificially so, to the wellbeing of another woman would not have been out of place.

Romance perishes in Scorsese's America. Women persist in their valiant, fated efforts to secure it, but they have been beguiled by an attractive yet sentimental and mythic idea that serves only to sabotage them. In fairness, it could be argued that Scorsese is depicting periods and places and his effort is to reflect faithfully how people thought, felt, and behaved in a way consistent with cultural demands.

Imagine an alternative: women, far from being preoccupied with romance, are interested in pursuing the kind of projects more readily associated with men, careers being the main one. In this scenario, women prioritize professional ambitions over all others. Romance is desirable, but not an alternative to a career. For men, in a preposterous reversal of expectations, the opposite is true: they *are* prepared to relinquish careers if romance presents itself as an alternative.

Absurd? Not according to Catherine Mosher and Sharon Danoff-Burg, whose research in 2007 found that men not only "tend to fall in love more rapidly than do women," but they are "more likely than women to prioritize a romantic relationship above achievement goals." Indeed, men were more likely than women to give priority to a romantic relationship when asked to choose between this option and their career, education, and traveling.

There are many other studies that have examined how the notion of romantic love and, indeed, the marriage that often follows is held dear by both men and women in Western culture. In *White Weddings*, Chrys Ingraham shows how "our culture's obsession" is cultivated and maintained by advertising, sitcoms, magazines, children's toys, and popular films. While Ingraham doesn't identify Scorsese as an improbable culprit, none of his films challenge what is effectively assumed to be a cultural norm: women obsess over romance; men prioritize their careers. But it is only an assumed norm and, even if it hasn't yet fully expired, its validity is a lot less secure than in 1980 when *Raging Bull* was released.

Romantic love is not something that springs to mind when the subject is Scorsese. No, Scorsese seems to have spared little time in exploring a theme that has inspired art and literature since at least the eighteenth century. Cinema audiences have become accustomed to peeping in on romances. Idealized, sentimental love affairs, whether brief or enduring, have qualities that excite and content us.

None of Scorsese's films challenge what is effectively assumed to be a cultural norm: women obsess over romance; men prioritize their careers.

What Scorsese has provided is a tradition of anti-romance that offers a provocative answer to the question "What Do Women Want?" To be in love, maybe. If this is the answer, it prompts another question: is this why women are their own worst enemies? Their futile quests for happiness in romantic liaisons have been their greatest impediment. Men, at least, have an excuse for their actions: they are incapable of genuine selfless love. It's in their nature.

During *The Last Waltz* The Band reveal that they were tempted into life on the road as a working rock group with a promise, "You won't make much money, but you'll get more pussy than Frank Sinatra." In the film, sixteen years on, they express no regrets.

11

CONCLUSION – PRICE OF MONEY

At the end of the game, you count up who's got most money; that's how you find out who's best.

It's a line from Robert Rossen's 1961 film *The Hustler*, but it could have been spoken by a succession of Scorsese's characters. His women obsess about men. His men obsess about being men, and they both obsess about trying to stay stable in unstable times. But being best is not an obsession; showing they're the best is. In Scorsese's America, the way to show it is with money.

For Scorsese, America didn't invent money, but it invented new ways to exhibit it, new uses for it. New meanings. Who would have thought people would squander their hard-earned cash on amusing themselves? Americans. Who would have thought you could steal money, then use those ill-gotten gains to steal more money? Well, a great many people, actually, though none with more panache than Americans.

Scorsese paints pictures of a society distinguished but also discredited by the pursuit of money; where men use money to buy other men, and beguile other men's women; and prove their own manhood. In some ways, it's a rewarding strategy. But only in some ways: everybody wins, yet no one wins.

This is no contradiction: Americans might not have originated the word winner, but they made it their own. To be an American is to be a winner. It's a birthright. Even when they're losing, Americans are winners.

"Show me you can dump like a professional," Eddie Felson instructs his protégé, Vincent Lauria. In the pool hustlers' argot, "dumping" is to lose deliberately for the purpose of misleading spectators or an opponent. Lauria is feeling sorry for his rival, who has a tracheotomy. "He's got a hole in his throat," he tells Felson. There's no room for mercy in the

"It's about money," Eddie Felson advises his protégé, Vincent Lauria. "The best is the guy with the most." Felson's obsessive quest for success against the background of cultural change in late twentieth-century America perfectly dramatizes Scorsese's vision. (© Kobal)

world of poolhall hustling. Well, not much. When Felson issues the pitiless advice, "you never ease off on somebody like that when there's *money* involved," Lauria pleads, "the guy's breaking my heart." Felson then disappears with the stake money, leaving Lauria to learn a painful lesson. He's lost the game, but has no money to settle his gambling debt. The guy with the tracheotomy has friends who give Lauria a few chastening punches. He pays for his mercy.

In *The Color of Money* winning and losing are like balls cannoning off each other, just as they were in *The Hustler* where the young hothead Felson – then "Fast Eddie" – loses a woman, but gains his "character" and so becomes a winner. Scorsese's film is a sequel, though, as Carrie Rickey of *The Philadelphia Inquirer*

> **To be an American is to be a winner. It's a birthright. Even when they're losing, Americans are winners.**

puts it, "a sequel in the same way that Leonardo's Last Supper is a sequel to his Annunciation." Leonardo's masterwork was completed in 1498, while his Annunciation was finished twenty-three years before. Scorsese's film was released twenty-five years after Rossen's, both films based on Walter Tevis novels.

Set in the late 1950s, *The Hustler* is framed by two games of pool between the upstart Felson and the hitherto unrivaled Minnesota Fats. Felson takes a beating, loses his money, and limps away with the word "loser" ringing in his ears. Loaded on his favored J.T.S. Brown bourbon, he befriends and moves in with fellow alcohol-lover Sarah Packard, gets his thumbs broken – for trying to hustle a group of guys who tumble to his subterfuge – and returns to the green baize under the tutelage of wheeler-dealer Bert Gordon, who intends to turn Felson into a winner.

In his zeal to change, Felson neglects Packard, who is mentally troubled and a borderline lush, anyway. When she commits suicide, it drains him of compassion, the very quality that was preventing his becoming a winner. In a rematch with Fats, he shows no leniency, or respect, and wreaks a bittersweet revenge.

When Gordon, whom he holds responsible for Packard's death, demands his cut of the winnings and threatens him, Felson snarls, "You tell your boys, you'd better kill me, Bert. They better go all the way with me 'cause if they just bust me up, I'll put all those pieces back together again and, so help me, so help me, Bert, I'm gonna come back here and I'm gonna kill you."

Felson becomes a winner, but at great cost. So, when he returns in *The Color of Money*, he is still possessed of the same mentality, though, at 61 (Paul Newman's age when he played Felson for the second time; he was a youthful-looking 36 in *The Hustler*), he has forsaken the cue and spends his days selling liquor.

Enter Vincent Lauria, a mirror image of Felson in his pomp: conceited, boastful, and utterly disrespectful, especially of opponents. Felson's competitive spirit is reawakened and he persuades Lauria to quit his job as a salesman and go on the road with him. A big pool tournament in Atlantic City beckons. But first, Lauria, played by Tom Cruise, has to learn how to hustle properly – make money by using deception without getting found out. Felson's main advice is: "It's about money: the best is the guy with the most." Almost word-for-word the same as Gordon's to him decades before.

Felson has long since ceased hustling pool ("I'm too old; my wheels are shot"), but offers himself as Lauria's stake-horse, or backer, as Gordon had once done for him. Lauria's sporting prowess is matched by his possessiveness, so, when

Felson tries to persuade him to go on the road, he realizes that his girl Carmen rather than Lauria is the person he needs to convince. When Carmen decides it's a good idea, Lauria listens. The three embark on a six-week pilgrimage to Atlantic City for the big "9-Ball Classic" tournament.

During the journey, Felson has a Damascene moment after he is outhustled by Amos, an African American player (in contrast to the 1961 film, in which black people are pool-hall cleaners, there are black pool players in Scorsese's film). It's as if he's been cannibalized. "How could I get suckered like that?" he asks himself. He leaves Lauria and Carmen, starts swimming, gets a pair of eyeglasses, and plays pool alone, hour after hour. His physical training resembles the torturous regimens of Jake La Motta or Max Cady. But why would a man in his sixties put himself through this? Perhaps he is just as obsessed as everyone else. After all, he lives in an obsessive society.

Emerging in Atlantic City as a competitor in the tournament, Felson pummels a barely adequate opponent to a humiliating defeat in an early round. "I didn't deserve that," declares the beaten rival, believing Felson should have eased up on him and allow him to escape with dignity. Felson is unmoved. "Yes, you did."

Weaknesses are there to be exploited, not tolerated, less still pitied; if his opponent had been a three-legged dog, Felson would have kicked him over. His cutthroat competitive impulse fully reinstated, Felson is drawn against Lauria in the tournament and dispassionately beats him to a place in the quarter-finals. Lauria, though, has learned his hustling lessons too well: he later informs Felson that he took advantage of long betting odds and got a front to bet money on his rival. "Then I dumped. I dogged about four shots." Lauria is interested only in money, which, in his eyes, makes him a winner. "There's other tournaments, right?" he asks as he hands Felson an envelope full of bills, suggesting that he was a party to the fraud.

Felson feels betrayed: he's been suckered again, this time by his own apprentice. But why should a veteran hustler feel offended? After all, he's $8,000 better off and is still alive in the tournament's final stages. Lauria has sacrificed himself in strict accordance with hustlers' protocol: the guy with the most money is the winner, not the guy with the trophy.

> "Hustling distributes its rewards strictly on the basis of individual talent and hard work, thus fulfilling two cardinal tenets of the Horatio Alger 'myth.'" NED POLSKY IN *HUSTLERS, BEATS AND OTHERS*

Lauria is actually not so well schooled as he imagines. In beating Felson, he's violated a code. It's specified in Ned Polsky's study from the early 1960s, *Hustlers, Beats and Others*. "When hustlers play each other," writes Polsky, "they know that basically they are just taking in each other's washing" (p. 69).

Polsky quotes a player, "That's not hustling – that's gambling." Skill, proficiency, and judgment are involved, for sure; but it's not true to the hustlers' code. Polsky provides the reasoning behind this when he observes, "Hustling distributes its rewards strictly on the basis of individual talent and hard work, thus fulfilling two cardinal tenets of the Horatio Alger 'myth'" (p. 79). Gambling is a different type of enterprise altogether.

As we've seen, the spirit of Horatio Alger inhabits several Scorsese films, most notably *GoodFellas* and the other compositions on mob life. Even in *Casino*, the central pursuit is less about gambling, more about how to base a rational industrial process on others' propensity to gamble. Hustling, like the deviant endeavors of Henry Hill, Sam Rothstein, and Frank Costello, as well as Jake La Motta's boxing or even Rupert

Pupkin's kidnap maneuver, is an American career. As Polsky writes, "For a number of lower-class youths, hustling as a possible ladder of social ascent seems very real."

When Polsky quotes a hustler, he might as well be quoting any of these Scorsese characters. "If I hadn't got interested in pool when I was a kid, I might have ended up a bum or in jail" (p. 80).

Many of Scorsese's characters actually do end up in jail; though their greatest virtue seems to lie in their pluck in trying to stay out. You need no special insight into human nature to understand why people want to avoid vagrancy or incarceration, of course. But Scorsese discloses how, in America, it's an obligation. This is a land in which success is to be sought at any cost.

Moral wavering, in fact wavering of any kind, is rarely in evidence: the purposeful pursuit of success in unpromising circumstances is one of the dominant themes in Scorsese's America. And little else instills a sense of purpose like money. This is one of three patterns that repeat themselves throughout Scorsese's work. With Scorsese, there seems, at times, almost an admiration for the heedlessness with which Americans pursue their aims, ambitions, and goals. In a different culture, the same quality might be condemned. Americans couldn't care less. They have created a nation that may not have the beauty of the Hanging Gardens of Babylon, or the magnificence of the statue of Zeus, but occasions wonderment just the same.

In the Introduction, I wrote of what David T. Courtwright calls "the hurricane of obsession" that sweeps through Scorsese's America. I also credited James Parker, who argues that Scorsese's films are usually set against the background of a collapsing order – I'll return to this shortly. The third pattern that adorns Scorsese's America is, as we've seen in previous chapters, how gender roles are defined and sustained and with what consequences.

Scorsese addresses all three – the pursuit of material success, the affirmation of manhood and womanhood, and the individual's attempts to get to grips with change – in a kind of value-neutral manner. He never explicitly reveals whether he thinks they are good or bad: they are just part of the reason we remain fascinated with America. While *The Color of Money* might not stand out as one of Scorsese's most resonant films, it actually includes all of Scorsese's major patterns as well as several of the themes I've dealt with in earlier chapters, and, in this sense, provides a paradigm.

The Color of Money deals with a subculture not unlike those depicted in *The Age of Innocence*, *Raging Bull*, and *Bringing Out the Dead*: it is enclosed in rule-bound patterns of behavior; ritualized. Breaches are punished or at least censured.

Scorsese is interested in associating each element of the male domain with its historical counterpart, a project that Paul Arthur describes as the "mapping of masculine prerogative."

Like the parlor, the boxing ring, and the streets of Manhattan, the pool table is a place where qualities will be assessed. They all provide contexts for the expression of thoughts that continually intrude on the minds of Scorsese's characters. If they don't want someone, they want something, whether it is proof of their mettle or the redemption of their souls.

When Scorsese probes the culture of the pool player, he reveals familiar people with recognizable motives. Felson sets his mind to his task; he is striving for what he calls "excellence" with the single-minded remorselessness of a young Howard Hughes trying to pry open the closed-shop movie industry. Lauria struts around the pool table as if he's on stage next to Keith Richards in *Shine a Light*. This is not because Scorsese continually draws on stock types, but because there is a consistency of *context*. "In Scorsese's larger constellation of themes," writes Paul Arthur in his article "Please allow me to reproduce myself," the pool hall, like the "rockers' proscenium becomes another enclosed space of male testing" (p. 49).

Writing in the 1960s, Polsky called the poolroom the "inner frontier, the new no-woman's land" (p. 26). There are many more such places in Scorsese's America, places where, as Arthur puts it, "male tribal rituals" are continually enacted according to unwritten rules and standards. Whether in the 1860s or the 2000s, men huddle, talk in codes, and act out their manhood, often mercurially as if to defy expectations, but usually within informal guidelines. Arthur, as we noted earlier in the book, believes Scorsese is not interested in leaving a superfluous record, but in associating each element of the male domain with its historical counterpart, a project that he describes as the "mapping of masculine prerogative."

It is, as I suggested earlier, one of the grandest, most pervasive patterns in Scorsese's *oeuvre*: how men exercise and extend the rights and privileges attendant on their gender. How their language, deeds, and symbols reflect their entitlement; how their sometimes acerbic, sometimes tender relationships with women are conducted with a wily respect for well-established arrangements. Scorsese's women are complicit in this. They might strike out, protest, deliver stinging rebukes. But they are all distressed damsels in one way or another.

Even Carmen, who is demonstrably more intelligent, practical, and farsighted than her male partner Lauria, gets sent off to buy liquor while games are in progress. And when Felson compares her man to a thoroughbred racehorse, he delineates their respective roles, "You make him feel good. I teach him how to run."

Scorsese's disregard for the changes in the status of women over the past three or four decades manifests in almost every film he has directed. Some might think "disregard" understates his approach: disrespect might be more accurate. When Arthur describes Scorsese as "a director whose work epitomizes the rough-hewn compact between modern urban masculinity and Hollywood genre traditions," he alludes to a conservatism that lies beneath the stylistic innovation and radical departures from filmmaking formalities.

In his 1996 review of *Casino*, Richard Alleva writes, "The idea of self-justification in defiance of convention, morals, and even reason is the burden of many Scorsese movies from *Mean Streets* to *Cape Fear*" (p. 19).

Many Scorsese men – not so many women – excuse themselves of their own actions by appeal not so much to a higher authority but to their conscience, that silent voice that guides rightness or wrongness. Alleva has Sam Rothstein in mind: the Vegas mastermind considers himself "the custodian of an incredibly complete money-making machine." A defensible belief. Rothstein's pride in his enterprise impels him toward what he fancies is his own destruction. Yet, as Alleva points out, he "refuses to knuckle under." He feels he is right and, even when he knows he might upset his mob confederates, he appears on his own tv show (fixing a steel plate under the driver's seat of his Cadillac as a precaution).

Alleva reckons Scorsese depicts Rothstein's motives only "sketchily," though he attends to detail when he portrays, for example, Travis Bickle, Frank Pierce, or Eddie Felson, all isolated creatures without reliable moral coordinates, yet all motivated by self-justification. Even in the documentary feature *No Direction Home*, Bob Dylan, as Arthur observes, "exhibits some of the wariness and disaffection of an asocial outcast" (p. 50).

Far from being facsimiles of each other, the characters are individual, even idiosyncratic. Yet each is tenuously attached to a social order, which is either changing or has changed irreversibly, leaving them behind or dislocating them in a way that leaves them unstable. Sociologists and psychologists use the term anomie to describe the condition; it refers not to the human individual but to the overall context that's liable to produce such instability, as we saw in Chapter 4.

Felson, like the others, is a cultural relic: he was out of time even in 1961 when *The Hustler* was released. The kind of pool subculture depicted in the film had disappeared probably in the 1940s, according to Polsky. By the late 1980s, a character like Felson would have been an anachronism. The prospect of revisiting his youth even vicariously is too much of a temptation and he opts for living through Lauria. Yet, like many other Scorsese men, he struggles to align his own principles of right and wrong behavior with those he feels and sees surrounding him.

Surviving remnants of an earlier time appear throughout Scorsese's films, sustained by either a fatuous longing to hang on to the past or an inventive plan to reinvent history. When Barry W. Sarchett sees in *The Last Waltz* "a perfect emblem of the nostalgic desire for a transcendent, stable referent immune to the contingencies of history," he alludes to Scorsese's yearning for permanence. The impossibility of having it offers Scorsese the opportunity to explore what happens when time moves forward and people don't want to, or, like Felson, are forced to.

Earlier, I suggested Scorsese's films were, as James Parker puts it, about "threatened or collapsing order." Scorsese doesn't picture a world in chaos: he situates individuals experiencing interior chaos when the rules and norms regulating their thoughts and behavior have changed – while they've remained the same. *Taxi Driver* is the most electrifying essay on this subject, depicting a state in which everything seems to Travis Bickle to be out of place, in which values have been inverted and standards of conduct have been ignored. His thoughts are calibrated with those of the America he left when he started military service.

Scorsese doesn't picture a world in chaos: he situates individuals experiencing interior chaos when the rules and norms regulating their thoughts and behavior have changed – while they've remained the same.

Expatriated in Europe where she has assimilated new standards and perhaps new values, Countess Ellen Olenska returns to New York where different rules operate, making her "something of an outcast," as Mark Burger puts it in his review of *The Age of Innocence*. "Her (subtle) dismissal of many of the social norms imposed on her further tests the patience of 'respectable circles.'"

Orders vaporize and reconstitute themselves everywhere in Scorsese's work. It's not possible to find a film in which some kind of cultural change, however minor, has failed to disturb the normal functioning of a person or familiar arrangements of a group. The consequent disarray, confusion, or disorder is both the dynamic that powers every plot and the background against which every plot is played out.

There is another kind of order that Scorsese addresses. "The structure of whiteness," as Christopher Kocela calls it in his article "Unmade men." He refers to the traditional cultural arrangements and dispositions of people that serve in "establishing whiteness as an American norm."

How does Scorsese deal with this? Kocela believes that Scorsese's mob films are all set against a background of the breakdown of an old ethnic order in which the strong Italian family occupies what he calls "a mythic place." Kocela begins by contrasting Scorsese's work with that of Francis Ford Coppola, who remains committed to a "cinema of fathers." In Scorsese's films, "the family is dissolved by the brutalities of ghetto life . . . father figures come to be replaced by local mob bosses or weak godfathers who cannot provide the centering influence of a Don Corleone" (para. 7).

While most of Kocela's essay concerns the HBO show "The Sopranos," he makes constant reference to the Scorsese films that are effectively forerunners of the tv series. Scorsese manipulates nostalgia about a disappearing ethnic identity; "the doom of its lost sons," as Kocela terms it. In contrast, David Chase's television series features Italian-American gangsters who harbor no sentiment for ancestral ties. "We do not learn from The Sopranos the language of ethnic sons deprived of their Italian godfathers" (para. 16).

Kocela means that, historically, Italians' most powerful advantage was their whiteness. "It gave them countless advantages over 'nonwhites' in housing, jobs, schools, politics, and virtually every other meaningful area of life" (para. 17).

Several Scorsese films reinforce this point. Time after time, black people are dealt with as dependable sidekicks or disposable flunkies. Von Morton, in *Boxcar Bertha*, is an example of the former, as we saw in Chapter 9; Stacks Edwards, who is shot in *GoodFellas*, is one of several examples of the latter, as we saw in Chapter 5. There is a near-reflexive attitude when dealing with African Americans, Asian Americans, or any other ethnic minority for that matter. Italians might

once have been marginalized – a point made in a reporto-
rial fashion in the documentary *Italianamerican* – but Italian
Americans developed and prospered in the mainstream. And
yet, as Bernard Beck, in another Sopranos-themed analysis,
writes, "Success, respectability, and familiarity have not freed
them from the taint of the Mob" (p. 25).

Beck argues that media portrayals, like those of Scorsese,
have contributed to strengthening the link between Italians
and organized crime. "Violence, legality, and respectability
remain central issues" for Tony Soprano: he retains a sense
of being ethnically Italian, but insists on being white, an
identity that he thinks confers social acceptability.

Soprano frowns at blacks, explicitly forbidding his daughter from seeing an African American boyfriend. He sneers
at Native American Indians and the "victim" status in
which they appear to revel. He spurns attempts to link his
business success with his ethnic background. He asks, "All
the good things you got in your life, did they come to you
because you're Calabrese?" (as people from Calabria, in
southwestern Italy, are known).

His emphatic answer is no. This is not the kind of response
we would expect from Scorsese's characters: they're much
more respectful of origins. This isn't because they are essentially different characters to Soprano and his crew: it's because
the ethnic order changed, dramatically, after September 11,
2001 (the HBO series started in 1999 but ran until 2007).

Scorsese's Italian Americans are self-evidently white. They
are also defiantly Italian. Unlike Tony Soprano, they have no
"disabling bouts of racial anxiety" about true identity in the
new America (he is in therapy). For Scorsese, the "enduring image" of Italians, as Beck calls it, is not something to
fret over, but to be ridiculed. In *Mean Streets*, for example,
Charlie approaches a girl who retorts, "You Italian?" When
Charlie asks "Why?" she laughs back, "You don't look it."

Betsy's colleague in *Taxi Driver* asks whether a guy with a missing finger who works on a newsstand is Italian, then defends his apparent prejudice, "If this newsstand guy's Italian and his fingers are gone, maybe he's a thief."

Once his boxing career is over, Jake La Motta, in his early forties, reflects on the prospect of incarceration in a prison in the South, "If you're a guy like me, you ain't got a chance in a place like that, especially if you're Italian."

Scorsese imagines the meaning of whiteness has changed. There was once certainty: it was a quality that was clearly authentic and fixed. In *Gangs of New York*, for example, natives loathe the "hordes of Hibernians" who live alongside them, but they at least acknowledge their human presence and consider them tenuously related by blood. But they effortlessly ignore blacks as if they don't exist, or exist in the same way as cattle: as possessions, to perform labor, or serve.

The Irish Americans in *The Departed* hate "guineas," ethnic Italians who have muscled in on what was once their territory. But at least hate is an emotion: for Chinese, there is freezing indifference at worst, condescension at best ("In this country, one guy brings the item, the other guy brings the money").

The meaning of whiteness has changed. So has the meaning of manhood. These are variables in the midst of constancy, the constancy, for Scorsese, being the obsession with the kind of success that money buys. Not money itself. But what it confers, grants, or bestows on its owners. And what it implies – success.

Scorsese's vision is certainly insightful and undoubtedly entertaining, though not, as we have seen, necessarily reliable.

At the start of this book, I argued that Scorsese has functioned as a kind of cinematic sociologist, someone who both chronicles and dissects society, revealing aspects that are occasionally laudable, but often lamentable. This is why sober evaluations such as Peter Thornell's, in a review of a collection on Scorsese's "philosophy," find widespread agreement: "Scorsese's insight into the human condition remains constant and penetrating, regardless of the subject matter through which he crafts his vision" (p. 87).

His vision is certainly insightful and undoubtedly entertaining, though not, as we have seen, necessarily reliable. He takes liberties with history, fashions his own version of women's attitudes and motivations, paralyzes cultural developments, and, on some occasions, gloats over actions that dramatize spectacularly but have woeful human consequences.

While his stance on civil rights and matters of social inequality are, as his documentaries indicate, worthy, his dramas frequently erase or render superfluous African Americans and other ethnic minorities. No one suggests that racism and other forms of bigotry have vanished from the American landscape; the racial epithets, put-downs, and the other kinds of insults that Scorsese includes in his scripts are still part of the popular vocabulary. But do they go unchallenged, as they usually do in Scorsese films? Probably not.

None of this makes Scorsese a bad social commentator; but a conservative, perhaps? One who is prepared to flout or defy filmmaking convention and who pursues unpromising subjects without fear or favor, but one who is unwilling or unable to let go of traditional values or hidebound beliefs? When he identifies injustice, unfairness, or the myriad other wrongdoings, he seems conditioned to celebrate them rather than probe their causes and excoriate them.

This may sound like criticism. But, I am ready to resist it on Scorsese's behalf. He is, after all, a professional filmmaker, not a social scientist. Even if he were, he still has a defense. My feeling is that he is not so much a conservative filmmaker as a maker of films about a conservative society. The spirit of rugged individualism that breaks through the bureaucratic restraints in *The Aviator* reminds us that Scorsese is ready to challenge the American status quo. With what? A kind of liberalism that's respectful of individual freedom but unwilling to discard frontier values that took shape in the nineteenth century.

And even if we accept what we could charitably call traditional conceptions of women, we're left to contemplate Scorsese's idea of romantic love, which seems, as far as he's concerned, unattainable. Maybe it is; but for the reasons Scorsese seems to suggest? Are women, even those weaponed and ready to seize their own independence, always so willing – no, enthused – when offered the opportunity to dump their aspirations and careen into a conventional relationship?

Over the years, Scorsese's films have accreted into an exceptional corpus. For sure, there have been corpora of art with comparable capacities to evoke images, as well as memories and emotions about America. The literary work of Herman Melville, Ernest Hemingway, and John Updike, for example. In visual arts, Andrew Wyeth, Norman Rockwell, and Andy Warhol spring to mind. The plays of Arthur Miller and the photography of Annie Liebovitz carry messages about the changing landscape, cultural and physical. Musically, George Gershwin, Cole Porter, and, more recently, Bob Dylan and Phil Spector have offered an index of American thoughts and values. (Spector, incidentally, reckons he was persuaded by John Lennon not to take legal action against Scorsese, who used Spector's 1963 track "Be my baby" by the Ronettes under the opening credits of *Mean Streets*, but apparently neglected to ask Spector for permission.)

But in cinema? Scorsese certainly has contenders in John Ford, Michael Curtiz, Oliver Stone, Robert Altman, and perhaps, in a quirky way, Frank Capra. Each has his cluster of ideas about the purposes, wishes, and aspirations of America, though arguably none has done so with the subject range or historical depth of Scorsese. He has discovered a way of exploring the wider conditions through his characters, their specific situations, and the courses of events they follow. In other words, he has framed his stories in a way that inspires, or perhaps induces, a sense of social context. Love his films or hate them, it is impossible to leave a Scorsese film without some notion of how America works, some conception of its purpose, some vision of what it means.

FILMOGRAPHY

Feature Films

1969 *Who's That Knocking at My Door?**
Writing credits *screenplay* Betzi Manoogian/Martin Scorsese

1972 *Boxcar Bertha*
Writing credits *screenplay* Joyce Hooper Corrington/ John William Corrington; *book* Bertha Thompson/ Ben L. Reitman, 1937

1973 *Mean Streets*
Writing credits *screenplay* Mardik Martin/Martin Scorsese

1974 *Alice Doesn't Live Here Anymore*
Writing credits *screenplay* Robert Getchell

1976 *Taxi Driver*
Writing credits *screenplay* Paul Schrader

---

* Originally, *Bring on the Dancing Girls*, 1965 then *I Call First*, 1967; later, *J.R.*, 1970

1977 *New York, New York*
      Writing credits *screenplay* Earl Mac Rauch/Mardik
      Martin
1978 *The Last Waltz*
1980 *Raging Bull*
      Writing credits *screenplay* Paul Schrader/Mardik
      Martin; *book* Jake La Motta/Joseph Carter/Peter
      Savage, 1970
1982 *The King of Comedy*
      Writing credits *screenplay* Paul D. Zimmerman
1985 *After Hours*
      Writing credits *screenplay* Joseph Minion
1986 *The Color of Money*
      Writing credits *screenplay* Richard Price; *book* Walter
      S. Tevis, 1984
1988 *The Last Temptation of Christ*
      Writing credits *screenplay* Paul Schrader; *book* Nikos
      Kazantzakis, 1951
1989 *New York Stories*, "Life lessons"
      Writing credits *screenplay* Richard Price
1990 *GoodFellas*
      Writing credits *screenplay* Nicholas Pileggi/Martin
      Scorsese; *book* Nicholas Pileggi, 1990
1991 *Cape Fear*
      Writing credits *screenplay* Wesley Strick; *original screenplay* James R. Webb, 1961; *book* John D.
      MacDonald, 1957
1992 *The Age of Innocence*
      Writing credits *screenplay* Jay Cocks; *book* Edith
      Wharton, 1920
1995 *Casino*
      Writing credits *screenplay* Nicholas Pileggi/Martin
      Scorsese; *book* Nicholas Pileggi, 1995

1997   *Kundun*
       Writing credits *screenplay* Melissa Mathison
1999   *Bringing Out the Dead*
       Writing credits *screenplay* Paul Schrader; *book* Joe
       Connelly, 1998
2002   *Gangs of New York*
       Writing credits *screenplay* Jay Cocks, Steven Zaillian,
       and Kenneth Lonergan; *book* Herbert Asbury, *c.* 1927
2004   *The Aviator*
       Writing credits *screenplay* John Logan
2006   *The Departed*
       Writing credits *screenplay* William Monahan; *original
       screenplay* Siu Fai Mak/Felix Chong, 2002
2008   *Shine a Light*

       Other Work Directed, Excluding Advertising
1959   *Vesuvius VI*
       Cardinal Hayes High School project
1963   *What's a Nice Girl Like You Doing in a Place Like
       This?*
       Writing credits *screenplay* Martin Scorsese. New York
       University project
1964   *It's Not Just You, Murray!*
       Writing credits *screenplay* Mardik Martin/Martin
       Scorsese. New York University project
1967   *The Big Shave*
       Writing credits Martin Scorsese. New York University
       project
1970   *Street Scenes 1970*
       Documentary
1974   *Italianamerican*
       Writing credits Mardik Martin, Larry Cohen/Martin
       Scorsese. Documentary

1978   *American Boy: A Profile of Steven Prince*
Writing credits Mardik Martin/Julia Cameron.
Documentary

1985   *Amazing Stories*, "Mirror, mirror"
Writing credits *screenplay* Joseph Minion/Steven
Spielberg. Episode in television/DVD series

1987   *Bad*
Michael Jackson video

1988   *Somewhere Down the Crazy River*
Robbie Roberson video

1995   *A Personal Journey with Martin Scorsese through
American Movies*
Co-directed with Michael Henry Wilson

1999   *Mio Viaggio in Italia, Il (My Voyage to Italy)*

2001   *The Concert for New York*, "The neighborhood"

2004   *Martin Scorsese Presents The Blues – A Musical Journey*,
"Feel like going home"
Writing credits Peter Guralnick. Episode in television/DVD series

2005   *No Direction Home*
Bob Dylan documentary

BIBLIOGRAPHY

Alleva, Richard (1993) "The Age of Innocence," *Commonweal*, vol. 120, no. 19, pp. 14–18.

Alleva, Richard (1996) "The master misses," *Commonweal*, vol. 123, no. 1, pp. 18–19.

Alleva, Richard (2005) "It's cold up there," *Commonweal*, vol. 132, no. 3, pp. 19–20.

Andrew, Geoff (2004) "Age of Innocence, The," p. 16 in *Time Out Film Guide*, 12th edition, London: Penguin.

Arthur, Paul (2008) "Please allow me to reproduce myself," *Film Comment*, March–April, pp. 46–51.

Asbury, Herbert (2002) *The Gangs of New York: An informal history of the underworld*, foreword by Jorge Luis Borges, New York: Thunder's Mouth Press. Originally published in *c.* 1927.

Ashe, Fidelma (2004) "Deconstructing the experiential bar: Male experience and feminist resistance," *Men and Masculinities*, vol. 7, no. 2, pp. 187–204.

Asma, Stephen (1999) "Descartes goes Hollywood: Using

movies to bring philosophy to life in the classroom," *The Chronicle of Higher Education*, vol. 45, no. 19, pp. B6–B7.

Asma, Stephen (2003) "Is 'The Blues' black enough?" *The Chronicle of Higher Education*, vol. 50, no. 5, p. B12.

Beale, Lewis (1998) "Of the spirit and Scorsese," *Kansas City Star*, January 18, p. J1.

Beck, Bernard (2000) "The myth that would not die: The Sopranos, Mafia movies, and Italians in America," *Multicultural Perspectives*, vol. 2, no. 2, pp. 24–7.

Berger, Peter L. and Berger, Brigitte (1981) *Sociology: A biographical approach*, Harmondsworth: Penguin.

Blake, Richard (1998) "Scorsese: A work in progress – *Martin Scorsese: A journey* by Mary Pat Kelly," *Commonweal*, vol. 119, no. 4, pp. 25–6.

Blake, Richard (2003) "Melting pot," *America*, vol. 188, no. 3, p. 30.

Blake, Richard A. (2005) *Street Smart: The New York of Lumet, Allen, Scorsese, and Lee*, Lexington: University Press of Kentucky.

Bliss, Michael (2000) "Affliction and forgiveness: An interview with Paul Schrader," *Film Quarterly*, vol. 54, no. 1, pp. 2–9.

Boorstin, Daniel (1992) *The Image: A guide to pseudo-events in America*, New York: Random House. Originally published in 1961.

Borkowski, Mark (2008) *The Fame Formula: How Hollywood's fixers, fakers and star makers created the celebrity industry*, London: Sidgwick & Jackson.

Brickman, Barbara Jane (2007) "Coming of age in the 1970s: Revision, fantasy, and rage in the teen-girl badlands," *Camera Obscura*, vol. 22, no. 3, pp. 25–60.

Bromwich, David (1993) "The Age of Innocence," *The New Leader*, vol. 76, no. 14, pp. 21–2.

Bromwich, David (2001) "How publicity makes people real," *Social Research*, vol. 68, no. 7, pp. 145–72.

Brown, Jeffrey A. (2002) "The tortures of Mel Gibson: Masochism and the sexy male body," *Men and Masculinities*, vol. 5, no. 2, pp. 123–43.

Burger, Mark (1993) "Scorsese hits paydirt with 'Age of Innocence,'" *Jewish Journal*, October 7, p. 7B.

Cantor, Paul A. (2007) "Flying solo: The Aviator and libertarian philosophy," pp. 165–87 in Mark T. Conard (ed.), *The Philosophy of Martin Scorsese*, Lexington: The University Press of Kentucky.

Carmichael, Stokely and Hamilton, Charles V. (1967) *Black power: The politics of liberation in America*, New York: Vintage.

Carter, Rubin (1999) *The 16th Round: From number 1 contender to number 45472*, New York: Penguin. Originally published in 1974.

Casillo, Robert (2006) *Gangster Priest: The Italian American cinema of Martin Scorsese*, Toronto: University of Toronto Press.

Castellitto, George P. (1998) "Imagism and Martin Scorsese," *Literature/Film Review*, vol. 26, no. 1, pp. 23–30.

Christie, Ian (2003) "Manhattan asylum," *Sight & Sound*, vol. 13, no. 1, pp. 20–3.

Christie, Ian (2005) "Fly guy," *Sight & Sound*, vol. 15, no. 1, pp. 18–20.

Christie, Ian (2006) "Scorsese: Faith under pressure," *Sight & Sound*, vol. 16, no. 11, pp. 14–17.

Conard, Mark T. (ed.) (2007) *The Philosophy of Martin Scorsese*, Lexington: The University Press of Kentucky.

Connelly, Joe (1998) *Bringing Out the Dead*, New York: Knopf.

Cook, Pam (1982) "Masculinity in crisis?" *Screen*, vol. 23, nos. 3/4, pp. 39–46.

Courtwright, David T. (2005) "The Aviator," *The Journal of American History*, vol. 92, no. 3, pp. 1092–5.

Cronan, Sheila (1970) "Marriage," pp. 213–21 in Anne Koedt, Ellen Levine, and Anita Rapone (eds), *Radical Feminism*, New York: Quadrangle.

Cummings, John and Volkman, Ernest (1994) *Mobster: The astonishing rise and fall of a mafia supremo and his gang*, London: Warner Books.

Dawkins, Roger, Ford, Hamish and Trahair, Lisa (2006) "Film theory," *Year's Work in Critical and Cultural Theory*, vol. 14, no. 1, pp. 311–35.

DeCurtis, Anthony (1990) "Martin Scorsese," *Rolling Stone*, November 1, pp. 58–65, 106, & 108.

Deignan, Tom (2003) "Sidewalks: One last thing about 'Gangs,'" *Irish Voice*, vol. 17, no. 1, p. 8.

Denby, David (2002) "For the love of fighting," *The New Yorker*, vol. 78, no. 40, pp. 166–8.

Dickens, Charles (2000) *American Notes for General Circulation*, New York: Penguin. Originally published in 1842.

DiGirolamo, Vincent (2004) "'Such, such were the b'hoys . . .,'" *Radical History Review*, issue 90, pp. 123–41.

Dollard, John (1937) *Caste and Class in a Southern Town*, New York: Harper.

Donato, Raffaele (2007) "Docufictions: An interview with Martin Scorsese on documentary film," *Film History*, vol. 19, no. 3, pp. 199–207.

Dostoevsky, Fyodor (1972) *The Gambler*, with *Polina Suslova's Diary*, translated by Victor Terras, edited by Edward Wasiolek, Chicago: University of Chicago Press. Originally published in 1867.

Dostoevsky, Fyodor (1989) *Notes from Underground*, translated by Michael R. Katz, New York: W.W. Norton. Originally published in 1864.

Doyle, Peter (2007) "Citizen Dylan," *Studies in Documentary Film*, vol. 1, no. 1, pp. 67–75.

Dumas, Alexandre (1995) *The Count of Monte Cristo*, New York: Signet. Originally published in 1844/5.

Durgnat, Raymond (1991) "The gangster file: From musketeers to *Goodfellas*," *Monthly Film Bulletin*, vol. 58, no. 687, pp. 93–6.

Durgnat, Raymond (1995) "Between God and the *GoodFellas*," *Sight & Sound*, vol. 5, no. 6, pp. 22–5.

Dworkin, Andrea (1992) *Woman Hating*, London: Penguin. Originally published in 1974.

Ebert, Roger (2008) *Scorsese by Ebert*, Chicago: University of Chicago Press.

Ellis, Robert (2001) "Movies and meaning," *The Expository Times*, vol. 112, no. 9, pp. 304–8.

Fein, Esther B. (1985) "The direct approach of Scorsese," *The Orlando Sentinel*, October 11, p. E1.

Fitzgerald, F. Scott (2000) "Bernice bobs her hair," pp. 108–33 in *Flappers and Philosophers*, Cambridge: Cambridge University Press. Originally published in 1920.

Freedman, Jonathan (2000) "Filling in the blankness: Response to Ferraro," *American Literary History*, vol. 12, no. 3, pp. 523–33.

Friedan, Betty (2001) *The Feminine Mystique*, New York: W.W. Norton. Originally published in 1963.

Friedkin, David (1994) "'Blind rage' and 'brotherly love': The male psyche at war with itself in *Raging Bull*," pp. 122–30 in Steven G. Kellerman (ed.), *Perspectives on Raging Bull*, New York: G.K. Hall.

Froehlich, Cliff (2005) "Martin Scorsese," *St. Louis Post-Dispatch*, February 27, A&E section, p. F03.

Galbraith, John Kenneth (1958) *The Affluent Society*, New York: Houghton Mifflin.

Gallman, J. Matthew (2003) "Movie reviews: *Gangs of New York*," *The Journal of American History*, vol. 90, no. 3, December, pp. 1124–6.

Gamson, Joshua (1992) "The assembly line of greatness: Celebrity in twentieth-century America," *Critical Studies in Mass Communication*, vol. 9, no. 1, pp. 1– 24.

Gamson, Joshua (1994) *Claims to Fame: Celebrity in contemporary America*, Berkeley: University of California Press.

Gay, Peter (1993) *The Bourgeois Experience, Victoria to Freud: The cultivation of hatred*, New York: W.W. Norton.

Gilbert, Arthur (2004) "Godfathers, GoodFellas, and Reservoir Dogs: Understanding international politics through crime films," paper presented at International Studies Association, Annual Meeting, Montreal, Canada.

Giles, David (2000) *Illusions of Immortality: A psychology of fame and celebrity*, London: Macmillan.

Gilfoyle, Timothy J. (2003) "Scorsese's *Gangs of New York*: Why myth matters," *Journal of Urban History*, vol. 29, no. 5, pp. 620–30.

Gill, Pat (2003) "Taking it personally: Male suffering in *8MM*," *Camera Obscura*, vol. 18, no. 1, pp. 157–87.

Goodman, Susan (1994) *Edith Wharton's Inner Circle*, Austin: University of Texas Press.

Greene, Richard (2007) "The Pupkin gambit: Rationality and irrationality in *The King of Comedy*," pp. 129–38 in Mark T. Conard (ed.), *The Philosophy of Martin Scorsese*, Lexington: The University Press of Kentucky.

Grenier, Richard (1993) "Society and Edith Wharton," *Commentary*, vol. 96, no. 6, pp. 48–53.

Grist, Leighton (2000) *The Films of Martin Scorsese, 1963–77: Authorship and context*, New York: St. Martin's Press.

Grist, Leighton (2007) "Masculinity, violence, resistance: A new psychoanalytic reading of *Raging Bull*," *Atlantis*, vol. 29, no. 1, pp. 11–27.

Halberstam, Judith (1998) *Female Masculinity*, Durham, NC: Duke University Press.

Hammond, David M. and Smith, Beverly J. (2004) "Death, medicine, and religious solidarity in Martin Scorsese's *Bringing Out the Dead*," *Logos*, vol. 7, no. 3, pp. 109–22.

Harper, Stephen (2005) "Media, madness and misrepresentation: Critical reflections on anti-stigma discourse," *European Journal of Communication*, vol. 20, no. 4, pp. 460–83.

Harris, Neil (1973) *Humbug: The art of P.T. Barnum*, Chicago: University of Chicago Press.

Haygood, Wil (2003) "The battle of Old New York," *Washington Post*, January 4, Style section, p. C1.

Helmetag, Charles H. (1998) "Recreating Edith Wharton's New York in Martin Scorsese's *Age of Innocence*," *Literature/Film Quarterly*, vol. 26, no. 3, pp. 162–5.

Hoffmann, Bill (2005) "FBI: Carson tormented by murder threats," *New York Post*, October 20.

Hooper, Nancy (1995) "Celebrities at risk," *Risk Management*, vol. 42, no. 5, pp. 18–34.

Hopkins, Philip (1999) "Dead man walking," *Irish Voice*, vol. 13, no. 44, p. 38.

Hornaday, Ann (2002) "Urban mythmaker: Director Martin Scorsese creates an old New York of blood and grit," *Washington Post*, December 18, Style section, p. C1.

Horne, Philip (2001) "Martin Scorsese and the film between the living and the dead," *Raritan*, vol. 21, no. 1, pp. 34–51.

Horton, Donald and Wohl, R. Richard (1956) "Mass communication and parasocial interaction," *Psychiatry*, vol. 19, no. 3, pp. 215–29.

Ingraham, Chrys (2008) *White Weddings: Romancing heterosexuality in popular culture*, London: Routledge.

Jaramillo, Deborah L. (2002) "The family racket: AOL

Time Warner, HBO, *The Sopranos*, and the construction of a quality brand," *Journal of Communication Inquiry*, vol. 26, no. 1, pp. 59–75.

Johnson, Brian J. (1990) "Reign of terror," *Maclean's*, vol. 103, no. 30, October 1, p. 55.

Johnson, Brian J. (2006) "Where every cop is a criminal," *Maclean's*, vol. 119, no. 41, October 16, pp. 67–9.

Justice, Benjamin (2003) "Historical fiction to historical fact: *Gangs of New York* and the whitewashing of history," *Social Education*, vol. 67, no. 4, pp. 213–15.

Kael, Pauline (1980) "Underground man," pp. 183–6 in Mary Pat Kelly (ed.), *Martin Scorsese: The first decade*, Pleasantville, NY: Redgrave Publishing.

Kauffmann, Stanley (1990) "Blood money," *New Republic*, vol. 203, no. 17, pp. 28–30.

Kelly, Mary Pat (1996) *Martin Scorsese: A journey*, New York: Thunder's Mouth Press.

Kelly, Mary Pat (ed.) (1980) *Martin Scorsese: The first decade*, Pleasantville, NY: Redgrave Publishing.

Kerner, Otto (1968) *Report of the National Advisory Commission on Civil Disorders* (Kerner Report), New York: Bantam Books.

Kieran, Matthew (2003) "Forbidden knowledge: The challenge of immoralism," pp. 56–73 in José Luis Bermúdez and Sebastian Gardner (eds), *Art and Morality*, London: Routledge.

Klawans, Stuart (1990) "Films," *The Nation*, November 5, pp. 537–40.

Knight, Deborah (2007) "*The Age of Innocence*: Social semiotics, desire, and constraint," pp. 93–107 in Mark T. Conard (ed.), *The Philosophy of Martin Scorsese*, Lexington: The University Press of Kentucky.

Kocela, Christopher (2005) "Unmade men: The Sopranos after whiteness," *Postmodern Culture: An electronic journal of interdisciplinary criticism*, vol. 15, no. 2, paragraphs 1–30.

Kolker, Robert (2000) *A Cinema of Loneliness*, 3rd edition, Oxford: Oxford University Press.

Kowalski, Dean A. (2007) "*GoodFellas*, Gyges, and the good life," pp. 31–52 in Mark T. Conard (ed.), *The Philosophy of Martin Scorsese*, Lexington: The University Press of Kentucky.

Kozloff, Sarah (2001) "Complicity in *The Age of Innocence*," *Style*, vol. 35, no. 2, pp. 270–88.

Kroll, Jack (1980) "Taxi Driver," pp. 186–8 in Mary Pat Kelly (ed.), *Martin Scorsese: The first decade*, Pleasantville, NY: Redgrave Publishing.

La Motta, Jake, Carter, Joseph and Savage, Peter (1971) *Raging Bull*, New York: Prentice-Hall.

Lasch, Christopher (1980) *The Culture of Narcissism: American life in an age of diminishing expectations*, London: Abacus.

Lasch, Christopher (1991) *The True and Only Heaven: Progress and its critics*, New York: W.W. Norton.

Lawson, R.A. (2007) "The first century of blues: One hundred years of hearing and interpreting the music and the musicians," *Southern Cultures*, vol. 13, no. 3, pp. 39–63.

Librach, Ronald S. (1996) "A nice little irony: *Life Lessons*," *Literature/Film Quarterly*, vol. 24, no. 2, pp. 128–44.

Linfield, Susan (1990) "'Goodfellas' looks at the banality of mob life," *The New York Times*, August 15, section II, p. 19.

MacDonald, John D. (1992) *Cape Fear*, formerly *The Executioners*, London: Penguin. Originally published in 1957.

Mackowski, Remi (1991) "'Cape Fear' no improvement on original," *Jewish Journal*, November 21, p. 9C.

McLaughlin, Eugene (2008) "Irish," pp. 213–15 in Ellis Cashmore (ed.), *Encyclopedia of Race and Ethnic Studies*, London: Routledge.

McMahon, Jennifer L. (2007) *"After Hours*: Scorsese on absurdity," pp. 109–38 in Mark T. Conard (ed.), *The Philosophy of Martin Scorsese*, Lexington: The University Press of Kentucky.

Maltby, John, Day, Liza, McCutcheon, Lynn E., Gillett, Raphael, Houran, James, and Ashe, Diane D. (2004) "Personality and coping: A context for examining celebrity worship and mental health," *British Journal of Psychology*, vol. 95, no. 4, pp. 411–28.

Marcus, Greil (2007) "The world premiere of *No Direction Home*," *Studies in Documentary Film*, vol. 1, no. 1, pp. 49–52.

Maslin, Janet (1991) "'Cape Fear' bears Scorsese stamp: Remake of thriller turns 1-note story into intricate symphony," *The Plain Dealer*, November 10, Arts & Living section, p. 1H.

Matthews, Pamela R. (1996) "Review: *Edith Wharton's Inner Circle*," *The Journal of English and Germanic Philology*, vol. 95, no. 3, pp. 462–4.

Mattie, Sean (2003) "Blood, justice, and American citizenship: An interpretation of *Gangs of New York*," *Perspectives on Political Science*, vol. 32, no. 4, pp. 215–20.

Merschman, Joseph C. (2001) "The dark side of the web: Cyberstalking and the need for contemporary legislation," *Harvard Women's Law Journal*, vol. 24, pp. 255–92.

Merton, Robert K. (1993) "Social structure and anomie," pp. 249–61 in Charles Lemert (ed.) *Social Theory: The multicultural and classic readings*, Boulder, CO: Westview Press. Originally published in 1938.

Miliora, Maria T. (2004) *The Scorsese Psyche on Screen: Roots of themes and characters in the films*, London: McFarland & Company.

Milne, Tom (1990) "GoodFellas USA, 1990," *Monthly Film Bulletin*, vol. 57, no. 683, pp. 355–7.

Morgan, David (1992) "Nowhere to hide: A lawyer faces his nemesis," *ABA Journal*, February, pp. 50–3.

Morrone, John (1989) "New York stories," *The New Leader*, vol. 72 , no. 5, pp. 20–2.

Mortimer, Barbara (1997) "Portraits of the postmodern person in *Taxi Driver*, *Raging Bull*, and *The King of Comedy*," *Journal of Film and Video*, vol. 49, no. 1/2, pp. 28–38.

Mosher, Catherine and Danoff-Burg (2007) "College students' life priorities: The influence of gender and gender-linked personality traits," *Gender Studies*, vol. 24, no. 2, pp. 21–33.

Muller, Jerry Z. (1997) *Conservatism: An anthology of social and political thought from David Hume to the present*, Princeton: Princeton University Press.

Murphy Kathleen (1998) "Made men," *Film Comment*, vol. 34, no. 3, pp. 64–6.

O'Brien, Martin, Tzanelli, Rodnathi, Yar, Majid, and Penna, Sue (2005) "'The spectacle of fearsome acts': Crime in the melting p(l)ot in *Gangs of New York*," *Critical Criminology*, vol. 13, no. 1, pp. 17–35.

Oestreicher, Richard (2003) "How should historians think about 'The Gangs of New York'?," *History Workshop Journal*, vol. 56, no. 1, pp. 210–15.

Orlando, Emily J. (1998) "Rereading Wharton's 'Poor Archer': A Mr. 'Might-have-been' in *The Age of Innocence*," *American Literary Realism 1870–1910*, vol. 30, no. 2, pp. 56–77.

Packard, Vance (1959) *The Status Seekers*, Chapel Hill, NC: University of North Carolina Press.

Palmer, Bryan D. (2003) "The hands that built America: A class-politics appreciation of Martin Scorsese's *The Gangs of New York*," *Historical Materialism*, vol. 11, no. 4, pp. 317–45.

Parker, James (2003) "Scorsese's low score," *The American Prospect*, February, pp. 42–3.

Petrakis, John (2002) "Mean streets," *Christian Century*, December 18–31, p. 40.

Phillips, Michael, Phillips, Julia, Bill, Tony and Dempsey, Michael (1976) "*Taxi Driver* by Martin Scorsese," *Film Quarterly*, vol. 29, no. 4, pp. 37–41.

Photinos, Christine (2006) "Transiency and transgression in the autobiographies of Barbara Starke and 'Boxcar' Bertha Thompson," *Women's Studies*, vol. 35, no. 7, pp. 657–81.

Pileggi, Nicholas (1990) *Wiseguy: Life in a mafia family*, New York: Pocket Books.

Pileggi, Nicholas (1995) *Casino: Love and honor in Las Vegas*, New York: Simon & Schuster.

Polsky, Ned (1969) *Hustlers, Beats and Others*, New York: Anchor.

Quinn, Anthony (2007) "Heroin chic? Just say no," *The Independent*, November 16, Arts and Books Review, pp. 6–8.

Raymond, Marc (2000) *Martin Scorsese and American Film Genre*, Master of Arts thesis, Ottawa, Canada: Carleton University.

Reese, Katie (2004) "Scorsese's *Cape Fear*: The triumph of stereotypes," *Picturing Justice: The on-line journal of law & popular culture*, January 6, *http://www.usfca.edu/pj/capefear_reese.htm* (accessed March 24, 2009).

Rickey, Carrie (1986) "Paul Newman in 'Color of Money,'" *The Philadelphia Inquirer*, October 17, Features Weekend section, p. 4.

Riesman, David with Glazer, Nathan and Reuel Denney (1969) *The Lonely Crowd: A study of the changing American character*, New Haven, CN: Yale University Press. Originally published in 1950.

Salamon, Julie (1990) "Scorsese's very good 'fellas,'" *The Wall Street Journal*, September 20, p. A12.

Sarchett, Barry W. (1994) "'Rockumentary' as metadocumentary: Martin Scorsese's *The Last Waltz*," *Literature/ Film Quarterly*, vol. 22, no. 1, pp. 28–36.

Schickel, Richard (1980) "Taxi Driver," pp. 188–9 in Mary Pat Kelly (ed.), *Martin Scorsese: The first decade*, Pleasantville, NY: Redgrave Publishing.

Scorsese, Martin and Cocks, Jay (1993) *The Age of Innocence: A portrait of the film based on the novel by Edith Wharton*, New York: Newmarket.

Server, Lee (2001) *Robert Mitchum: Baby, I don't care*, London: Faber & Faber.

Shannon, Christopher (2004) "Catholicism as the Other," *First Things: A monthly journal of religious and public life*, January 1, pp. 46–52.

Siegel, Ed (1985) "Fame game becoming America's newest pastime," *Boston Globe*, March 18, National/Foreign section, p. 1.

Sikov, Ed (1983) "The King of Comedy," *Film Quarterly*, vol. 36, no. 4, pp. 17–21.

Simmel, Georg (1903) *Die Grosstädte und das Geistesleben* [*The Metropolis and Mental Life*], Dresden: Petermann.

Simon, John (1991) "The mob and the family," *National Review*, January 28, pp. 63–5.

Smith, Gavin (1998) "Street smart: Excerpts from three Martin Scorsese interviews," *Film Comment*, vol. 34, no. 3, pp. 68–74.

Smith, Gavin, Lyons, Donald, and Murphy, Kathleen (1993) "Artist of the beautiful," *Film Comment*, vol. 29, no. 6, pp. 10–25.

Sounes, Howard (2001) *Down the Highway: The life of Bob Dylan*, London: Black Swan.

Stern, Lesley (1995) *The Scorsese Connection*, Bloomington: Indiana University Press/British Film Institute.

Stevens, Peter F. (2003) "'Clear the streets': The Irish of Boston resisted the 1863 draft by rioting in the North End," *The Boston Irish Reporter*, vol. 14, no. 2, p. 12.

Stowe, Harriet Beecher (1981) *Uncle Tom's Cabin: Or, life among the lowly*, edited by Ann Douglas, New York: Penguin. Originally published in 1852.

Swensen, Andrew J. (2001) "The anguish of God's lonely men: Dostoevsky's Underground Man and Scorsese's Travis Bickle," *REN*, vol. 53, no. 4, pp. 267–303.

Taubin, Amy (2005) "From there to here," *Film Comment*, vol. 41, no. 6, pp. 30–3.

Tevis, Walter S. (1959) *The Hustler*, New York: Thunder's Mouth Press.

Tevis, Walter S. (1984) *The Color of Money*, New York: Thunder's Mouth Press.

Thain, Gerald J. (2001) "*Cape Fear*: Two versions and two visions separated by thirty years," *Journal of Law and Society*, vol. 28, no. 1, pp. 40–6.

Thomas, Deborah (2003) "*The Age of Innocence*, Martin Scorsese, 1993," *CineAction*, vol. 62 (June 22), pp. 22–33.

Thompson, Bertha (1937) *Sister of the Road: The autobiography of Box-car Bertha*, as told to Dr. Ben L. Reitman, New York: Gold Label Books. Reprinted in 1988 as *Boxcar Bertha*, New York: Amok Press.

Thompson, David and Christie, Ian (eds) (1990) *Scorsese on Scorsese*, London: Faber & Faber.

Thompson, Kirsten Moana (2007) *Apocalyptic Dread: American film at the turn of the millennium*, Albany: State University of New York.

Thomson, David (1999) "An offering to the ghosts of

wildness past," *New York Times*, November 7, section II, p. 23.

Thornell, Peter (2007) "Review: The Philosophy of Martin Scorsese," *Library Journal*, March 1, pp. 86–7.

Torrance, Kelly Jane (2007) "Telling stories through film," *The Washington Times*, November 30, section D, p. 1.

Turan, Kenneth (2002) "Murder, revenge, rage . . . and apathy," *Los Angeles Times*, December 20, p. E1.

Viano, Maurizio (1991) "GoodFellas," *Film Quarterly*, vol. 44, no. 3, pp. 43–50.

Vidal, Belén (2006) "Labyrinths of loss: The letter as figure of desire and deferral in the literary film," *Journal of European Studies*, vol. 36, no. 4. pp. 418–36.

Vito, Gennaro F. (1992) "Editorial comment," *Journal of Contemporary Criminal Justice*, vol. 8, no. 1, p. iii.

Walkowitz, Daniel J. (2003) "'The Gangs of New York': The mean streets in history," *History Workshop Journal*, vol. 56, no. 1, pp. 204–209.

Willett, Cynthia (1996) "Baudrillard, 'After Hours,' and the postmodern suppression of socio-sexual conflict," *Cultural Critique*, issue 34, pp. 143–61.

Williams, Raymond (2005) *Culture and Materialism: Selected essays*, London: Verso.

Wilmington, Michael (2006) "Eastwood's and Scorsese's heroes," *Chicago Tribune*, October 25, Tempo section, p. 3.

Wood, Robin (1986) *Hollywood from Vietnam to Reagan*, New York: Columbia University Press.

Worsnop, Richard L. (1992) "Mafia crackdown," *CQ Researcher*, vol. 2, no. 12 (March 27), pp. 265–88.

INDEX